DAYS IN THE SUN

DAYS IN THE SUN

by
MARTIN ANDERSEN NEXÖ
Author of "PELLE THE CONQUEROR"

AUTHORIZED TRANSLATION FROM THE DANISH BY
JACOB WITTMER HARTMANN

PUBLISHED IN NEW YORK *by*
COWARD-McCANN, INC.
IN THE YEAR 1929

914.6
N567d

1256

CONTENTS

DAYS IN THE SUN

I

SPAIN

En Route

WE said good-by to Italy with tearless eyes and put off. No doubt the country is beautiful, but it is a little too picturesque, a little too idyllic. Its importunate beggars are too smilingly amiable; the whole nation laughs and crowds around you—for tips. The countless tourists have transformed it into something resembling a bedraggled poodle performing idiotic tricks.

The whole land has been embroidered over, bedeviled, as it were, by all the painters, poets and philosophers in the world. John Smith painted that pine tree; that fragment of a wall was poetically interpreted by John Smith; and what has *unser Goethe* not said and Byron not done in these places! Every spot is tagged with its slip of paper, its erudition, its reminiscences; and if a wretched modern writer turns off the beaten path a little, after the manner of his profession, at once a score of great departed shades will rise up from the ground—like trolls in the legend. As in China, you dare not spit for fear of hitting an ancestor, nor draw a breath freely for sheer tradition.

We have cast loose, and Italy hardly matters at all. The millions of bright reflections in Naples Bay are swallowed by the Gulf. Messina comes and goes without leaving a trace on our unfettered spirits, which already dwell in Spain.   Palermo drops deep in its golden horn and disappears; Sicily itself vanishes, the snowy top of Ætna being the last thing to go down in the waves.

It is lovely to be sailing; there is nothing but ocean on all sides as far as the eye can see.   Mile after mile of watery surface passes in under the ship's bow and glides out astern, but far off on the horizon new wastes of water appear as fast as we can eat them up.   Apparently we are making no progress at all, and yet the ship is jogging along and the screw turning—it must be something like this to wade through eternity.

The sun rises from the sea and goes down in the sea day after day.   The same sheet of water constantly moves in under us, blue or mother-of-pearl in color, indolent, slothful, in long swells which lie across the watery surface like great sleeping mollusks.

Occasionally, a faint speck appears in the north or south horizon—a promontory on the coast of Sardinia or Africa; but its effect is distant, immaterial, by no means disturbing the impression of an eternity slowly gliding by.

The Mediterranean!

At times of a sullen green, opaque and viscous, like molten bottle-glass.   Again it shines like an opal in its pale milk color; or the whole surface breathes hot indigo.   Or, it may be a crystal in its reflections, and so transparent, so nearly ethereal, that our shadows pass right through it and distinctly fall upon the glinting back of a gray shark following us faithfully a few fathoms down.   Great numbers of big jellyfish cruise in the clear and vibrating element in rhythmic jerks; silver-scaled fish and long sinuous threads of mucus dart out frightened to either side of the ship's keel.

We are on board a dirty Dutch freight steamer. We have canned food three times a day, sleep in little canteen rooms right over the screw, surrounded by open cases of raisins, dried prunes, groats, and dried fish—and for these accommodations we have to pay three hundred gold francs.

Every time I turn in my sleep, my head collides with some sharp projecting iron, the name of which I cannot ever guess. But what is the use of complaining? A man of character should know what he is doing even when he sleeps.

Not that we sleep very much. When the first petals of the dawn come swinging down toward us on little white waves, we are already up and doing, are reading the log, finding our bearings on the chart, and perusing the horizon with our big field-glass. We absorb this new world with all our pores—and consume mountains of canned meat into the bargain. The sea air uses you up, said the sailor as he vomited.

"Such days, such nights!"

The sun stands in a cloudless sky for days, exerting all its huge energy fruitlessly over the insatiable sea, and when it drops fatigued beneath the horizon, the ocean spreads itself out in golden loveliness as if to hold it back; it shines in shameless colors and draws off far to the west like a flood of golden hair. And the sun takes a strong grip of this fair golden hair as it goes down. And then there is a flood through the sea, a blushing modesty as if the sea were ashamed of its splendid nakedness; it faints pale away, with a golden bloom breathed upon it. And from the east the evening wafts a veil of soft gray chiffon, spreading it indulgently over the naked one.

Heaven and sea are gone. Only our little ship remains set in a surface of pale silver, which begins at no great distance to fade away into a bright chaos of gray on all sides. Shades of lead and slate stand like dark nuances in the bright gray of cement and pearl; the smoke-stack's smoke hangs like a skein of raw silk over the heavy mercuric hue of our wake. There is gray in all shades and tones, nothing but gray! Gratifyingly soft, monotonous and yet rich, it rolls in upon us like a tone-poem without tones. It is like the crooning melodies of the common people all over the world; the primal mist must have looked like this.

With the coming of night, however, the sky dissolves into a vehement, almost aggravating purple, which makes the pulse beat audibly again. And the sea flows black and turgid as tar.

These nights, with their gurgling and swishing under the ship, the faint tick of the log and the sonorous snoring of the crew, under the forecastle! And the great marvelous calm of the firmament, while the ship hammers away with its heavy engine-thump, which sounds like a grave-digger working in a large closed alcove. . . .

On the morning of the fifth day, Spain shoots forth like a violet rocky wall, rising straight out of the sea, its upper edge covered with clouds. As we approach, the highest cliffs recede; blue glens open up and green valleys, entire promontories step forth from the mass and advance into the foreground—until they finally reveal themselves as capes projecting several miles out from the coast proper. And although the cliff had seemed to drop right down into the sea, we discover a broad and fertile lowland in front of it. This is the famous Huertas, the most fruitful plain on earth, constituting a belt along the coast from Barcelona to beyond Malaga in the south, a distance of more than a thousand miles.

There is a white gleam above the clouds, and as they recede with the advance of morning, we behold the mighty snowy ridge of Sierra Nevada some two or three hundred miles to the southwest. All day long we have the "snow tops" before us in the same general direction and at the same distance, so remote and immense are they. But on the following morning we can distinguish the various country towns along the southern slope of the mountain chain, all of Alpujarras, so famous for its fruits and hams and its ten centuries of Moorish history. And beyond it, over on the northern slope of the chain, I know Granada lies, madly captivating, with the Alhambra, the Vega, the gypsies.

About noon, we slip into the port of Malaga.

Malaga is the same pleasant town it was six years ago, an agreeable blending of old and new; Moorish ruins, Andalusian odors, new streets with pavements of wooden blocks, modern cement quays. It is all fine but not particularly characteristic, with its two hundred thousand industrious inhabitants, who are suspected all over Andalusia of coquetting with the English and of having uttered contemptible words to the effect that their seaport is as good as the Alhambra of Granada. The foreigner who has seen both will find it about as sensible to quarrel over this question as to dispute which is higher: the soprano's high C or the cathedral spire at Seville. Probably something is wrong with the Malagans: do they not afford perfect proof of this in their proposal that their harbor be made a free port—after the fashion of their neighbor Gibraltar?

While our steamer is stuffing its iron belly with figs, raisins, sweet Malaga wine and many other commodities, we go ashore to look around and call for our mail.

We have arrived at the height of the export season; the port is bustling with activity. All the fruits of Spain seem to vie with each other here, to bid us welcome, and we are picking our way between tuns of wine and olives; cork receptacles filled with grapes; chests of dates, raisins, lemons, oranges and almonds; mats of figs; sacks of hazel-nuts and walnuts—and many other products. Sometimes a receptacle has burst open owing to careless handling, and the navvies offer us some of the contents as we walk by.

Further up the quay we see crowds of women and children on their knees, surrounding large mounds of oranges. They gossip and sing as they take the fruits, which a few men are sorting, roll them into silken paper and pack them into long cases. In their many-colored rags, the women seem a wreath of poppies and corn-flowers edging a pile of gold. It surprises us involuntarily to find these lovely fruits, which at home in Denmark are so dear and so much desired, treated here as if they were hardly more than potatoes. The freight cars run down to the edge of the pier, the compartment doors are opened, and the oranges are dumped into baskets or on the bare ground, wherever they may chance to fall. Lean, sinewy men, bare-footed, a red cloth bound about their heads like a turban, run to and fro, throwing the contents of the baskets over the top of the heap so that the oranges roll down between the naked legs of the women and children, sometimes continuing their course over the black ground like flames in the darkness.

We have had no mail for three weeks, so long is it since we gave Malaga as our post office address to the folks at home; and it is with trepidation that we hasten to the Consulate.

Consul Schulz, a pleasant old German, shakes his gray head smiling and hands us a newspaper in its wrapper.

One newspaper! Such is the Andalusian post office! There should have been letters too. Possibly some widow or other has gotten our post because she stands in well with the letter carrier. And since the public scribe—who usually writes and reads her letters for her—cannot interpret these Danish letters, she is convinced they mean a legacy of millions, and proceeds to make debts and live on them all her days. Such is life. But newspapers! Who can possibly enjoy them as much as we do?

Apparently foreigners are fully in charge of the business life of this town "of almost English industry." All the big commercial houses have French or English or—particularly—German names.

Our national pride induces us to cast about for signs of Danish enterprise, and when we behold a Danish flag waving over a seaman's pothouse in one of the harbor streets, we take the liberty to enter. Better talk to a saloon-keeper than to no one. Mine host is a full-blooded Spaniard; he has bought the flag for one crown from a ship-thief and has raised it aloft as bait for Scandinavian sailors. We give the thing up as a bad job and drift along at random, drinking Muscatel wine and eating Malaga grapes, ascending the high cliff Gibralfaro, with its Moorish ruins, where now only the poorest people live. The women up there say dreadful things to us, believing that we cannot understand them, and laugh to themselves. And when, in order to curb their arrogance, I show them that I have understood, they become all the worse and shout still more abusive things after us. I grow angry and use an evil word myself; they bend down to pick up stones. We hurry down the mountain side, pursued by oaths and pebbles.

II

THE WHITE CITY

AGAIN we have left terra firma. Having left
Malaga about midnight, with as little noise as
had heralded our coming, we passed Gibraltar at dawn
and made for the west. The coast of Africa lay to
the southward; behind us the rocky fortress sank into
the waves foot by foot; a heavy sea and a cold wind
indicated that we were moving into the Atlantic. Only
two hours ago we were over the submarine threshold
that connects the ranges of Andalusia with those of
North Africa, erecting an invisible but effective line
between two seas: the blue and smiling Mediterranean,
whose temperature (fifteen to seventeen degrees
Réaumur) made it possible for us to bathe every day
even in November; and this corner of the Atlantic
Ocean, a fretful porcupine that was lashing us with its
current, its waves, its cold winds, and making us put
on heavy clothes and freeze nevertheless.

The heaven was bright, almost pale blue, without
the limitless depth usually seen in southern skies. And
instead of the steep violet coastlines of the Mediterranean, with mountain tops rising one behind the other
as far as the eye could reach, Spain, to the north,
presented its bare undulating fields and a coastline,
now flat and sandy, now towering in yellow cakes of
chalk, chewed off by the sea.

Toward noon the sea became better-natured. The

9

first sign was a hotter sun; it stood like an evil eye in the cold sky and blazed away. The wind groveled on its belly before the sun, crept over the waves prostrate like a dog, and finally abated altogether. The waves collapsed into long swells, weaker and weaker, as the air came down warm and enervating over them. The heavens changed from white to blue—then to an azure drenched with purple; the sky seemed to be absorbing added depth from the infinity of space. It shaded imperceptibly to violet, to lilac. It became flaming, red as blood, a heat-emitting fiery ether; it became the sun itself, standing like a dead spot in the white-hot masses of light, the only object the eye could bear to look at. It was the sun that bedizened the whole vault of heaven with bright lights and rich warm tones, but the sun itself stood like a mighty cocoon up in the sky. But on gazing at its dull surface, all soon became a bright milky white, and the eye could perceive no forms, only a huge stinging blaze of light.

Ecstatic brightness took possession of sea and sky, a very fire of gladness. It must have penetrated the depths below, for the flying fish came up, floated over the water for a second's silver gleam, and disappeared again. A single tuna fish would show itself like a huge black disk, or pass on leaving a trail like long lines of rocking-horses. Now and again a column of water would shoot into the air—then disappear—in fine white spray. That was where the big whales were.

Many steamers proceed in our direction, or pass us, or head southward along the coast of Africa. Right under the lee of Spain there is a steamer with its bow way up on shore. A busy little tug is jerking at it tirelessly, not making the slightest progress—as a gnat nibbles at a dead chafer. The Danish flag over the stern shines like a poppy in the sun.

Far out ahead are countless columns of smoke, great pines rising skyward like hundreds of factory chimneys. This is one of the highways of the ocean. Under the smoky pine nearest us rises a hull coming our way. It passes us, disappearing in its own wake—and again one, and another, and so on forever. Great ten-thousand-ton steel monsters push their panting masses forward with the aid of twin screws, spew forth ugly yellow water from their sides, and drag along a wake of cinders, kitchen-garbage and shining coal dust over which the choking smoke pall hangs suspended blue-black like a stormy sky. These are the great coal ships for Gibraltar, Malta and Port Said.

There comes a festive glow over the water; polished ivory and gilding, bright brass trimmings and the twinkle of countless moon-like portholes. The four chimneys of this great hull emit no smoke, only warmth. The two promenade decks, one above the other, are filled with fashionably-dressed ladies and gentlemen strolling about or reclining in deck chairs; black-clad waiters dart to and fro among them. We hear the orchestra from the saloon as the ship passes us by. Over the white water of its wake hover lovely sea-gulls which catch in the air the bits thrown to them from the after-deck by little children with golden locks and bare knees. It is a steam packet proceeding to India with English military officers and government officials on board; it passes by like a glad vision and is gone from sight in half an hour.

Many little steamers are met, are overtaken by us—or they overtake us. About half of them are Scandinavian—mostly Norwegian, but some Danish and Swedish—engaged in foreign carrying trades. The flag is dipped three times! A greeting to these nameless northerners who here in foreign service earn a scanty sustenance for their wives and children, and some pickings besides for exacting shareholders at home—and in return enjoy the privilege of looking in at home again every three or four years and begetting a new mouth to be fed with the others.

In little floating colonies of some twenty men each, they move about over the seas, tidying up the ship by day, taking their watches by night, and ready to turn out at a moment's notice; in this lies all the romance of sea life. Sometimes they discharge and take on new cargo all in one day, and sail by night; discharge and take on again the next day—and they keep this up all the way around the Mediterranean. They rarely go ashore, and when they do, it is likely to be at night; their incursions seldom extend beyond the seamen's resorts along the water front and the little abutting streets.

"Tell me something about the country in there," a sailor said to me one day. "I have been sailing the Mediterranean for eighteen months and have not been on shore once!" When he had taken to the sea, he had believed that sea life was vastly more than an eternal round of watches and tasks in quiet weather, and unending day and night watches in storms and gales. Any young man who goes to sea for adventure soon finds that he faces only the regular grind, interrupted by an occasional rough spell. The forty-five or fifty kroner in wages which he gets each month are

barely enough to support wife and children in decency.
Yet huge wages are now being blamed for the decline
in Danish navigation.

Steam cuts paths over the ocean. As far as the eye
can reach, before us and behind—down to the merest
shreds of smoke left by ships now miles beyond the
horizon—there is the same endless line of boats,
plowing the same narrow course. It is as if their
long Indian file extended around the globe.

Further out, on the great waste of waters, sailing
vessels are moving in every direction. A majestic ship,
all four masts bulging with white sails, skews toward
us like a dazzling iceberg. Little cutters with lateen
sails cruise in every direction like white birds grazing
the water's surface with the tip of one wing. Our
Dutch captain points out a schooner from Svendborg
and a sloop from Marstal. All sea-faring nations are
acquainted with these two types of boats, the former
famous for its harmonious lines, the latter for its
peculiar poop.

Far out on an horizon of ineffable clearness, two yellow spots appear. For a time, they are two water
lilies. Then they detach themselves and rise slowly on
slender white stems out of the sea. They tremble in
the sun-flickering distance like two stamens, and behind them a great yellow calix appears. One stares
and marvels at this vegetation which recalls the slow
growth of grasses, and proceeding just as slowly; we
are filled with expectation, not with impatience. The
sea is a narcotic, and the deliberate tempo, the unceas-
ing chugging of the ship, beating monotonously like
a ruminant's pulse, induces a sense of peace and quiet;

just as the growing things beyond impart to us something of the great patience of eternity, so endlessly
slow is their growth.

New plants appear by the side of the others. Rare
forms and colors sprout from the depths and blend
with the mighty white bed of the flowers. It is the
sea blossoming. The outlines become more discon-
tinuous: battlements, towers like minarets, domes.
The vision wavers before the eyes, distant, unreal—a
far-off castle with golden cupolas rising from the blue
sea on a dazzling pedestal of chalk. The white mass
dissolves into countless surfaces as you watch it, and
the city spreads out like a water lily in an ocean of
blue, swaying on leaves and stems, with the dome and
the two slender spires of the cathedral leaping like
corolla and stamen into the purple-drenched air. We
have been steaming along for six hours since catching
our earliest glimpse of the first faint dots. So clear
is the air.

As we cast anchor in the Bay of Cádiz and our
glances wander over the city which spreads in dazzling
splendor before us, the blood pounds in our veins.
These unaccustomed outlines; this marvelously pure
white, mingled with the bright green of spring, though
it is now December; the whole dazzling mass, framed
in the deep indigo of the sea and the heaven's bright
mixture of purple and gold and blue; this revealing
under its snow-white robe of its many colors so faint,
so delicately suggested as in no other city you have
seen—this indeed must be the fairy tale that drew
your incredulous smile when you were still a child.
Here is the wondrous fable born from the sea itself,

now raised jubilantly aloft in sunlight and color, in
dazzling gold and blue!

In the year in which Methuselah died, a number of
bold young Phœnicians sailed a little beyond the end
of the world—which then ended at Gibraltar—and
founded the city of Cádiz. They built the city on a
small island which, connected with Spain by a narrow
sand bank, extends into the ocean like an attenuated
neck.

Cádiz soon became an important mart for staples.
It was the intermediary in all maritime commerce between the Orient and England, the Baltic Sea and
northern France. Gold, amber, purple, metal ores,
precious stones and woods: all the treasures of antiquity passed through this city. The city grew, increasing in wealth and beauty, and acquiring a peculiarly feminine lust for power, which made it surrender
its charms successively to the most powerful races, first
to Carthage, then to Rome. Cæsar fortified the city
and made it a military port; it became the center of
world commerce, the queen of the seas. For a brief
moment the wavering focus of civilization flickered
over Cádiz before it passed on to Córdoba and Seville.

The Moors did not succeed in drawing any profit
from the city, closely surrounded as it was by deep
waters. It dropped back into the sea, to emerge after
a thousand years, when the new world began to be exploited. Again Cádiz became the middleman, between
two worlds this time. Great shipyards grew up;
every banking and commercial house in the world had
its branches there. Merchants swarmed through its
streets when the commercial flotillas returned from
America: Russians, Jews, Hindoos, Berbers, blonde

Nordics, sly Greeks, slave traders of giant stature from western Africa, and Moroccan pirates, on the lookout for the arrival dates of ships with cargoes of gold. Gold tinkled in many tongues. Its glitter was reflected in every racial pigment.

Gold enough here for him who knew how to grasp it! The gold and silver received by Cádiz from America in the course of a single year (1790) was valued at upwards of thirty million dollars. Gold became so common a commodity in the town that even dogs, despising their golden chains, are said to have preferred liberty. Only human beings continued faithful to the precious metal.

With the sudden boom in steam tonnage about the year 1880, Cádiz suffered a setback as the warehouse of the Old World. No harbor could boast a more favorable situation. It lay hard by the Straits with their swift currents and their hostile winds, which often made it a dangerous business, full of financial risk, for sailing ships to continue their journey to the far-flung and rich coasts of the Mediterranean Sea.

But the steamer, unlike the sailing ship, is not limited to destinations by the open sea, with its wide waters and regular winds. The steamer can sail against the wind and against the current, can negotiate narrow straits and sail up navigable rivers, discharging a little cargo in one place, then in another, serving as a connection between any port and all the rest of the world outside. The steamer made transshipping, middlemen, staple-marts unnecessary. This was the end of Cádiz as a trading center. It suffered its final blow when Spain lost its colonies in 1898, which deprived the city of its significance as a forwarding and receiving center between the colonies and the motherland.

The population of the city declined in the course of thirty years from one hundred to sixty-five thousand inhabitants, who now live on memories of past greatness. It has hardly a better connection with the outer world than a Jutland country village of two hundred souls; there is one mail train a day, which always arrives two hours late. The Madrid morning papers do not get to Cádiz until the following day and subscribers seldom receive them—because of the lateness of the mail train—before the morning of the third day.

Life moves slowly in Cádiz. The city is like a delicate old smile framed in white locks, a white bonnet nodding behind an old-fashioned flower-pot. Over much of the city you may amble as you do in the closed villa streets back of Frederiksberg in Copenhagen, where pensioned clergymen and teachers live in retirement. There is the same peaceful light over the houses, the same vegetative quiet everywhere. Here there is no clanging, grinding, nerve-racking electric tramway, no hoarse croaking of factory whistles, no thundering trucks of labor. The constant tremble in the air which is characteristic of a modern town, the ceaseless vibration of pavement and walls, the destructive hum of millions of noisy objects, the surging crowds—these things are not for Cádiz, whose few sounds can be heard far off like the sounds of a village in the open country.

The Gaditano sits within his four walls and regards his city as the liveliest in all Andalusia, so accustomed is he to its quiet. Cafés and squares—these natural gathering places of the southerner—are empty; the promenades, with their entrancing trees, are never used. But among the common people, who are the same everywhere and under all conditions, there is noise and ferment as in any other city.

Cádiz is surrounded on all sides by the sea, which holds the city locked in an iron clasp, and prevents it from expanding its boundaries when the population increases in boom periods. The high bastion rises steeply from the water and extends around the city like the curves of a giant serpent; the serpent's entrails thunder with the sounds of moving artillery while a gorgeous deserted promenade winds along its back, as broad as a highway and adorned with ancient field-pieces which receive their periodic coats of stove polish. On one side there is a broad delightful view of the bay and the continent; on the other you have little glimpses of clean, narrow streets in which men stand about like draped statues, while women float along like oblong prayer books, pale, black-clad, serious. They give signs of life only when they encounter a stranger; then they stand still and burst into shrill laughter. So far is the city now from being the metropolis of former times when all races moved and haggled in bright confusion in its streets.

Few cities are as quiet as Cádiz; none so clean. Excepting the poorer quarter around Santa Elena, where vermin-infested groups of women, mounds of garbage, and mangy, hairless, masterless dogs combine to produce a genuine southern metropolis, the city is meticulously clean, almost old-maidish in its neatness. The asphalt pavement of the narrow alleys is as spotless as a scoured kitchen and the houses are a stainless white from ground to roof, with green shutters or glass-covered balconies all the way to the top. Clean, cool, still, swathed in shadows—such is the city below us, with its pillared courtyards in which fountains play and palm-trees, nerias and plane-trees remain green all year round. These courtyards are often roofed with glass and furnished with rugs and lounges—cool refuges in the summer heat.

But you will look in vain for real yards for washing, drying, or bleaching in this densely built city, where every block of houses is a single compact mass; that is, you will look in vain until you take an opportunity to ascend one of the five thousand towers of the city and let your eye wander over the flat roofs. Every house has its flat roof with a stone coping around it and a little tower as outlet for the winding staircase. Here is the yard, the laundry, the bleaching place, sometimes even the garden and the workshop too—a whole city spread out under a merciless sun and blazing white in color. Five thousand cubes, some a little higher, some a little lower, all in some way related, seem from your point of vantage like a great cross-section of a beehive floating on translucent waters, adorned with little ivory towers, white linen and blazing red pelargonias. The whole invites you to meander through it, to leap over the narrow crevices which mark the streets, and to gain the opposite shore —if only the sun were not so hot that you cannot remain very long on your tower. But it is lovely here in the evening when the heaven flames and the ocean moves in upon you from all sides like molten gold, once more enriching this city of white.

The sand bank one mile long and a stone's throw in

width is the umbilical cord which connects the city with the mainland. On the left, the waters of the bight lazily lap a smooth beach of bluish clay. On the right, the waves of the Atlantic Ocean roll on before a row of lovely dunes, a yellow-green porridge of sand and water, to break on the shore and thunder against the gay white coastline.

Between the dunes there is a gypsy cabin, made of old rags, leaves of aloe and rusty sheet iron. A little ten-year-old boy in a bare shirt approaches us begging, scratching great white streaks in the blackish brown of his loins, which are richly dotted with insect bites shaped like little angry craters with a red spark in the center of each. When he is ready to give us up as a bad job, an old woman, in a curiously shrill voice, eggs him on to renewed effort from the village below.

All roads lead to Rome, they say, but this one really does. Its course takes it through Seville, Salamanca and southern France, and the whole length of it was built by the Romans themselves. Its masonry, restored in spots, still gives evidence of the Roman skill.

Gradually the tongue of sand widens into a flat, bare, marshy stretch ribbed with canals that increase in number and width until they take up more space than the land. Between the canals the black soil has been trodden into a single beaten trail by many hoofs and feet. You may follow it as you might follow the thread of Ariadne, and it will lead you farther and farther into the labyrinth of lean islands on which cattle are grazing and over which an occasional pyramid towers. This country extends in every direction, as far as the eye can see, resembling with its canals, its curious pyramids, an acrid marsh on which some nomad race has left its tents, when driven out by its successors. These pyramids, upon closer inspection, remind you of dirty snow, and if you taste of them you will find they are made of salt.

For this apparently fruitless region is one of Spain's great natural resources; these are the salt fields of San Fernando. This confusion of fragmentary canals covering miles and miles of area is connected by narrow sluices with the long main canals, which in turn are connected with the sea, so that in exceptionally high tides every dike can be filled. Work ceases only in winter and the salt-dikes fill themselves and empty themselves four times every twenty-four hours as the water ebbs and flows. But in May, when the sun bakes all things hot and no rain has fallen for months, the actual work with the salt begins. The sea water is prevented from flowing out and is left standing at a depth of about three feet in the dikes. In the course of ten days it will evaporate completely, leaving behind on the bottom of the dikes a layer of salt two inches thick, not unlike hoarfrost in the fields.

After crystallization is complete, the salt is shoveled into great heaps, loaded on the backs of donkeys, and piled into great pyramids along the large canals. Flat scows next deliver it to the ships lying in the bay. To northern eyes it is like the shoveling of snow from a skating pond, a strange thing to be happening under the tropical sun.

As soon as the salt has been removed, the canals are filled again and this may normally be repeated from four to six times in a single summer. But if rain should fall during the process of evaporation the salt will not deposit and the harvest is ruined. The strong sun, the summer drought and the saltiness of the sea here create most favorable conditions for the winning of salt. But only a few of the salt fields are still in use; the rest of the vast excavated region now lies fallow, frequented only by shrimp-fishers and sea birds. It has been choked by the dead hand of the state.

One is hardly surprised to learn that salt here, in the place in which it is produce ', costs the consumers four times as much as in Denmark, because the state collects more than two million dollars in taxes every year from this indispensable foodstuff. In Spain, many sources of wealth are disorganized in this way. Ridiculous as it may seem, it is actually a paying business to steal a few pots of salt in the midst of the wealth of the salt fields; and an expensive system of inspection is maintained in order to prevent such thefts. The surfaces of the pyramids are hardened so that in many cases dynamite has to be used in order to break off the salt.

The city of Cádiz must of course live; its whiteness is not enough. It no longer affords even a port for mariners, but seeks to mulct them in other ways, by means of octrois, duties and extortionate prices of provisions. Freight rates are thus made more prohibitive and shipowners usually prefer to dispatch their ships to the Mediterranean, sending them to the more recent salt fields of Sicily and the northern coast of Africa.

Meanwhile, the fields at Cádiz are permitted to harden and grow old, and are no longer able to repay in dry bread the interest of all the human labor that has been put into their excavation.

III

SEVILLE

GREAT cities nearly always have some peculiarity
which is invariably associated with them, imparting to every recollection of them a color and a mood,
sometimes even a slightly repellent flavor. There is,
for instance, the beer which flows sticky and odorous
of malt through München's gutters. There is the
penetrating noise of human voices echoing through
Naples day and night. In Rome, it is a soft murmur
of waters behind every wall; and who can behold
Venice in the mind's eye without picturing the *Campanile* as dominating the scene? The *Campanile*
towers over every memory of this city, though the beholder may remember quite well having seen the tower
in ruins at his feet.

There is something pleasing in the thought of a
tower which can evoke a whole city, floating like a song
over its hundreds of thousands of inhabitants, and remaining on its base though we know it has collapsed.
And every city has a tower to which such a place may
be assigned. Copenhagen has two such spires: that
of the Church of the Redeemer, and that of the City
Hall. But, in spite of their architectural beauties, not
all these towers have life and meaning in their
masonry; not all greet you from a distance as a sharp
far-seeing glance of the city itself, or constitute a lofty
background for every square, every petty alley.

In Seville, there is *La Giralda!* You can see *La*

Giralda thirty miles away in the flat region surrounding the city; and the peasants who work the blood-red earth in that part of the country point to it as they say with luminous eyes: "Look, there is Seville!" The tower flashes in the sunlight with its gayly colored tiles of *azulejos;* and beneath it, hazy under the horizon, lies the city celebrating. Some day in the future, when they have saved up enough money, then—long live joy! Long live happy Seville!

Up the narrow Guadalquivir, ships from Scandinavia, Germany, and England pick their course, crawling over sand banks with the waters of the stream and warping their way between rich flat meadows. On these meadows Gerion once grazed his celestial flocks, but he was obliged to consign them after a few days to the Elysian fields because too long a sojourn on our lowly sphere would have made them burst with fat. These meadows are now the property of the great cattle-breeding establishments which supply the many arenas of Spain; wild bulls with mighty horns graze on them. All tourists give this region a wide berth, and the only contact these animals have with human beings is when a horseman with a long pointed lance rides in among them in order to test their thirst for blood. He makes off as fast as he came, and the animals will gore the grassy ground in their impotent rage. Whenever a ship passes, they stalk down to the shore, stand still and bellow their challenge to the vessel. The jovial seamen—ordinarily so ready for fun—find no merriment in this. Each man will turn aside, count up his earnings in his own mind, and turn his eyes to *La Giralda.*

Thousands of foreigners who come here from all the

corners of the earth to *La Feria*—the Easter Fair—
and the great festivals of the Resurrection, which are
considered the most magnificent bullfights in the world,
lean far out of the windows of their railway compartments and shout their joy on beholding the shining tip
of the tower in the distance.

La Giralda is 350 feet high. A bright beacon of
joy, it sends its light afar, a message to the traveler.
At my foot lies a cliff on which it means happiness to
be shipwrecked at least once.

La Giralda means "the weathercock," "the weather-
vane." At the very top of the spire stands a bronze
figure—a woman! She is fourteen feet high, weighs
three thousand pounds, and represents Faith—and she
turns at the slightest wind!

What a symbol of the city at her feet!

Seville has a dazzling history and—like that of almost all the other cities of southern Europe—the tale
goes far back into antiquity.

From the beginning of history, this city has sparkled
in joyous sunlight, always festively clad, always celebrating and celebrated, always under the protecting
wing of the mighty Sun-god and the beautiful Goddess
of Love. Each year, as the sun reached the zenith of
his course, the image of the Goddess of Love was
borne through the streets of the city by the most distinguished beauties. Young girls who did not make
sacrifice without reserve to the goddess were sen-
tenced to death, but legend tells of only two such re-
calcitrants in all the periods of history—the sisters
Justa and Rufina. After a time, the gay population
transformed the two chaste sisters into saints. To this

day they are the patron saints of Seville and are wor-
shiped with that austere awe which men always accord
to that which is inaccessible to them.

The Mother of God has now assumed the obligations of the Sun-god in addition to all her other duties,
and of all the thirty incarnations in which she appears
at the present day, none is closer to the heart of the
Sevillano than *La Virgen de la Aurora,* the Madonna
of the Early Dawn. The Sevillano prefers not to go
to bed before her mass has been rung to announce a
new day.

Seville holds few reminders of its Roman period:
some slight remnants of city walls and baths; an aqueduct, which has been put into operation again; old
coins, which may be gathered by the handful wherever
the plow has drawn a furrow—as in all the places in
which the Romans once lived. Then there is the
splendid amphitheater *Italica,* a genuine Italian ruin
with great blocks of marble strewn about, with golden
maidenhair shuddering in the subterranean crypts, and
agile lizards flitting through every crevice in the
masonry. The festive mood of those old times has remained, that eternal cheerfulness which made this a
charming summer resort for jaded pleasure-seekers
even in the days of ancient Rome.

Nor did joy die of starvation during the terms in
which the city served as the royal camp of the Vandals,
and later of the Goths. Only, with the oncoming of
Moorish rule, a new era set in for Andalusia, in agriculture and industry, in art and science—all of which
flourished. A great irrigation system criss-crossed the
country with meshes as fine and as effective as the veins

in the human body. The hills were cut open and their precious minerals taken out; silkworms were bred; excellent universities were established; and the luxurious imagination of the Oriental fertilized the soil for the miraculous fairy-tale castles which shot into the air: the Alhambra, the Alcázar, the mosques of Córdoba and Seville.

Even merry Seville began to work in a sudden spurt of industry; it worked with gold and laces and silks. The silk industry alone is said to have employed 150,000 persons. From the mouth of the Guadalquivir, trading ships sailed forth, bringing to a Europe in darkness the tidings of Andalusia, a land of light, where industry, learning and tolerance prevailed; where Jews, Christians and Moors lived side by side in harmony.

But Moorish rule disappeared from Europe, leaving no more trace behind than a fair dream might leave. Seville shook off its enterprise like a nightmare, stripping itself in a trice of the effects of six-and-one-half centuries of civilization, and again proceeded to celebrate its feast days.

The Alcázar and *La Giralda* still stand; so do some of the Moorish walls which then encircled the city. The streets still have an oriental narrowness and their general direction is perpendicular to that of the sun. The houses are plastered white and are shut in, with cool yards growing narrower at the top in order to shut out the sun's rays.

But the Sevillano himself reminds one in no way of the Moors, neither of the active, highly-cultivated Moors of the Middle Ages, nor of their present-day

incompetent posterity, who sit with their legs crossed,
tailor-fashion, in the gutters of Morocco, basking in
the sunlight, gazing at nothing.

Only the homes are reminiscent of the Moorish
harem, for there the ladies of the upper class continue
to sit, lost in vague reveries, putting on fat. A whole
week may pass before you see a better-class Sevillian
woman walking through the street; and the city may
even appear—in spite of its reputation for beautiful
women—to be the city most devoid of beauty in the
world. On Sunday evening, however, beauty opens
up all its sluice-gates, and every *porte-cochère* is filled
with the charms of luxuriant females. At five o'clock,
the promenade along the Guadalquivir is swarming
with elegant glass coaches on rubber wheels, and in
each coach reclines an obese Sevillian dame, wide-eyed
and voluminous in silks and laces—a formidably
corseted beauty of the harem.

On the other six days of the week these rather portly
beauties—quite stylish in appearance, however—idle
about at home all day with hair unkempt, dressed in
calico kimonos, their only exercise a trip from living-
room to balcony, or vice versa. The Sunday outing reminds one of the weekly outing of the seraglio except
that in this instance onlookers are not driven away but
stand about in great numbers, representing all classes
of society. The Seville promenade is perhaps the only
one in the world which is meant for all the people.
Splendor here walks naturally and simply by the side
of modesty and poverty as if these qualities had arranged a meeting in this place. Here a mass of wan-
dering rags may be as proud as if the rags covered
a Spanish grandee. A dazzling beauty may have her

charms extolled to her face, but she receives such rude-
ness by no means ill. The wretched poor lap up the
splendor of wealth with an undisguised innocence in
which there is as yet no trace of proletarian hatred.
But they do not wallow in the dust before it; it has no
power over them. This perhaps is the reason why they
do not hate it.

The Sevillano lacks curiosity about all useful things.
But his mind is open enough for whatever may divert
and distract him, and the flow of human beings through
streets and squares produces a dual impression of careless loafing and restless bustle. Thousands of strangers
come to Seville every year; but the city still laughs with
childish amusement at each one. Wherever a foreigner walks, the natives, rich and poor alike, stand in
line, shouting harmless pleasantries to each other,
uttering fragments of English or German to the foreigner's face, even rudely jostling him if they can.
No one is too insignificant and rarely is any one so
dignified as not to take part in this popular sport.

If you enter a shop, it will be filled at once with
busybodies, and those who cannot force their way in
will stand about in the street. The tradesmen—if a
Sevillian shopkeeper may be dignified by this name—
will at once proceed to question the foreigner in the
interest of the onlookers; his nationality, how much
money he has, the purpose of his journey. Only after
reminding him repeatedly can you have any service.
"What a bunch of savages!" I once said to a book-
seller as I pointed to the curious crowd. *"Somos así;*
that's the way we are," was his somewhat brusque
answer.

And why criticize? They crowd about not to annoy

you because you are a stranger, but to be amused themselves. The stranger is the fuse that kindles pleasure. Why should this displease him? Among themselves no one is more pleased than he who serves as the butt of the joke.

When a city has many vaudeville theaters, you may be sure that city has little real merriment. The two hundred thousand inhabitants of Seville have no such theaters and do not need them. Their laughter is so easily aroused that it can be started with no cause at all. Introspection is a stranger to them. Ibsen, Björnsen, are regarded in Seville simply as comic writers who manage to keep a straight face while making sport of northern European pompousness and hypocrisy.

Seville is the home of bulls, bullfights, and bullfighters; the city of dancing, of fans, and of castanets. Late in the evening you can pick your way through the narrow streets, lured on by tinkling music, and land, not in a dance hall, but in a church with the priest standing before the altar celebrating mass, assisted by a solemn male choir. Whenever the chorus has sung a few stanzas in its dismal Miserere, there is a spasmodic interlude of castanets, tambourines, cymbals and triangles, sounding a dance of such seductive savageness as to dispel all piety and draw sparks from the eyes of the most demure madonnas. Then once more pious meditation possesses the wide spaces of the church, evoked by gloomy strophes, only to yield again in its turn, like an alternating shower-bath of flesh and spirit.

We had long been eager for an opportunity to witness Sevillian dances. The opportunity finally came.

The dance was given in the cathedral itself. For one entire week we saw ten boys dance before the high altar each evening in laudation of the Immaculate Conception. They were dressed in the costumes of pages of the Seventeenth Century and they sang and clicked their castanets as an accompaniment. It was so lovely that it was easy to understand how dance-loving Seville is so strongly attached to the unique church festival of *Los Seises,* which no other church in Catholic Christendom has permission to celebrate, and which several popes have tried in vain to stop.

Your merry Sevillano regards only one thing as sacred, and that thing is pleasure. Whatever subdues pleasure provokes his derision. What piety he has in his own spirit inspires him with blasphemous aspirations, which grow as his fear of God increases. Nowhere in irreverent Andalusia is there so natural and easy a union of the fear of God and contempt for Him in the same person as there is in Seville.

During our stay we lived at the house of two elderly ladies, sisters, and very poor. At every step we took they commended us to the protection of a saint. One day they besought us to go first to the cathedral before taking our day's trip, to pray the favor of the Madonna of Kings, patroness of excursions. This Madonna could perform great miracles. Indeed, a priest had once lifted her robe to see what she was made of and the Madonna had stricken him blind on the spot. "You see, she was only of wood," they explained, and laughed.

It was Seville that hit upon the idea that the confiscated Capuchin monastery would be devoted to the purpose least foreign to its original destination if it

were turned into a piggery. For can you not smell a
Capuchin further off than a pig, and is there any great
difference in color either? Every Sunday the Sevillano
journeys out of town to look over the hundreds of pigs
who now wallow in the cloister cells fattening hams
which, when soaked in wine and cured with herbs, will
bring a dollar the pound.

When the Teutonic custom of visiting cemeteries
and spending a few hours with the dear departed
reached Seville a few years ago, it was regarded simply
as a lark. All the respectable families, whether they
had relatives who were buried in the cemeteries or not,
would take their lunch baskets to the churchyard where
—as far away as they could get from the graves of
their loved ones—they held such feasts of joy that the
city authorities forbade the amusement.

In spite of its magnificent climate, Seville has the
highest mortality rate of all the large cities of Spain.
Other cities combat their death rate with sewerage
systems and sanitary measures; Seville has only its in-
destructible joy of life to oppose to death. The city
has also the highest birth rate, and suicide is unknown.
But these three facts, if we may trust the political
economists, are an unmistakable sign of cultural back-
wardness. Seville must have a low death rate, low
birth rate and more suicides before it may be counted
blessed with European civilization.

The rate of illegitimate births is also highest in
Seville, 17.4 per cent., as compared with 2.6 per cent.
for Barcelona. Priests elsewhere say this is an indication of moral corruption. But priests in Seville itself
say no such thing; they maintain that the city is the
foremost in Spain. Are not its women recognized as

the most beautiful in the country? Has not the city a cathedral which compares with the most celebrated churches in the world in its majestic beauty; and is it not esteemed by many architects as superior to the Church of St. Peter at Rome? Is there a population anywhere which places heavenly matters so confidently in the hands of its priests as does the population of Seville? Or is there anywhere a population which clings more tenaciously to its observance of the church holidays?

Seville has one hundred and thirty feast days each year and the other days can hardly be called real work-days. But even these one hundred and thirty days are not sufficient to give expression to the city's joy, and the streets resound nightly with songs and tinklings, and the call of the blood.

Night in Seville is too beautiful to be described!

It is now December. This is winter: the Andalusian winter, with sunlight and a blue sky. But the sun cannot reach into the narrow streets and deep courts; it is miserably cold inside the houses, and all living things take refuge on the public squares and on the banks of the Guadalquivir. In the narrow streets, poor women on their knees are scrubbing the sidewalks and the lower parts of the walls. This process is part of the weekly cleaning-up. Dogs and children wallow in garbage heaps which have accumulated, at every point where streets radiate, and form something like a little playground. An athletic young man is walking from house to house, ringing each doorbell and asking— whether this letter belongs to you. "You see, I cannot read," he adds by way of excuse, and proceeds to ring the next doorbell. His feet are bare and he has a big blanket wrapped around his head as a protection from the cold.

Men dash out of all the houses, their cloaks held tightly over their mouths as they hurry down the street. When they meet an acquaintance they make a swift gesture with their hands as they rush past. If a stranger should ask them the way, they would utterly discard their Spanish courtesy and make no reply. Congealed breath hangs from their mustaches and drips down unnoticed on the gorgeous velvet of their cloaks, their cigarettes are poised neglected on their ears, and their glances are fixed with terror. They have barely a shrug for the political notices posted at the corners of the street. They hurry along, taking up as little space as possible, their cloaks held tightly to their mouths, pursued by an invisible—perhaps an imaginary—enemy: tuberculosis.

But in the patches of sunlight in front of señorita's bedchamber, the gnats perform their dance of blood, so far removed are they from actual cold. And as she steps out on the balcony to catch a glimpse of a sighing admirer, the spots on her face announce the source of the blood-thirsty enthusiasm of the little beasts.

But no sighing worshipers are to be seen—it is too cold. Hunger cannot dampen the Sevillano's love of life; neither can care; only one thing can cool his ardor: weather! On a day like this the Sevillano has no eye for the ladies; he passes under their balconies without a glance and refuses to halt except in some public square where the sun can bake him. There he will find a sympathetic group of men, warm up, begin to talk a little, and finally blossom forth in all his

native simplicity—a true sunflower. He will allude
with a sickly smile to "that damned polar winter of
Arabia," where the night is six months long and the
day also six months long; and to Old Castile, the
coldest place on earth. In his boundless joy at having
recovered himself again, he is ready even for excesses;
he will visit a café and drink thick chocolate from
diminutive cups, or invite his best friend to a pastry
shop and share three cents' worth of candy with him.

A crowd of women come strolling out of the silent
semi-darkness of the streets. They wear thin black
shawls with long fringes, are bareheaded and have
paper flowers in their black hair. Some of them are
very pretty, but poverty is not in the habit of breeding
beauty here more than elsewhere. Some are pock-
marked, some have lost an eye, many have wide plasters on both temples; every one of them has distended
nostrils and watchful eyes, seeking a prey for her
laughter. They trip along, a flock of bluejays, babbling and laughing. They crack jokes on the dandies'
thin legs, throw the donkey-driver from his saddle as
they go by, gather in groups about the foreigner, and
throw kisses to the fat priest who quickly disappears
with a suppressed chuckle behind the heavy curtain of
the church door. Everything is a source of laughter
for them, a limping dog, a coffin, a sneezing beggar.

They do not timidly cover up their mouths, but open
them wide and eagerly suck in all the air's ingredients
of sunlight and cold, contagious substances and stench.
Their high-arched, provocative breasts offer defiance
to the world and to all lung troubles. "Come, I shall
press you to me, even though you be Death himself,
and I will then cast you off like an empty lemon." This

is the challenge of their bearing. They pick up little naked children, kiss them all over their bodies and hand them about from arm to arm. At the sight of a handsome man they will gnash their teeth passionately —but they will sling mud at a beautiful woman.

These are *las cigarreras,* the tobacco workers, the soul of Seville. They constitute an army of about five thousand, whose oldest member is past a century; the youngest, fourteen.

When speaking to strangers, the Sevillano passes lightly over the tobacco girl, but in the depth of his heart he admires and worships her with a sort of complacent awe. She is care-free, naughty, godless; she is ruthless in her passion, witty, mobile of mind, skillful; she is the incarnation of all the frivolous qualities of the city, elevated to the nth degree. The Sevillano could not deny her without casting a stone at his own house, and no Spaniard would do that.

In his innermost spirit, every serious Spaniard is filled with the conviction that revolution is the only solution for anything, and he feels keenly the disgrace of continuing to stagnate in inactivity. But thanks to the tobacco girl, Seville has no need to be so much ashamed of itself. The tobacco worker is always ready for an insurrection; it is her hand that throws the first stone; it is her mouth that utters the kindling cry of battle. She is the bubbling spirit of unrest, the provocative element of disturbance within the state. And whenever the cork pops out, it is she that serves both as the report and the foam; she is everything that is terrifying to women and delightful to men.

When Alfonso XII visited Seville about forty years ago, and the republican population of the city, filled with shame, showed his majesty the customary honors, the self-respect of the city was saved by the five thousand tobacco girls, who received the king with merciless laughter when he visited the great tobacco factory. On a later occasion, being unable to arrive at a satisfactory agreement with the powerful director of the factory on the wage question, they carried the hearts of the working people by storm with their convincing and logical action. They simply slung a rope about their director's body and suspended him down a deep well. More than once *las cigarreras,* crawling on all fours, have picked up the offal of the streets as their only weapon against the swords and revolvers of the mounted police. And it is largely due to the behavior of these insolent creatures that it is now impossible to secure admission to the great church festivals without first obtaining a certificate from the priest of the church.

But all these things require no forgiving. The people themselves, who have been maltreated both by the state and the church, and who find their revolutionary tendencies and their love of blasphemy so well embodied in these pock-marked, one-eyed Valkyries, are—contrary to all tradition—decent enough not to leave them in the lurch.

The tobacco girl is the spoiled child of the nation for another reason also: her economic function. The Spaniard associates with her the fragrance which he values above all things—the smell of nicotine. How highly the Spaniard estimates tobacco may be judged from the fact that a beggar is just as certain to receive alms when he asks for a penny for tobacco, as when he states that he is starving.

All the remarkable qualities possessed by alcohol in Denmark are assigned in Spain to tobacco. Tobacco appeases hunger and stimulates the appetite; tobacco keeps you awake or puts you to sleep; tobacco acts as a laxative or as an astringent—all depending on your immediate needs. "Where's a cigarette?" is what people say when some one falls sick, as in our country they would say, "Where's some whiskey?" Moist tobacco leaves are spread over cuts and wounds.

The first thing a Spaniard does in the morning after opening his eyes is to fumble in the dark for a cigarette, kindle it and then stick it to his lower lip. There it continues to hang, sending aloft its little blue rings of smoke while he speaks, when he coughs and sneezes, sometimes even when he eats and drinks. It is the sacred flame that never dies. Its last spark is the fire that passes on to kindle a new cigarette; and he resorts to the cigarette between every two mouthfuls of food. The cigarette is attached to his lips all day long. Often he smokes in bed until he falls asleep and wakes to find the cigarette, ready for lighting, under his nose the next morning.

It is a mighty poor smoker that will simply puff out the tobacco smoke in the usual pusillanimous manner. Any one with pretensions to manhood will exhale the smoke through his nose as through a discharge pipe; professional smokers, however, inhale the smoke and then sit with their mouths open playing the smoke to and fro with their tongues.

Some persons believe it possible to attack a national evil by imposing a tax on it. In Spain the right to supply tobacco has been conferred on a few capitalists, chiefly foreigners: this is the Tobacco Company, which must give the nation in return an annual bonus of eighteen million dollars. Although climate and soil are excellently adapted for the raising of tobacco, the peasant is not permitted to plant the seed even for his own use. The Company spends an additional twelve million dollars in order to enforce this provision and to guard the borders of the country against smugglers. After obtaining these thirty million dollars, additional funds must be applied to the purchase of raw materials and to the process of manufacture; profits have to be assured to retailers and the Company itself must secure a handsome income. It would be no exaggeration to state that the amount that goes up in smoke annually in Spain is much more than fifty million dollars.

There is smoking in the theaters during the performance; in banks, post-offices and municipal bureaus. Every one down to the merest clerk has his cigarette in his mouth. The barber smokes while shaving his customer; the waiter carelessly flicks off his ashes while serving at table; the public speaker will halt in the middle of his most incendiary utterance to take a puff at his cigarette. During mass, the priest will slink away behind the altar to light his cigarette, and the same priest will carry his lighted cigarette through the streets, concealed in the wide sleeve of his robe. Children receive a regular allowance of tobacco from their parents; old women sit in the sunlight outside the villages, chewing the butt of an old cigar. Everybody smokes, in spite of the tax. Those that have no money go about collecting moist cigarette butts; and it is not unheard-of to have men, garbed in long cloaks, following you for a quarter of an hour hoping that you may throw away your cigar.

Red flags flap in the wind wherever *las cigarerras* go. Idleness and long glances follow in their wake. They issue forth in bands from Triana, Macarena and other suburbs, clicking their tongues, scratching their black hair and laughing. Down by the river, all their merry bands unite to enter a huge structure that cost more than two million dollars to build. This edifice is surrounded by a deep moat, the inner defenses of which are guarded with little sentry towers having long, narrow loopholes, while on the ground floor of the building a military detachment is noisily evident. The building reminds one of a penitentiary. It is regarded by the government as a sort of dynamite cache; it is the tobacco factory.

In the great arched foyer the sentry is busy examining a few workers who are about to leave. They stand with their arms raised over their heads while the guard goes through their pockets.

We pass up a broad stone staircase into the interior of the building proper, from which double doors lead into the various wings. The guards here are women, gigantic creatures that could be produced only in the south. The leader of the guards, to whose care we are assigned, appears to have been intended—judging by her physique—for the felling of oxen with a single blow, or for holding on her lap the most rebellious of tobacco girls while she frisks her to see whether anything has been stolen.

From all sides comes a subdued, vehement buzz as if the air were full of wasps. When our leader opens one of the great doors the effect is that of lifting out a sluice-board in a weir. A heated gust of noise and stench envelops us, deprives us of all air, all mental concentration, almost of all consciousness. We find ourselves, without knowing how it came about, suddenly staring down a tunnel five hundred feet long, in which four rows of women are seated side by side, close together over their tobacco troughs.

As they look up, their faces shine white in the brown mist of tobacco, and the noise ceases as with a single stroke. They stare at the stranger with wide-open eyes and mouths, while their fingers roll the cigarettes with a speed that affects our eyes like the flicker of a moving picture. Now two heads incline to meet and a whisper shoots along the rows. One can follow it like an undulating wave, until it encounters the saint's image at the end of the tunnel, where it rebounds and again passes down the rows—suddenly to be thrown into our faces in the form of a saucy question uttered in a burst of laughter. Once more the bustle bubbles over, the composite racket of hundreds of laughing, chatting, scolding groups, surging up in shrill falsettos while the robust female guardians pass through the rows to maintain order.

It is here that the merry mood of Seville gives forth its gayest blossoms; they sprout from the envenomed soil in dazzling bloom. Under this single low barrel-vault, fifteen hundred women are working. Many thousands of pounds of tobacco cover tables and troughs, but there is not a single opening to admit fresh air. The tobacco dust blinds our eyes and the exhalations of tobacco and of human beings will not permit us to breathe. Although I am a hardened smoker, I had such a pounding headache after a few moments spent in this place that I thought my eyes would pop out of my head. My mental powers weakened; I was no longer capable of grasping my environment, of collecting it and retaining it in an image; I was inspired with one thought only, to get back into the open air.

Suddenly a peculiar sound meets my ear, frightening every thought out of my head. It is the well-known thump of a cradle moved by a human foot. And sure enough, there is a cradle, close by us, almost hidden under troughs and work-tables—an old wooden cradle, its rockers worn shiny. The woman who is moving the cradle with her foot is pale, with white plasters pasted over her temples to deaden her headache. There is brown tobacco dust in her hair and over the white cradle linen, and edging the little distended nostrils of the child. But the child sleeps peacefully in spite of the noise and the venomous air. There is even a faint glow of red on its cheeks, and a smile bursts forth at every moment through the distorted features of the mother's face, illuminating them like sunlight on a white-washed wall.

There are other cradles along the length of the tunnel—not less than forty. In some, the children are sitting up and playing with tobacco leaves as if they had already learned the business. As I bend down over one of the little ones, and it is frightened, a woman is heard to say: "Don't you even know your own father?" They all laugh loudly, but the mother in question regards me attentively for a moment and then shakes her head with a smile.

Some of the children really have a father, who helps them eat up their mother's earnings; these are not the most fortunate of children. Others have only a mother, and this mother affords them the advantage

of training them early in life for their future occupation. The children give evidence of the most affectionate care, and if they survive the intolerably venomous stench, they will no doubt ultimately occupy a place
by the side of their mothers and pedal cradles as their
mothers have before them, nurse babies, and roll three
thousand cigarettes a day—provided they are girls.
But if they are boys, it will be their ineluctable duty to
hang about the street corners smoking incessantly until
they have reached the ultimate proficiency—which
means two hundred cigarettes per day. If they attain
an even higher level, they will be entitled to take their
places in the ranks of those young men who wait every
evening outside the tobacco factories, shouting to the
girls as they come out, and who are dragged along
with the raging torrent of humanity out into the darkness of the suburbs, where you encounter them shuffling
about in the dawn of the next morning, looking like
blue specters.

There are angels who can live on attenuated ether,
as well as bacteria that will flourish only in deep
sewers; but is there any creature anywhere that has
the vitality of man? In defiance of all the laws of
hygiene, here sit three generations of women side by
side, lulling to sleep the fourth generation. We are
shown a fourteen-year-old mother who is just giving
the breast to her screaming first born; and near her,
an old woman one hundred and six years old, who for
the last eighty has been working in the tobacco factory.

Christmas is coming; in a few days the holiday will
be at hand.

On the Danish steamer which lies at the wharf, taking on a cargo of iron ore, you hear the last mortal

screech of the Christmas geese, while in the narrow
streets of Seville peasants are guarding their flocks
of turkeys. Occasionally, an electric tramcar creeps
along, gently driving these fowl ahead of it into the
nearest public square.

Christmas is at hand; I have felt it all week in the
growing restlessness which replaces the usual care-free
spirit of the rest of the year. The word Christmas
(*Navidad*) is on every man's lips in this country and
in every man's thoughts. The stiff Spaniards in dignified drapery who daily gather to fume over the change
of cabinet or the latest bullfighter, now amble about
as excited as if they were really looking for work. Or
they may stand alone in front of some wall counting
out their change and assembling it from the various
pockets of their vests. If they converse at all, it will
be on the subject of money and *Navidad*. I have even
seen them do, these last few days, what is ordinarily
left to the women; in full public view they kneel down
for hours before the Madonna or before some other
saint in the cathedral, murmuring the word *Navidad*
to themselves. The beggar says *Navidad* as he puts
out his hand; my washerwoman stammers words of ex-
cuses as I catch her in the act of charging me double
prices; and all the women who are gathered with huge
bundles before the entrance of the government pawn-
shops have only the single word *Navidad* to exchange,
accompanied by nods of understanding.

The whole world is so completely involved in
Navidad, in the approaching Christmas feast, that you
imagine you have never before witnessed such powerful and all-embracing piety.

Suddenly you remember that *Navidad* no longer

means Christmas at all, but "the lottery"—the great
Christmas lottery.

It is early morning, time of the arrival of mail from
Madrid. Streets and squares are full of people; in the
Calle Sierpes—the Corso of Seville—they stand round
the yard of the post office like a solid wall. And suddenly the tension of the last few days is released, engulfing the city with hosts of blind men, women in rags,
half-naked boys; all have their little wads of lottery
tickets in their hands, and the air trembles with shouts
of *"Navidad! El gordo! El gordo!"* the shouts rising like rockets on all sides. *El gordo* means: the
luscious morsel, the fat meat, the big killing!

Here comes a dirty priest, and here a mountainous
female, her face covered with flour dust—each of
them buys a little ticket, paying two hundred dollars
a piece for them. The Commandant of the city comes;
so does the Civil Governor; the Archbishop, the bank
director; so do all the other notables. Each buys his
two-hundred-dollar ticket and makes off for the nearest
church to sprinkle it with holy water. The priest himself seems to feel less need of holy water; instead, he
spits on his tickets three times, for luck.

And the shopkeepers come also. They have clubbed
together in groups of ten, because they can raise only
twenty dollars each, and the government will sell only
whole tickets, not, as in Germany or Denmark, half-
tickets, or quarter-tickets, or even one-eighth-tickets.
Among the workingmen, a hundred of them may club
together to purchase a single ticket, and the poor of
the city form stock corporations with a thousand members, each investing twenty cents (one peseta).

Soon the government selling stations are all sold

out; then follows the stage of petty jobbery between man and man, in which large or small fractions of a single ticket pass from hand to hand at prices that are constantly increasing. All trade, all business enterprise, centers about the lottery; if any one really does any serious work, that is, if he steals something or commits some other offense, you may be sure that *el gordo* is behind it, the fat morsel of over five million pesetas ($1,000,000) for which the whole country, standing on its toes, is gaping and gnashing its teeth. With a tension that is driven to fever heat by means of artificial excitation, the days pass until Christmas Eve, the hour when the drawings are made. Now certain ones will be transported to heaven; thousands will collapse in despair. And the Christmas holidays will drag by in dull apathy until Twelfth Night—the Festival of the Three Kings—when the first drawing of the new year is made, and life again becomes worth while to mortals.

There are three drawings every month in the Spanish lottery, all a matter of tense excitement to the whole nation. But no drawing is so exciting as this one on Christmas Eve, for which forty thousand tickets at two hundred dollars each sell like hot cakes. This drawing costs the people of the country about eight million dollars; to many of those who play the lottery, the loss of their investment is not more serious than the drooping of an eyelid; but some sacrifice the warm feathering of their nests; others, the nest itself. Of this sum of eight million dollars, about three million remain in the national treasury, while the rest is distributed by the wheel of fortune in the form of winnings that are so large as to pour oil on the fire of

the Spanish gambling spirit.   In addition to a few
thousand bonuses running from one thousand to about
four thousand dollars, and thirty-four small takings of
from ten thousand to twenty thousand dollars, the
Christmas lottery offers the great prizes of 50,000,
100,000, 200,000, 400,000, and 750,000 dollars—and
finally, *el gordo,* the fat morsel of a whole million.

Just as other governments devote themselves to the
task of stimulating the principal business activities of
the country—England its trade, Denmark its agriculture—so the Spanish government is concerned chiefly
with fostering the gambling spirit of the people, and
by lotteries alone has encouraged a turnover of about
one hundred million dollars a year.   By the Spanish
government, this is counted a genuine achievement.

It is a simple and a grateful task.

Every Spaniard has a thirst for surprises, which
produces in him a fabulous activity of mind; his character is like a great heart, alternating between violent
excitement and profound dejection.   To maintain himself in health, he needs a constant succession of hot
and cold shower baths, a leap to the point of the
greatest hope and a plunge into the deepest despair.
Life must offer him strong stimuli, and likewise complete lassitude; he is not addicted to habitual afternoon siestas, and a complacent life of porridge is repellent to him.   The sun must blaze hot and love must
come to the point of using the knife.   He is little concerned with alcohol, for he is not interested in dulling
his spirits; he seeks his forms of excitement chiefly
in the domain of mental irritations—he is a born
gambler.

There is the peculiar direction taken by the practical gifts of the Spaniard, particularly the practical gifts of the Andalusian. The Spaniard has little desire for material enjoyments; he has no appreciation of placid comforts and despises the way to their attainment: the method of slow, peaceful progress. The peseta coin which he finds in the street or obtains by begging is a far more agreeable object to him than the ninety-nine righteous pesetas gotten by personal exertions, for this peseta he finds is for him a symbol—as it were—of happiness, which comes from without, which must seek him unsought. For this reason his plans have very little continued direction; he never works for a distant goal, or for long intervals, but only by spurts—that is, only until the great lottery number falls due. For there is no doubt that he will be the lucky man some day.

A locomotive driver and a locomotive fireman, who were playing the lottery together, were driving a passenger train northward to Madrid on the day before Christmas, the day of the great drawing. During a stop at a certain station, a stop that was to last a few minutes, they obtained a list of the successful numbers. They learned that their number was one of the lucky ones, whereupon they abandoned the locomotive at once, leaving the train and its hundreds of Christmas passengers to take care of themselves.

Progressive newspapers in Spain write savage articles attacking the Christmas lotteries and the national fever that comes with them; they draw the darkest picture of the Spanish gambling nature and predict disastrous consequences to the economic future of the nation. But after every drawing, these same newspapers will give to their readers precise reports of the persons that have won the prizes, even though the amount may in some cases be not more than fifteen thousand dollars, divided among ten individuals. These papers have a perfect system of espionage, the excellence of which is a matter of great pride with them. No paper in Germany or Denmark that reports some wretched political trifle one day ahead of its contemporaries could be more ridiculously proud of such a scoop than the Spanish paper which has succeeded in getting the names of the winners ahead of its rivals. The telegraph system is resorted to, and your paper may inform you as follows:

Malaga, January 14, 17 o'clock.

Your correspondent in this city has succeeded in ascertaining that the two tenths of the 75,000 did not fall—as was reported by another newspaper in the capital—to Coachman Cenizo and his brother—but to a hotel keeper and his male servant. There has been no denial of the six tenths which we succeeded in revealing yesterday. Of the remaining two tenths, one is said to have fallen to the lot of a sailor; but we regret that we have not been able to learn anything about the second winner.

(Latest telegram) The final tenth—we are now happy to be able to report definitely—was won by Policeman Number 14, Don Enrico Manuel Barato.

In this country, it is not alcohol that piles up jail sentences, but gambling; and most of the penalties imposed on prisoners when they transgress the prison regulations are for gambling.

"It can't be wiped out, do what you will!" the prison inspector of Granada said one day, as we stood on a balcony over the prison yard. "We have severe penalties for all kinds of gambling among the prisoners, we confiscate any object that they might want to gamble for or that they might use as an aid in gambling; but all penalties and measures are useless. Just look over here!" he suddenly interrupted himself, seizing me by the arm.

Two prisoners were sitting on the ground in the corner under the balcony, their faces turned toward each other, their legs spread far apart, the soles of their feet touching; without eyes or ears for anything else, their eyes were fixed rigidly upon a circle that had been drawn on the ground in the space enclosed by their legs. And what was it they were looking at?

"Why, you see," said the inspector, "each one of them has just caught a louse, and they have put the lice in the center of the circle and the man whose louse first succeeds in getting out of the circle has won the bet. Can you tell me what to do with such creatures?"

"Keep on confiscating!" I said, with a slight smile.

But he did not understand me and continued seriously:

"What use? Their ruling passion makes them inventive. But—to change the subject—have you been at the Officers' Club lately? You really must go— nothing but gentlemen; any one of them would rather blow his brains out than cheat at cards. So you may feel quite secure on that score. I'll introduce you to the members to-night—but you must be ready for real business. Be sure to bring real money with you!"

IV

CÓRDOBA

WE have been in Seville for a whole month, but our stay cannot last forever. Shortly after the opening of the new year we make up our minds, drive for the last time through this city which has held our senses slave, and take our seats in the train for Córdoba.

The time for the train's departure has come, but the train does not budge. A quarter-hour passes, a half-hour; people are still arriving and getting into the train but there is no passenger here who glares at the newcomers from his seat, none that claps his hand on the compartment door to keep out the new arrivals, or who trips them up as they toilsomely clamber in with their baggage.

"There's room here, come this way!" they cry to the helpless one, though all the seats are taken. And if he hesitates, some one shouts:

"Get in, get in; my dear man, I'm only going to the next station and don't mind standing a bit." Hands ready to serve seize his luggage and stow it under the seats and the man himself follows after—hot, dripping with perspiration, his back to the other window. He was the last-comer; he insists he will stand, nothing is so good for him as standing; in fact, his physician has ordered him to stand! But the other passengers will not consent; just because he is the last to come he shall not stand—after all they are not rowdies! And they oblige him to take a seat by all getting up themselves.

We feel a secret itch—we always do when we travel on Spanish railroads—a longing for a row. And we are a little ashamed afterwards of the strange stirring!

Every new passenger at once joins in the conversation, which touches on all subjects twixt heaven and earth except the lateness of trains, a matter which concerns no one.

Finally the bell rings and the train rolls out of the station. A man dashes over the platform, jumps on to the train as it moves, and clings to the last car. He climbs along the outside of the cars to the door of our compartment, and enters. He is hot with rage at the poorness of the service. Has it not always been understood that this train was not to leave less than an hour after its schedule? He shows us his steel watch, gesticulates as he scolds, but the other passengers give him tobacco and calm him with their good-natured sly digs. Is he an Englishman then? Was his father perhaps a watchmaker, that he should concern himself so with minutes?

The compartments are separated from each other only by low partitions open at the top. We can look through the whole car. On the floor, and on some of the seats, hand baggage has been piled to the ceiling: bags and great sacks and rough blankets. Some of the travelers have brought bed linen and great leather wine-pouches and monstrous traveling bags; these are the people bound for the northern provinces to look for work. They dress like Swedish peasants, in tight-fitting jackets of black velvet, but they have sandals woven of vine-tendrils on their feet and around their necks huge folded blankets, which they pull forward as far as possible, so that the tips touch the ground. Sometimes a collar has been sewn on one hem of the four-cornered blanket, which is provided with a hook to fasten it about the neck like a rudimentary cloak. Every one smokes; and whoever rolls a cigarette for himself first offers it to every one in the compartment.

All are restless—like eight-year-old boys. They toss from side to side and take every position except sitting in their places. They lean far out of the windows, lie on the tops of the benches, crawl over partitions from one compartment to another; talk to themselves or emit hollow bellowings of contentment. Ear-splitting conversations are carried on from one end of the car to the other. Like all southerners, they have powerful lungs and are talking chiefly of money; but the sums mentioned are not to be taken seriously.

I can tell by their clothes and their skins that some are workers from the city or country, while others are petty officials and tradesmen, or teachers. Otherwise, they are marked by no differences of language or manner; the man in working clothes will conduct himself with as much refinement as the gentleman. There is no relationship of inferior or superior in their attitude toward each other; they all move on the same familiar level. They show something approaching reserve with regard to us only.

An old woman in rags, carrying many bundles, wishes to leave the car at a small provincial station. A well-dressed gentleman gathers all her things next to the door of the compartment, then gets out himself and takes out her bundles one after the other. Finally he takes her in his arms, lifts her out and carries her for a few steps before he sets her down, laughing, on the platform. He comes back to the compartment. The old woman looks after him with tears in her eyes and says aloud to some youngsters, possibly her grandchildren, as they greet her: "How kind he was to me, an old wretch—and yet he never lay by me!"

Although we have barely entered the new year, it is warm as summer and the dust whirls up from the road-bed and tickles our nostrils. Whenever we sneeze, the well-dressed persons say: "To your health!" while those with the blankets say: "*Jesús, María y José!*" which exposes their rural origin. But they address each other as *caballero* and hospitably offer one a share in their frugal meal: some bread and a piece of apple or melon. A leather pouch containing wine cir-culates over the partitions; it passes from mouth to mouth, the consumers holding it above them at arm's length, as the liquid curve descends into their mouths.

We proffer our lunch baskets to those around us, which immediately puts us in good grace. With their great curved knives they cut off little slices of our pastry and eat of it, but they definitely decline meat and eggs.

"*Carramba!*"—they say to each other—"the deuce you say! are these people Englishmen? They are al-most as well behaved as we are."

"No, we are from Denmark."

"From where? Denmark! I know! That is a province in northern Spain?"

"No, it is a country by itself far to the north of northern Spain."

"But they speak Spanish there, do they not?"

"Not at all. They speak Danish."

"Are you speaking Danish now?"

"No, it is meant to be Spanish."

"Excellent Spanish," they hasten to assure me courteously. "But—isn't it France? or North America?—England perhaps?" The expressions of their faces show that they have exhausted their whole map of earth.

"No," say I, offended, "it is an independent country, and a country with rich soil—a real tub of butter. If you used butter in your porridge as other civilized nations do, you would not be ignorant of Denmark: the entire civilized world takes the spread for its bread from us. And we have a real king of our own."

They do not say outright that I am lying abominably, but their glances give them away. Fortunately I can prove my statement. I produce a Spanish newspaper and run through the telegrams. Here you have it in print: "King Oscar of Denmark desires to abdicate in favor of his eldest son." The sheet goes from hand to hand, until it finally reaches, in the third compartment from us, a man who is able to read. He reads the item aloud, and there is a moment of silence.

"How big the world is after all," one of the men says, "and how remarkable!" And again all the tongues are loosed.

My national pride has sustained a severe shock, but I seek to collect myself. Once before in Granada a postal official was also completely ignorant of my native country; and yet, the things I sent home by mail arrived in due course. In fact, I cannot be certain that I have ever met any one that really knew of Denmark except a few German tourists who thought that we spoke German at home. Our most important contribution to world economy, our butter, is obtainable in all southern countries under the trade name of "Flemish butter"; and our great Danes stroll up and down in these parts, always being taken for German dogs. In Venice I have seen Englishmen and Americans melt with sentimentality over the songs of Christian Winther, set to the music of Johann Peter Emilius Hartmann; but the inside of the title-page bore the remark: "From a German Romanza." British school textbooks of history describe King Canute the Great as an English king, who conquered Denmark and Norway. And in German histories of German literature, the "Golden Horns" figure as the earliest monuments of the German language! The great nations are like whales; they open their jaws and consume everything without a thought; floating bottles and tin cans as well as fishes and mollusks. They are not very discerning in their taste; otherwise we might season ourselves with a slightly bitter flavor to ward off their attentions. At present, we can only hope that they may find us indigestible and later eject us more or less intact.

So I consoled myself; and I made up my mind not to tear the bandage from the eyes of my compatriots at home, but to let them live and die confidently believing that the rest of the world expects great things from us and regards us as the most enlightened people on earth.

While Denmark leads its shadowy non-existence apart, another little country constantly attracts attention to itself, Switzerland. Every day it is mentioned in progressive newspapers and by progressive politicians, for its situation and its institutions. It has a halo of ideals—ideals of the future. Depressing this is for the Dane, sallying forth into the world, with mind and heart full of homespun self-eulogy. So it is. We cannot change things.

The Spaniards, too, are a self-confident nation, but they do not care for the judgment of the world. They too are the most excellent and enlightened people of the earth, but they take no pains to explain why. They simply state their characteristics—*basta!* And each of them acts precisely as he pleases, indifferent to the judgments of others as if none existed his superior or his equal.

While the train rolls along, the door of our compartment is opened by one of the passengers, who steps out on the running-board. He has an acquaintance in one of the cars ahead, and crawls along the outside of the train to meet him. The conductor tries to stop him, but he will not listen. The man sitting opposite me deposits his dirty feet on the seat next to me time and time again. The conductor tries to stop him, too, nor will he listen either. I soon learn to say nothing on such occasions, but I do indulge in a motion which throws his legs to the floor, whereupon he calmly hoists them back. I decide finally to use vigorous methods, to make evident to him—by means of an exaggeration of his own act—how inconsiderate he is; I place both my feet in his lap. At once he removes his legs from my seat and sits up respectably—but only to make things more comfortable for me and my feet!

Meals are frequent, but they eat very little at a time. The food is frugal—dry bread and a little fruit; at most, some tomato pickle is spread over the bread. They use no other relish. One or two have a bite of bacon-sausage or eggs. Whoever drops a piece of bread will pick it up hastily, kiss it two or three times and then devour it. I have observed the same touching apology among the peasantry in Denmark. If a fruit or piece of meat falls to the floor, it will be kicked under the bench; it is not valued, and the floor is very dirty. But bread is sacred.

We leave the flat Sevillian landscape behind us. The soil begins to roll and undulate. We no longer meet familiar people at the stations; those who enter the compartment here have sharper features, more reserved expressions, more conservative clothing. They carry balls of living chickens, tied together by the legs, their heads reaching out on all sides like flowers in a huge bouquet. Sacks of flour are thrown in, as well as lambs, tied together in pairs by their hind legs. A few dogs secure admission, establish themselves under the seats and sniff about our heels. The men wear knee-breeches, sandals, jackets that do not reach below the belt, and rakish hats; they are smooth-shaven and frequently pock-marked; there are a number of gypsies among them.

As soon as I travel in the mountains, I begin to make mistakes in my judgments of age; time appears unable to create definite generations here. Young and old are equally old-fashioned in costume and manners, equally young in bearing and gesture. You have color of hair and skin, and wrinkles only, to serve as guide to your guessing, and these are deceptive. Those two old men sitting opposite us are as active and slender as men of twenty, but their close, short-cropped hair is sprinkled with gray, hinting of half a century; and the few white specks in their eyes inform me that they are much older still.

"How old are you, *Caballero?*" I ask one of the pair, intending to flatter him. I am quite sure he is an earth-digger.

"*Compadre, amigo!* I am seven species and five marks (eighty-nine years old), and my son here is exactly six species (seventy-two years old)." He points smilingly at the other old man who nods with child-like respectfulness.

"You must have become a father when very young," I exclaim, after having calculated with great difficulty the age equivalent of the moneys he had mentioned.

"There are people who go about it even much earlier. Up in our village a couple have just been married; he is sixteen and she thirteen. They were lovers for several years and their parents were anxious to have them married before anything should go wrong; but it was impossible to do so, because the law did not permit it. She was over twelve all right, but of course he had to be sixteen. There was nothing else to do but proceed at once from the marriage ceremony to the baptism, which shows clearly enough what the whole law is worth."

"Aren't such early marriages quite exceptional?" I say.

"Not when I was young; but now they are not favored. People say the children are not worth much. This fellow turned out very well, though; I vouch for him in every respect." He took his son gayly by the shoulders and shook him. "But true, there is not much juice or energy in young people nowadays."

"I don't suppose a sixteen-year-old husband can support a wife and child very well?"

"Neither can a forty-year-old in Spain—at least not

by honest labor.   You need first to cut off twenty-five
thousand of the highest heads.   But it will come—the
revolution will come—you will see.   We will have a
republic, and the authorities will come to me and my
friends and say: If you please, you have tilled the
count's soil for all these years, while he has devoured
the crops; now it is yours, and you may eat up everything that grows on it!   If you wish to send your children to the university, you may; the doors are open.
Or, if you wish to take a trip to the Alhambra, or up
to Madrid, you have only to take the train.   For the
task of the new government will be, not to seek
strength for itself from the bread that we supply, but
to help us get our own food.   Come and see!   Come
and taste!   It will be a fine life."

His offspring nodded in agreement; he had sat with
a question on his lips for some time, but remained respectfully silent.   Now he hastens to break in: "Do
you know Kropotkin?   He must be from the same
country as you?"

"No, but I know his works.   Have you really read
Kropotkin?"

"I have not read him, for father and I cannot read.
But my son-in-law reads him to us at home in the village, at the revolutionary club of the farm-workers.
They are good books, particularly *La Conquista del
Pan* ('The Conquest of Bread').   He is a man, I tell
you; here's his picture."   He takes a Spanish anarchist
paper from his pocket and shows us Kropotkin's picture.

"Yes," says the father, "if we only had men like
him.   But our big men sell themselves for money.   We
are left without leaders.   Our roots are sound.   The

top of the tree is rotten; that's the trouble. The Spanish people are the finest in the world, but they have the worst government."

"But there is an old proverb that says that a nation always has the government which it deserves," I interpose.

"Old proverbs say a lot of things, Señor. But we also have a new proverb: If plant lice get into the vines on our hills, we dig out the vines with their roots, so that the eggs of the insects may not float down in the rain water and damage the entire valley. That is what our new proverb says; but the old proverb taught us to do nothing against the vine lice, for they had been inflicted upon us for our sins. Well, so long, my friend, and a happy voyage!"

They leave the compartment. I follow their slender forms as they trudge along under their heavy burdens through the lime-dust of the road, until they disappear behind an olive grove.

The far south of Spain inherits from the Moors a love for dazzling whiteness. When you sail through the Straits of Gibraltar, equally brilliant are the white cities on both sides; the exception is Gibraltar itself, which has been toned down into an English mole. Cádiz is a pinnacle of whiteness; nothing, not even snow, can make an effect of a purer white than this city.

As you travel northward, white alternates with dismal earth-color. Seen from above, even Seville is already less white. Its houses are not topped with flat roofs, as in Cádiz, where white linen is dried on wide roofs with white balustrades. In Seville, most of the buildings are covered with gray tiles, and the total impression is of clay.

But down in the streets the city is still white. From the depths of the narrow alleys, one's glance ascends over blindingly white sun-lit wall spaces, framing fragments of blue sky. The white penetrates the interior of the houses, where ceilings and walls are whitewashed and where insistence on whiteness goes to such excess that the women in their daily house-cleaning devote most of their time to mixing kalsomine and applying it with a brush.

Along the road between Seville and Córdoba, the villages stand like great lumps of clay, crude efforts to relieve the crusty level of the soil. We stop in front of such an uncanny cake of loam, the only life in the picture the vivid red and blue dresses of the women. I have committed the grave error of praising the lining in a merchant's cloak, which forces the poor man to urge me to accept the cloak, which he had absolutely no idea of giving to me.

"You like it," he says, as he takes it off quickly; "very well, it is yours." He folds up the coat neatly and hands it to me.

"No, thank you," I stammer in great embarrassment, "I didn't intend it so—"

"But don't you like it—how? Do take it; it is not of the slightest value, not the slightest! It is a poor coat, a miserable coat; I am very sorry I cannot offer you a finer one—"

And as I refuse to accept it, he simply walks over to my baggage and deposits the coat upon it in a manner and with an expression which indicate that he will tolerate no further resistance.

I am fulfilled in one of my dearest wishes, for the possession of a Spanish cloak, and a beautiful and valuable cloak at that, with lovely red and green lining. The man is serious, the offer is not a mere matter of form. But what shall I give him for it? Money will not do, and as for my watch—I could not part with so much in exchange. But I shall think up something, before we leave him; something that will cost me nothing and yet have value in his eyes. I smile at the generous merchant and he smiles in return, but hardly as benevolently as before. That would really be asking too much.

There he sits gazing at me so curiously—wondering perhaps that I have no breeding at all. But I do not understand. I am not a Spaniard. Then he shivers as if freezing; it should be my duty to say now: "My wretched cloak is at your service." He could then keep the cloak without any further ceremony. But I do not understand; I have come into possession of a cloak and do not intend to part with it so readily. Is it not a silly thing to give something away and then expect to get it back? How really too easy to enjoy a reputation as the most courteous and most hospitable people in Europe on such an inexpensive foundation!

I talk to my wife sleepily about the lovely cloak and discuss my inability to make some gift in return. Her only reply is to suggest what a lovely beret she could have made for herself out of the velvet lining. I make protest against any division of the spoils, and we prepare for a sharp family scene when the train suddenly halts at a village station. Our generous merchant leans over to read the name of the station, jumps up, takes his hand-bag, absent-mindedly throws his cloak over his shoulders and dashes out. He came near missing his station, is our thought as we gaze after him disappearing through the exit. It has not occurred to us till now that the cloak has gone with him. Of course his act was mechanical, due to his haste; he will return with the cloak as soon as he notices his mistake—the Spaniards are such honest people! We catch another glimpse of him at the station, making for the forward cars at the other end of the platform.

There is no time to mourn our loss, for a crowd of village youngsters suddenly fills the platform, surrounding two gendarmes and a tall, smooth-shaven man carrying a tripod. I conjecture that a criminal is being taken to prison; but when he and his escort approach our compartment and my fellow travelers catch sight of him, they start from their seats as if they had suddenly caught fire. *"El verdugo*—the hangman! *Carramba,* not in here! Not in here!" they yell, as they hold shut the compartment door. But the gendarmes enter by force, while the passengers grab their things and make off, mumbling, over the partition, to the other end of the car. Each gendarme takes a corner, while the hangman sets down his tripod and seats himself upon it. He has paid no attention to any one, but now sits, well bent over, rolling his cigarette, his elbows resting on his knees.

This tall, awkward person with his enigmatical expression and glance that seems to sound the infinite—where have I seen him before? Oh, yes—I have seen him in Seville, where he often walked through the streets, carrying his tripod, a sort of mania with him, I thought.

Suddenly I recall that in Andalusia the hangman is more despised than the lowest scoundrel. No one will offer him a seat or touch him. He must not even sit on the steps or on low walls where others might sit down after him—he is unclean. He must carry his own stool with him everywhere.

The people at the end of the car beckon us to come to them; but I pretend not to have seen them and instead offer the hangman a cigarette. He looks up hastily, discovers that I am a foreigner and suddenly loses his eager interest. "No, thank you," he says with a quiet smile, as he drops again into revery. I put the cigarette on his knee and offer him my own to light it with—that is a kindlier act than the offer of a match. And he goes so far as to light his cigarette without dignifying me with a word or glance. The gendarmes signal to me with their eyes that I had better have nothing to do with him.

I try a number of Spanish courtesies, without result; he disregards me. Then I fold up my traveling blanket and ask him to sit on it. "Your chair must be pretty uncomfortable if you use it all the time."

"I suppose you do not know who I am," with a bitter smile.

"I know," I say.

"In your country, are hangmen not outcasts?" He raises his head as he asks the question.

"One hundred and twenty-nine applicants asked for the job when it was vacant a few years ago."

"*Caraja,* that's the place I'm going to!" he bursts out in a sudden attack of sardonic humor. "You say the job was advertised? Had the whole family died out? The place is never vacant in Spain; and if it should be, no one would try for it, not even criminals. But we have plenty of people in this trade; I alone have three sons who want nothing so much as to become my successors; for the present they must live on the jobs I cannot take."

"But why don't they look for some other occupation?"

"Why? Because no one would like to employ the hangman's children, or make use of utensils fashioned by our hands; they will not even have us buried in the same soil with them. I married off my daughter very well; she married the assistant to the executioner of Madrid; he will surely advance some day, when his superior shuffles off, and it's a good post. He is the son of a hangman, too, from the neighborhood of Bilboa, a splendid fellow, who would have made a great career with the women had it not been for his trade. Things being as they are he had to come all the way to Seville to get a wife from me. I did not have quite so much trouble; I married the daughter of the executioner at Malaga; the jobs were not so far apart then as they are now."

"And is it true that you must be escorted to the execution place and back again, as the people would stone you if you were not protected?"

"Yes, the people always side with the offender— the Spanish people are very proud, you know. And in a way the authorities stick to the offender too—not so much nowadays any more. But about twenty years ago they used to seize me after each execution and imprison me, with heavy chains. They would take me before a judge, and I would be asked: Do you admit that you have killed Don Fulano?—Yes!—Why did you commit this act?—Because of his great sins!—

Have you any right to punish sinners?—The justice of man has judged him and commissioned me to carry out the judgment. Then they would remove my chains and escort me back to my home."

"I suppose this farce was gone through with in order to pacify the rage of the mob and give some protection to you?"

"Yes, that's it! But when the people were in unusual rage over the execution, there was no authority to protect me—as if I were the guilty one and the whole thing had been done by me! Once they nearly tore me limb from limb. It is not so bad any more; only in the remote districts do the people ever attack me. But everywhere they have nothing but derision and contempt for me; in their eyes I am worse than a leper or one afflicted with cholera. If only the authorities would treat me as a human being! For, after all, I am a part of the government!" Once more his face assumed its previous expression of enigmatical reserve, as if many thoughts were brooding behind it.

"What are your feelings when you are engaged in your work as an executioner?" I utter this question reluctantly, almost with aversion.

"Feelings?" his features become bitter. "Feelings? Must a hangman have feelings? Why don't you say plainly, just as other people do, that a hangman is so blood-thirsty that he cuts off a chicken's head every day on which he has no execution to perform, and sucks out its blood? Feelings? When I was still a young man, I sometimes considered myself to be the representative of divine justice, and I thought my trade a splendid one. But at times I shared the views of the people, and sympathized with the criminal; then it was hard for me to do my job. There were often times when I should have liked to be in the sinner's place. Then my knees would fail me, like a pregnant woman; but the thought that my prisoner might not be willing to change with me made me attack him like a beast of prey. No, the hangman is not a human being. And yet, I have often stood on the scaffold with thousands of lustful eyes fixed upon me and my only feeling was that if a reprieve should arrive, there would be only two people who would really be happy—the condemned man and his executioner—in spite of all the noisy protests of the crowd. And while I was consigning a man to death as a warning and as a penalty, other men were making use of the excitement to pick each other's pockets; once they did not even scorn the hangman's coat and stole all my pay, unclean though I was."

"Do you ever feel any desire to reverse the job, as it were?" I ask.

He makes no reply, but his sidelong glance at the gendarmes shows me that he has grasped my question immediately. No Spaniard can have failed to understand me.

"It would be very difficult for me to find any expression for the things I have felt," he says cautiously, after a short pause. "But Espronceda has spoken for us—for me and my kind. Do you know his poem 'The Hangman'? I can recite it for you."

It is not a boast when a Spaniard offers to recite for you. Every Spaniard is eloquent and has oratorical resources; when he can neither read nor write, he will yet be capable of a melodious and rhythmical delivery

in verse. He still sat bent forward, his elbows resting on his wide open knees, when he began his recita-
tion; he swayed gently with the beat of the rhythm.

THE HANGMAN

An outcast I and scorned by all mankind,
. I am the victim of their crimes,
Bear well, they hate each other not,
Their hate with rancour fraught is vent on me,
  For whom betimes
A grave offense they've chosen to requite.
  'Tis mine own hands
  Must needs mete out
The scourge decreed to quench their spite!
Let him, they said, bear all our stain,
Let him eat his bread in blood and pain!
And may he bear upon his brow
  The mark of shame,
  Reward well earned,
  Cursed be his name
  By all men spurned!
  And e'er they left me,
They cast the cloak of crime around me,
And hardened to my pleadings they confound me,
  Ignored the tears I shed.

The judge who speaks God's solemn curse
In hallowed precincts is God's creature;
But who shall say the hangman is not worse
Than others are who bear man's lowly feature!
  God's image well befits
  E'en him who lowly sits!
As of old to savage beasts they hurled
With greedy lust their guiltless victims,
So now they bring to me the outcasts of their world,
And I, their tool, must sting in retribution!
  Righteous are they,

Accursed am I,
And I without crime,
A criminal am I
For their execution.
From a scornful judge my mead I take, and why?
Is not the task he pays me for performed
At his behest?

He had been sitting still, rocking himself gently,
with the rhythm of the poem; but now he jumped to
his feet. His delivery of the verses became terrifying,
bringing the sweat to my brow—a rage that gnashed
its teeth, a vehemence that meant blood. Only the
voice of a Latin could rise to such a vibrant roar of
harshness and malice.

Cracking the bones of his quivering frame,
The wheel, the culprit its helpless game,
His sinews snapping under the battering blows
Of the ax descending; this agony, his throes,
        Are my delight.
And as his head is severed from his trunk,
        It rolls away
        From the bleeding stump,
Tinging with blood the sand at my feet.
As the surging crowd like floods overflowing,
Burst out in anger at the blows I repeat,
At the jubilant scorn that glows on my brow,
        As I laugh at them,
        At their Judas' pay,
        It never swerved me.
        With their wrath
        They have served me,
Those cruel souls have trained me farther away
From man's gentle ways to torture and to slay.
        O wretched path!

The hangman yet is greater far than any king
That ever trod upon the laws of right.

They stood in awe when dropping down the rope
He rode * the culprit's back as on a swing,
      To flatter the gallows' might!
And if his foe the king commanded him to slay,
      Rich the pay!
      Indeed the day!
Then drunk with joy and filled with terror,
The hangman's face a radiance bore,
And on his lips a smile then broke once more,
Though in his eyes flashed lights of horror.
      Those hands beware!
      By the hangman's hand
      Falls the crown of kings,
      On the throne you'll see
      The hangman stand.
And the rabble that grants him this elevation
Is filled anew with consternation
      To have him standing there!

Could these people forget, at this moment, that the reciter of these lines was a leper, an outcast from human society, the hangman? They crawled closer to us, hung far over the partition gesticulating, murmuring the verses under their breath, as he recited them. And the hangman had turned toward them; his face was a purple red; his neck swollen; the back of it dripping with perspiration; he looked as though he were about to be seized with a stroke of apoplexy.

In me is scrawled our earth's long story,
In words of blood by fate dictated.
E'en autumn leaves betray my mission gory.
But has the vulgar lust of man been sated?
      As age succeeds each age,

---

* *It is related, by persons old enough to remember, that the hangman was sometimes obliged, when the rope did not tighten about the culprit's neck, to climb up on the gallows, lower himself on the rope to the man's shoulders, and tighten the rope by applying his weight and resorting to jerks and impacts.*

And passes slowly into endless time,
        Will my loathsome trade
        By man be stayed?
Is it only the memory of a life bygone?
But the truth remains and vain the dreams of races,
Of lofty clouds and sunny spaces,
For I still rule, the scaffold is my throne.
        A thousand specks of blood
        Now stain my cloaks,
        A single crime
        My garment soaks,
        Here still I stand.
A faithful ghost from out the past,
I move with other ghosts and last,
        Without hope.

My child, why wert thou born of hangman's loins?
Thy life is blameless, clean, and without guile.
A boundless blessing seems the fate that joins
To mine thy soul which nought can e'er defile.
        How sweet thou art!
Thy smile in sleep is far from pain and care,
        And thine, a mother's heart!
        Woe, woe is thee!
Wilt thou not give thy love to thy young child?
Then be less gentle—thou wilt a better mother be—
If thou wouldst truly show a courage bold,
Then smother him with thine own bed's pillow!
        How, weepest thou?
        Shall on him too,
        Upon his brow
        My mark accrue?
        Mind thou the day
He'll find himself the one accursed,
As I—and then—what shall betide?
        An outcast, or a culprit, at our side!

They weep and laugh and clap their hands in applause. *"Espronceda!"* they say with voices that are

caressing, "our *Espronceda!* And what verses of
blood and fire! What infernal verses!—*Hombre!*"
they shout, affectionately, stretching their hands out
beyond the partition toward the hangman.

But the hangman pays no attention. He picks up
his three-legged stool, opens the door and steps out on
the running board. The train is passing between signal
towers and switch-houses, a water-tank and piles of
coal; before it reaches the platform, the hangman has
jumped off.

Out in the street we see him again. He walks on
ahead of the two gendarmes, followed by a host of
children and grown people, screeching and shouting at
him. In the midst of the crowd we can discern three
or four of the hangman's fellow-passengers, joining in
the cat-calls. Their emotion a few minutes ago was
genuine; they were moved by the verses, burning
verses—long live the hangman! But in this mob
that reminds them of insurrection, revolution; why
shouldn't they join it?—Down with the hangman!

It is about fifty miles from Seville to Córdoba; the
same blue sky vaults over us; and the same sun is
shining—but the resonance chamber is lacking. The
people here are not the same as in the other cities of
Andalusia. This is apparent as soon as we leave the
train. Here there are no bunco-steerers, no greedy
hotel omnibuses nor importunate cabbies. There are
droves of beggars. They lie along every street—
brown, ragged, a rag instead of a hat tied around their
foreheads—their muscular arms held out for alms; if
we ask them to help us with our baggage and take us

to a hotel, for which service we are willing to pay, they turn their backs contemptuously.

Once Córdoba meant to the world what Paris does now; it was the city of beauty, of art, of science, of progress—a focus of civilization. It was the first city to lay pavements or put up street lanterns; in its most flourishing period, ten centuries ago, it had about one thousand public schools, fifty hospitals, a library with half a million volumes, nine hundred baths and six hundred mosques; the latter required, as counter-weight, an equal number of taverns. The population was fully one million souls, with an annual municipal budget of about thirty million dollars. The city spent fabulous sums on its adornment. In its day it was celebrated for its overpowering splendor; Córdoba secured a hegemony of the spirit both because of its entrancing beauty and because of its learning and freedom of thought.

A peculiar feeling assails me as I stroll through the site of such glorious memories—a sense of futility and emptiness. Churchyards are not very stimulating, though they hold the dust of great celebrities. Worse, Córdoba is a neglected churchyard; the grassy mounds have been trodden down. Only here and there a corner of some tombstone still peers forth.

You have the Guadalquivir at Córdoba, but you have no big steamers on its yellow waters as at Seville, and the streets that run down to the river have no levees at the lower end to prevent floods. Not even a small vessel could navigate the river at this point; it is not a river, but insignificant dirty water, flowing sluggishly over a bed of exaggerated wideness and between sullied banks. On one bank, the poor quarter serves as the river's edge; the sewage of the city trickles in green slimy rills over the spotted walls; on the other side, the bank is formed by dry sand and heaps of garbage. The whole is a monstrous scene of gray ennui, with an occasional picturesque ruin of a Moorish water-mill for relief.

A splendid old Roman bridge leads down to the city. It is the only artery of traffic that crosses the river, and yet its heavy stone back bears no living current of humans. It is like a fabulous gray monster that has flung himself straight across the stream ages ago to die in peace. In spots, the tooth of time has gnawed a little at his loins of twenty centuries, but only to demonstrate the dead beast's immortality.

In all Andalusian cities, you are bound to meet the type of cloaked Spaniard who will stand like a hermit in the midst of bustle, leaning against a palm or a wall, arms crossed, glances idle. You may see him standing as you leave your house, and two or three hours later you return to find him still in the same position. Outwardly blasé, completely indifferent to the affairs of practical life, he will seem to have developed in the purest form that contempt for temporal possessions, of which every Andalusian has at least a trace. Such types remind you vividly of the kindred Moors of the northern cities of Morocco: the expression betrays the same descent, and in spite of the difference in the conditions of their lives, they do tend to revert to the Moor. Fruitless to indulge in speculation as to what might not have been achieved by the Moors had they not been driven from Spain. They had already begun to decline and would probably have become precisely what they are now—an extinct crater.

These scattered descendants who, in spite of isolation from their kin, lead lives so closely resembling those of their cousins across the straits, are all the evidence.

Córdoba has many of these Moorish scions. Stiff as monuments, they grace the squares of the city, representing in themselves both the present and the past.

We wander about this endless confusion of narrow, twisted streets, meeting not a soul, although the city is recorded as having more than fifty thousand inhabitants. We walk single file, following the gutter, which is in the center, and can easily touch the houses on both sides at the same time, with our finger tips. It is shady and quiet, and the sky over our heads is blue; occasionally we hear steps in front or behind as we walk, only to discover that they are our own footfalls. We can hear our own hearts beat in the curious quiet which reigns here between these closely shuttered rows of houses.

Of what are we reminded by this voyage of exotic loneliness? There is the arrow on the street corner, still indicating the direction traffic must take in this one-way alley—the deep ruts in the pavement blocks—worn by the busy wheels of the past, by striding feet and rolling wagons—is this not Pompeii? Of course it is Pompeii; the only feature lacking is the echoing sound of the iron-studded boots worn by the custodians who circulate among the dead house-walls at Pompeii.

We walk on and on without meeting a soul, turning repeatedly, never able to see more than the length of two houses ahead. Always the same strip of blue sky above us and always the same immaculate gutter under us, framed by two flagstones. This constitutes the width of the street, and an ell above the ground the houses are provided with a deep groove to afford space for the hubs of the wheels. At times the masonry recedes to offer such a groove, in other places it appears as if the wagons themselves had worn it down.

In Seville, great mountainous women lean over all the balconies, while the men fill promenades and squares with their babble and their idleness; you can travel about here for hours without seeing anything more than a starved cat. But lovely views may be enjoyed on both sides, through the vaulted horse-shoe portals with their wrought-iron gates, views of marble courts with green plants and fountains, pillared arcades and sun. And above, in the sunlight, over the roofs of the houses, hangs a bit of garden whose almond trees blossom though it is now the twelfth day of January.

As we amble along with no hope of ever escaping from this intricate labyrinth, we are suddenly halted by a battlemented wall with a marble basin by its side —the Mosque. In the basin, where a donkey is now wetting his decayed teeth, true believers once washed their feet before they disappeared under the horseshoe entrance.

Behind lies the Orange Court of the Mosque, full of sunlight and fragrance and splashing waters. You may sit in the shade of an Arab arch-way, drinking the stillness of the oranges until you slip into a dazzling sunlight nap.

But behind the Orange Court is the famous Mosque, the greatest miracle of the architectural world; it waits for you.

Entering the Mosque of Córdoba cannot but be an

unpleasant surprise. You pull yourself together, mindful of all the praise that tourists have sung of it, mindful of what the Mosque once stood for—and then you are moved by the idea of actually being in it.

The Mosque is large, but its effect is not magnificent; it can indeed hardly ever have made an impression of magnificence. One's eye roams about in every direction, but it never encounters a vast space or a mighty wall, nothing but columns and columns, cutting off one's view at no great distance, like tree-trunks in a dense forest. And as you go on, your eye finds new series of columns; green columns and blood-red columns, black columns, white columns, red columns and bright pink columns, columns of jasper and porphyry, breccia and delicate alabaster—until you finally get to the walls. In a space not more than six hundred and fifty feet in length and five hundred feet in width, you have about a thousand columns. The columns are not larger than those you would find on the veranda of a private residence; they are not thicker than the waist of a boy attending confirmation lessons, and it is not particularly difficult for you to touch the capitals, from which arches radiate in red and white masonry, two or three imposed above each other, in every direction, from trunk to trunk, like a network of branches.

No doubt every one who enters the Mosque makes the simile of a forest, and this effect was no doubt intended by the ancient architects. But it is no such impression as of a path through a beech-wood which Gothic cathedrals so often give. Here you have only a young forest whose trees have been cut back so that their heavy masses of foliage rest directly on a man's head.

The vaulting is oppressively low—there is no head-room at all. And if there are any additional spaces at the sides, you accept them merely because the guide-book tells you they are there; the guide-book figures impress us, not the magnificence of the composition—there is no sense of composition about the whole thing. If you should cut away three-fourths of the whole structure, or rebuild it four times its present size, you would have secured a different area and a different number of columns, without attaining any change in the effect on the eye.

The Mosque in Córdoba, like all the other examples of Moorish architecture in Spain, seems not the result of a single great idea, but of a thousand isolated little notions, each delightful in itself, all stitched together like the squares of a patchwork quilt.

This lack of unity is apparent even from the outside of the Moorish architectural monuments. Viewed from without, the Alhambra seems an aggregation of diminutive huts, half buried in the ground, with a general air of planlessness—as if it had been gradually added to, piece by piece. As a matter of fact, this actually was the method in which the Moors built; the Alhambra and the Alcázar were built room by room, with no other connection between them than the door which leads from one apartment to another.

The genius of the Moorish architects is most apparent in their infinite wealth of detail, their inexhaustible supply of decorative ideas. Their luxurious imagination transformed the heavy walls of castles and mosques into light fairy webs, and the rich and intricate stucco which constitutes the walls and ceilings of the halls of the Alhambra, the delicate pink on the surface, with a ground of gold, purple and blue, to this day produces the effect of an airy tent made of delicate laces, with the sky shining through. You face a wanton excess of vitality—even in the most inaccessible corner, every square inch is covered with decoration; and every capital, every tile has an ornamentation of its own, differing from all the others.

The Mosque of Córdoba was said in its day to have excelled all other buildings in rich imaginative decoration. To-day it bears the marks of rude acts of vandalism, particularly those perpetrated by Charles V, who also destroyed portions of the Alhambra and the Alcázar. In the middle of the Mosque lies a large Catholic chapel, with a truly terrifying altar that has been thrown together out of units of marble and metal; the original wooden frame-work of the building, made of inlaid cedar, has yielded in many places to plaster of Paris; the red and white color of the arches is no longer produced by an alternation of vari-colored blocks of stone, but by bricks covered with paint, or white-washed; the neat stuccoes of the walls have been obliterated by the use of kalsomine.

Lately a beginning has been made at the restoration of the Mosque, and after some years it may again look like its original self.

But in its present form, the Mosque is a sadly mutilated temple, fascinating details visible only here or there, such as the Mirab Chapel, with the niche in which the Koran had its place.

V

GIBRALTAR

THE traveler in Andalusia should visit the southernmost tip of Spain to enjoy the contrast afforded by the British rocky fortress of Gibraltar.
This chunk of Anglo-Teutonic culture lands into its
tropical oriental environment like a pugilist's fist thrust
into the dark eye of a lovely woman.

Leaving the railway center of Bobadilla, the tracks
lie directly to the south through one of the most savage
and beautiful mountain regions of Andalusia, Sierra de
Ronda. Wild, rocky precipices and depressions rich
with verdure, tunnels, viaducts and dizzy bridges are
passed in rapid succession; mountains suddenly tower
above us—we almost imagine we are at the bottom of
a deep well—only to emerge again at the next moment
at a height with far glimpses of cities and flat tilled
fields.

Painters who visit the south for other purposes than
to train as theatrical scene-painters, who mean to study
nature on a large scale, or the peculiar manifestations
of popular life, should certainly go to Andalusia rather
than to Italy. For instance, there is the mountain
across Sierra Nevada from Guadix to Granada,* with
its deep-set cities, a journey that seems to reveal a new
world and whose monstrous fields of snow and abysses
of blue may force a terrified perspiration to the
painter's brow. There is Granada itself, unique

* *See the final chapter:* "A Vision of Sudden Death."

among cities for its streets and its bustle of people, its Alhambra and its natural beauties. There is Loja, six miles to the southwest, Alhama, Antequera—curious Moorish cities blessed by nature. And a little to the south there is again the Sierra de Ronda, through which we are now passing, a disjointed region which increases in majesty and wildness until it reaches its culmination in the vicinity of the city of Ronda.

Ronda lies in the midst of a great rocky plateau, on a dome-like mountain top cloven in twain by a deep cut. A great arched bridge spans the top of the crevice, connecting the two sections of the city in its bold leap. Looking down from the bridge, you gaze into an awful depth with the Guadiaro foaming at its bottom, dashing over the rocks like disheveled floods of hair. A moist coolness comes up to you, and occasionally a slight mist of spray refreshes your face.

There is a rare view from the promenade which passes all around the city. Up and down the hills there are strings of olive-groves and vineyards, broken by wheat-fields and orange-groves, or by cliffs of naked coral-red and hyacinth-blue. A circle of mighty hills envelops the horizon like a frame.

We are obliged to hurry and content ourselves with a cursory view of the city, but each detail of my visit six years before is made to live again. No region or people in Spain ever made so full and strange an impression on me as this.

I had come in August and September. At that season, every fruit market in Andalusia affords a beautiful and varied sight; but Ronda's market-halls excel them all in their abundance, in fragrance, and in fruits curved tense with bursting juices. It seemed as if every

variety of fruit had absorbed one of the colors of the
solar spectrum and was yielding it up again more
dazzling than before—so great, so indomitable was
the riot of color which roared from the hall like a
warm breath of gold and fire. Inside, the people were
making curious gestures and shouting like mad, screaming to themselves as they went about their tasks. Their
throats emitted melodious, short calls and bright coo-
ing laughter, recalling the screams of stags; here and
there one of them would throw a knife-blade at the
woodwork where it stuck trembling. Did his mind's
eye behold a jet of blood rush forth, a hotter red than
that of the tomato or the Spanish pepper? Did he
hear a cry of terror more piercing than the ardent
yellow? I am a Nordic, but I should have found it
quite pardonable if all these persons had drawn their
knives and run amuck in true Malay fashion. I think
I might have joined them. For all these colors held
me by the throat and I expected them all to burst at
any moment, spurting their juices into my eyes like
living blood, so monstrous was the general tension.

Can a gray, misty, drizzly-cold northerner ever
come to understand the Andalusian temperament? I
hardly think so. It may infect him or carry him away
with it; he may stagger about like a new-born calf,
finally stumbling to the ground; he may suffer sun-
stroke and become half-witted; but the ecstasy of the
sun will remain strange to him. How can he, who must
shut all his love in his heart and entrench it there
against many forces—all hostile to his petty Eros,
stifled by feather-beds and thick walls and double windows—how can he ever understand the great Eros of
the south: the sun's heat which bursts and radiates in

all the objects of creation, engulfing not only the Eros of human beings, but all their being and nature, so that one may read from the motion of a little finger, from the bearing and manner of a child or an aged man, the same accumulated tension of the blood that may be seen in northern countries only in a pair of eyes madly in love?

*   *   *

The mountain ridge that runs down through Loja, Antequera and Ronda, shelters an extensive section of old Spain. The colors, celebrated in ancient books of travel, not ever wholly credible, are here before our very eyes. Here the *bandolero*—nowadays half a smuggler, half a highwayman—is still the hero of the villages and may find an asylum in any peasant's house. Still they throw stilettos; you see young men practicing the art, outside the villages, using olive-trees as targets; but the eventual target is the eye of an adversary; even to-day faithless women have their stomachs cut open by their lovers' crooked knives. All these things still happen; only we pay too much atten- tion to them and forget to notice others.

Ronda has a note of blood. Although the city has only about thirty thousand inhabitants, its bull-fights are among the best in Spain; if a second-rate per- formance should be presented to the eyes of these mountaineers in Ronda, they would tear down the arena or set it on fire with their own hands. The region serves as a great reservoir of supply for pro- fessional bull-fighters, since every one—man or woman —is an amateur in the art, an *aficionado*. They are acquainted with all the technical terms, all the tricks of the trade, and no sooner do they catch sight of a little calf far off in the fields, than they produce their red cloths and begin to wave them.

There is something feline about these lean, sinewy mountain-dwellers of Andalusia, especially in the hills around Ronda. There, the mountaineer walks quickly, without a sound; he knows nothing of nervousness, though he is nothing but nerves; he can never have enough of the sunlight, and even in the hottest season, he lies outdoors on a blazing hot blanket, at midday. He is voluptuously idle and tirelessly persevering. His glance, which usually evades your eye and yet follows you persistently, imitating your every motion only half awake, will suddenly grow sharp, energetic, aggressive; he measures your place, your distance; he transfixes you calmly. He is peculiarly cruel, a characteristic of all Andalusians, due perhaps to the fact that this land of the sun has not enough sunlight after all to please a race that comes from still hotter zones! At times the surface may be covered with an opaque stratum of the veneer of civilization; but here it is exposed, having yet another shade of red to add to the general effect.

There is something like the challenge of a beast of prey in these powerful, gaunt men, who have not the good-natured curiosity of the Andalusian of the plains, nor the proud kindliness of other mountain-dwellers, but the cold reserve or haughtiness of the Arabs. They still retain the Oriental's scorn for the European barbarian; they treat the stranger with contempt, regarding him as so much empty air, and it is difficult to secure admission to their houses. The Spanish self-respect here rises to an arrogance that impresses the cultured traveler as baseless; for it is an arrogance based neither on money nor intellectual conceit, but on the possession of that which is common to all of them —their fine bodies.

The women are tall and sarcastic; their hair is darker than that of the other Andalusians—a bluish black—and their oval chins often have a soft blond bloom, imparting a peculiarly fair tone to their faces. A woman of these mountain regions takes little care of her children, but instead lavishes affection on them; all day long you may see her with her own child in her arms, or another's, caressing and cuddling it, with an occasional savage pinch which makes the child burst into tears. Women like these can tame the wild tiger, though he be armed to the teeth, can make him talk, can turn his savage mutterings to soft-cooing tenderness, subjugate him quite if she will. He will lie at her feet like a great lap-dog, humble whether she caress or kick him—his knife in his sash, his rifle in his hand, her foot on his neck. This will go on only until at twenty-five or thirty she begins to fade; then he will rise in his dignity and harness her to the yoke. His capricious Venus changes swiftly into a patient beast of burden; but he—by virtue of his eternal youth —will proceed to seek another mistress.

To the south of Ronda the mountains flatten a little, become more peaceful, until the landscape passes imperceptibly into the great cork-forests of Castellar. The crooked, peeled branches of the cork-oak have an uncanny grin as they loom through the half-dark of the forest, and as the train rolls by one has the fantastic impression of an armory of naked skeletons, carrying green branches over their heads for protection.

We are back in the plains of the south. Loquacious

valley-dwellers worm their way into the train; immediately they offer me their tobacco pouches; they shout deafening commands to each other, which graze my ear destructively, toss restlessly in their seats and laugh loudly; their eyes are overflowing with benevolence.

We have arrived in Algeciras, the terminal station.

The name sounds Arabic, and the city looks as if it has been asleep for centuries, since the days when the Moors were driven from Andalusia. Its color is white, and the town has flat or slightly inclined roofs of grayish green azulejos; the houses stand close together, like old nags blinking in the sunlight; their shutters tightly closed. In the cool patios, women babble away and spin on their hand-power spindles; the men recline in the sunlight on the benches of the Alameda, wrapped in their long cloaks. Their faces are large, with a massive, open forehead, soft, black, full beards, and nut-brown skins; the women have the great rounded outlines of odalisques and their faces are the color of raw cream.

The gutter dirt is in no danger of being washed away; children and red pigs wallow in it to their heart's content. All are equally naked, natural and round; there must be enough dropsy and pork and bacon and rickets for a whole host of Raphael's angels in this place.

Twenty minutes across the bay, we find ourselves in a scene entirely different.

Half way across, the water loses its deep blue color and gathers a scum of coal dust, a gray, dry sheen in the sunlight. Steamships and sailing ships are moving about in all directions, cutting smooth furrows in the dusty surface, which displays, before it closes again, a bit of sea-bottom lying many feet below; yellow sand, violet slag, polyp-like rock formations.

This gray inlet, open only to the south, is a fine natural harbor. We glide into a forest of masts and steamer chimneys; the air resounds with the flapping of the flags of all nations; thick-bellied sloops sway lazily on the flood as they disgorge their black cargoes. Immense iron giants come rushing in, swallow four or five ordinary shiploads of black fuel in as many hours, and strike off again for the Orient or America. Coal and coal and coal again, everywhere! The air rings with iron and steel, anchors being thrown out or heaved, steam windlasses rattling away at the job. The huge cranes of the scows sing like great black swans at ship's side, cautiously burying their heads of steel in cargo and rising again in long gliding curves; out beyond, above the scow, they open their steel beaks and drop mouthfuls of coal—big as carloads, again and again the cranes repeat! Short whistles alternate with long drawn roars; a packet steamer is sounding its siren—three sharp vulture-like croaks which make you start in terror, while they continue to reverberate gloomily from coast to coast. A word of command may be heard in English, the start of a Norwegian chanty; naked negroes flash their grins over the railings like lightning in a summer night, and revel familiarly in the black coal, like creatures who have at last grasped rapturously their Providential purpose.

Gibraltar is a fortress—the English declare it is the one impregnable fortress in all the world. Their confidence does not prevent them, however, from requiring you to surrender your penknife when you set foot

on shore nor from shoving you in through the gate
with an invitation to get out of English territory before sundown. The period can be lengthened on the
application of your consul or some other reputable
citizen, to be sure.

The city is a free port, but it is governed exclusively
on military lines, under regulations far more severe
than a prison's. At sundown (five o'clock in the evening, in this month of January) a cannon is fired; five
minutes later the gates are closed; and the city remains completely cut off from any contact with the
ocean or outside world until seven the following morning. The citizen who has not finished his errands in
the outlying parts by sundown must make up his mind
to camp outside the walls. At half-past nine a second
gun is fired, after which only the tip of your nose may
peer from your downy bed. Even during the day you
may not stroll about unaccompanied. Grim constables
and sentries watch your every step; military cards of
admission are required to visit the most ridiculous
places; if you set down the address of a laundress in
your note-book, vigilant eyes will interpret it as a plan
of the fortifications. So, newly come from free Andalusia, where the lack of red tape and military pomp
makes life and breathing such great pleasures, we can
hardly draw a breath, so constrained are we by these
mechanical regulations; such provisions appear to us
justifiable only in war time. Your stay inside the
walls is made even more irritating by the firm tread
of guards on their incessant rounds, and troops of various arms of the service, marching up the street, down
the street, drawing up, wheeling round corners—all
dictated by the inscrutable laws of some form of higher

insanity. Along the sidewalks and on the balcony stand cool-blooded Britons, of the kind not to be impressed either by the cruelty of a bull-fight or the beauty of the Alhambra, yet they drink in with an expression of delirious enjoyment this flood of rolling drums, calls of command and mechanically moving legs.

Upwards of thirty thousand people live on this rock. Six thousand of them are English soldiers and officers, to which we must add the English officials and many private English families. But the great mass of the population—all of the lower class and most of the middle—is as southern as the climate. Indian, Jewish, Turkish and Spanish shops stand side by side as soon as one walks away from the main street, with an occasional saloon for the English sailors, or a German or Scandinavian shipping office. On the market-place you will find togas, Jewish kaftans and the white burnous of the Arab; the English language is murdered by offenders with every accent; cursing, swearing and cheating is carried on in Babel's tongues. Coolies, negroes, Spanish and Italian day-laborers do the rough jobs in and around the ports. Each race prays on its own holidays; the Hindoos close their shops on Friday; the Jews on Saturday. There are oriental flat roofs, and Andalusian balconies and pillared Moorish courts with fountains. The backs of donkeys carry all the luscious tropical fruits of the south through the streets.

But the careless oriental calm, the indifference, the complacent *laissez faire*, the unconventional, the inactive, the care-free animal-like existence which is so much the temperamental attraction of southern nations, is not to be found here. You will not find here arrogant pride, thoughtless generosity, the unselfish spirit of sacrifice, nor proud contempt of the petty tradesman's morality. Here no one will get off his donkey to offer a tired traveler his seat, or rather, everybody does it—for money. If you ask a man to show you the way, he will first mention his fee and then speed you on your quest.

Yes indeed, Anglo-Teutonic civilization may be proud of its victory; it has crowded all the light and care-free way of the sun from the people and molds them now in the image of solid Anglo-Teutonic money-making utilitarianism. You fancy sometimes you are at a masquerade: costumes, faces, voices, gestures— everything seems genuinely oriental, but behind the mask stands John Bull always formal and correct. One day I was in Gibraltar. A man came dashing down the street with a policeman after him. The policeman was waving his arms wildly: "Stop, thief!" An Arab tripped the fugitive. He fell to the ground and was made a prisoner by the policeman. At home in Denmark I know people would probably have done the same thing; but in Spain or Morocco certainly they would have tripped the policeman.

Gibraltar is a fortress. Officers' dwellings with sentry-boxes, officers' clubs, barracks, soldiers' saloons, soldiers' missions and garrison churches lie one next to the other as far as the road runs. And after the road passes out of the open gate in the city wall, you come to the strand promenade, which runs on and on, past drill grounds, arsenals and huge barracks. Under rich foliage, of an African richness, French and Swiss nursery-governesses play with little English babies—

faces of peaches and cream with angel curls; raw-boned, red-cheeked Englishmen drag their flat feet and bow legs by the side of dark-eyed Spanish señoritas whose gait is like the rhythm of music; respectable English women move about on their respectable feet, either alone or accompanied by youths in the uniform of cadets. They impress you as an emanation of beef and porter; if they do no more than open their parasols the action is performed as with a slight explosion of energy; the indifference in their eyes expresses the perfect impregnability of the fortress in which they live.

Their matter-of-fact gait, their gray and brown dresses, the whole monotonous expression of their faces, has a painful, almost a stifling effect in this bright and sparkling sunlight. But they suit well this armored rock, with its long row of cannons down the whole length of the promenade with the pyramids of bombs and shells that adorn the park grounds and render superfluous other art products fashioned by human hands. They are on solid ground; their bases are stone block and cement, in the belly of which is a second row of cannons, capable of covering the entire sweep of the bay.

Rising above this double row of teeth in the armed jaws of this monster, the rock attains some fifteen hundred feet, in the form of a long narrow book that has been opened a little and set with its back pointing upward. This rock is accessible from three sides, the fourth side, which is inaccessible, is made up of rows of houses, each one with its toes on the necks of the houses immediately beneath.

But they do not go all the way to the top; the hill

gets too steep for them. Dry grass and underbrush take their place; the trail, fringed with lean agaves, winds in a short zig-zag between great bluish rock surfaces and clumps of bushes as it leads upward past still more great guns, resting on circular turn-tables, hidden in the bushes, camouflaged by paint to match the colors of the rock.

The naked rock curves out still more like a giant's wrinkled brow, furrowed by long diagonal ruts which collect the rain water, which then drains through drilled holes into great cisterns inside the rock. Some day it will be pumped up again to serve as pale ale, when the great Mediterranean war breaks out and this bare rock becomes the stage for world history.

All Englishmen are firmly convinced that this will sooner or later happen. They have hollowed out the rock in long galleries, extending—one over the other— often three stories at a time. From the outside you can see only three rows of holes, half hidden by bushes, cannons gazing out of them like peaceful nesting birds. Being a Dane, I am interested in all things military, and I succeed—with great effort—in obtaining a card of admission, valid, however, only for the lowest gallery.

The path digs farther and farther into the cliff, ending finally as it seems directly over my head. I am before a black, iron-latticed hole in the side of the mountain with a detachment of guards camped about it; I hand my card to the noncommissioned officer and am admitted. He comes with me. The others carefully lock the door behind us.

We go through a high-arched passageway blasted out of solid rock; for a while we walk along in darkness, but suddenly a sharp blaze of light from one of the port-holes brightens our path. Darkness again until we come to the next port-hole. At several places the corridor widens into great apartments, along the inside walls of which there are provision chambers and water-tanks, ammunition piled in neat heaps against the walls, cannons standing in all the port-holes. The heat outside is unbearable, but here it is cold, with icy draughts blowing through the corridor. The harsh breath of these nether regions makes me shudder and I quicken my steps as I approach each new port-hole, to get as much as I can of the light of the outside world. Each new port-hole reveals new landscapes—a succession of new fields of operation for these long-throated guns. Under us and over us the rock ends in an almost perpendicular wall for hundreds of feet in each direction, against which the enemy's balls would glance. Even the loop-holes are provided with steel curtains that may be raised or lowered after each discharge, so that the soldiers may not be disturbed, in taking aim, by the effects of the hostile projectiles.

We have seen all the sudden views the loop-holes afford of the bay; the flat tongue of land which rises but a few yards from the sea and connects this rock with Spain lies four hundred feet below us. We can see the guards at the Spanish boundary and, nearer, the English sentries, and between the two boundary lines the white churchyard and the neutral zone. You could spit directly on the heads of the men under us, so steep is the descent. The English have mined their part of this tongue of land, right up to the steep wall itself; they have only to press a button and the whole thing goes up in the air; its place will be taken by the sea—God knows for what sane end!

You long grateful for the sunlight. Let it burn you a little, so glad, so delighted with everything and anything would you be to escape from these rocky entrails. Everything shines with a strong light—the landscape, the bay beneath you, with its hundreds of ships and boats. I look down on their decks; they are like big toy boats. The naked negroes are simply little fly-specks. I can also hear the song of steel and iron to which I have become hardened during the last few days. It floats upward to my present height like a long-drawn-out melodious tremor. The coast batteries lie dazzling white in the bright sunlight. The promenade dances along the foot of the cliff with its long row of guns. The cannons themselves are like black ants, about to crawl straight over the boulevard and out into the sea.

The hour of the evening promenade has come; the broad stream of human creatures is moving over the road; I can discern red and blue parasols and silver-mounted saddles—a distinguished company! I glow with satisfaction that I have not become a worm doomed to wallow in the earth's vitals; I turn my thoughts humbly to the apes that dwell on the summit above me and decide to pay them a visit.

The trip is a hard one leading you through a number of guard lines, posted all around the cliff. Finally I succeed in reaching the top and seating myself a-straddle on the backbone of the rock. But I can see no monkeys. They are probably disporting themselves on the perpendicular rocky wall that faces the Medi-

terranean. I regret that I am unable to join them and
content myself with my seat gripping the rock as
tightly as I can with my feet, and staring about in all
directions.

On the other side of the strait lies Africa, with the
second pillar of Hercules, Ceuta; beneath my feet is
the Strait, with its white sails and long streaks of
smoke; I have the Mediterranean on the east and the
Atlantic Ocean on the west. Northward lies Spain
with its richly colored naked mountains—I can see
half of Andalusia, from Cape Tarifa across the cork-
forests all the way in to Jerez, the rocky plateau of
Ronda, the coastal regions skirting Malaga with the
Huertas and the cities, and the white battlements of
the Sierra Nevada more than one hundred miles away.

There is a hollow clang of activity in the inside of
the rock, as if the monster retched. If it should now
discharge all its two thousand cannons, at once, would
I be able to retain my seat? Would I be shaken off my
saddle? In spite of these two thousand modern gul-
lets of fire and in spite of the fact that there is room inside the rock for one hundred and fifty thousand men
with provisions for two years, while six thousand men
are said to be sufficient to hold the rock against attacks by an army of one million—in spite of all this
the whole savage business does not really impress me.
Though the English may regard this rock as a lion in
repose, standing guard at the southernmost tip of Europe, eyes fixed on the wild hordes of Africa, I can
take it no more seriously than a dog on watch in a little
coal-yard. It reminds me even more of a ruminant, a
plain ordinary ox.

At the bottom of his heart, John Bull probably knows there is nothing serious in his pathetic figure of a lion guarding Europe from savage hordes; he knows very well that civilization actually is simply the commercial spirit, and that this spirit of commerce has very excellent means of disposing of all the wild hordes south and east. For, though the proverb may tell us that it takes three Jews to fool a Greek and three Greeks to fool an Armenian, the entire destiny of Armenia is encompassed in the pocket of a single Anglo-Teuton gentleman.

The Englishman means to retain for himself the leadership of this exalted civilization; and for the purpose he needs this rock. He has figured the thing out something like this: in case of a crisis, the navies of the powers allied against him will cast their anchors in the Bay of Gibraltar to bombard this bare rock and be sunk by its two thousand cannons, leaving his hands free to act in all the rest of the world. It is to be hoped that his opponents will have sense enough to carry out their part of this arrangement. One Englishman, with whom I discussed this matter seriously, did admit that the rock would be of much greater practical value if it were portable, and could be used as a sort of flying battery.

But the Englishman defends this rock, in spite of the obvious foolishness of doing so; sometimes he even defends it with great warmth, as one always defends an object in the purchase of which one has been stung. The rock as it stands has cost England far more than three hundred million dollars, and it costs more millions annually to maintain it. Even so, there are

Englishmen who are so timid as to believe that the rock will have to undergo a thorough overhauling before it can really answer its purpose.

Spain also—although it shows not the slightest concern over the fact that its own great resources are undeveloped and may be exploited by foreigners at their own free will—is hypnotized by this bare rock. Since Spain has lost its colonies, it keeps its eyes turned on Gibraltar ceaselessly, as the key that will open up a great future in foreign fields, or encourage a great boom within the country, a boom which the country needs very much; now it is the center from which destruction and disaster threaten.

When Spaniards are alone they actually go so far as to speak of reconquering Gibraltar at the first opportunity. In public, it has even been proposed to purchase it (!) or, if possible, exchange it for the second pillar of Hercules, Ceuta, for Ceuta also has little monkeys jumping about on its pinnacle and furthermore, Ceuta is seven hundred feet taller.

But England has practical sense enough to prevent her from burying her millions in northern Africa after she has dug them so solid and expensive a tomb at the southern tip of Europe.

VI

TANGIERS

HOW near is Tangiers—and yet how far and strange! From the summit of Gibraltar I can distinguish its houses, and from the minaret in Tangiers the Muezzin was able to observe the great naval battle of Trafalgar; it is possible for a bee to fly from continent to continent, from Europe to Africa. And how remote are the characteristics of the two places! A living oriental bazaar, a motley fairy tale from the Arabian Nights, taken bodily out of the book and populated with fabulous characters of all kinds, with dervishes and pashas, eunuchs and ladies of the harem. There lies the city on its hills, house against house, whitewashed and dazzling in the sun of Africa, without windows, but with flat oriental roofs. The towers of azulejos show you where the mosque stands; the zig-zag Moorish fortress-walls indicate the limits of the city on the desert side.

Yet how old and familiar it all is! Who is there that has not dreamed through all this in his soul, that has not built for himself curiously colored fantasies that become all the richer because it was impossible for them to assume definite form.

Pilgrims come singing all the way from Mecca, with sacred relics on their bosoms and cholera in the folds of their mantles. Bedouins and Berbers cross the strait armed with long-barreled carbines or crescent; camels float down from the hills and the wind blows dry and stifling off the desert; one swears by Allah on the market place; one prays to Allah in the mosque.

I crossed the straits in the little steamer, anchored a bit up along the shore, got into a smaller boat, from which I transferred to straddle the back of a naked negro who carried me ashore.

My official entrance into Tangiers was the one familiar in all southern cities. A band of burnous-clad bandits tugged at my garments from all sides and fastened themselves on my hand baggage. I dragged my body from the landing-dock up through the gloomy crevice in the walls where the customs agent was nodding sleepily, his lance in his lap, and then on through the strange streets. Each of the bandits was trying to drag me to his own hotel, promising me gold and the ownership of earth if I should go with him. "Come with me, sir, take no notice of these loafers; I shall lead you to the best hotel in the whole town," said an elderly one-eyed rascal. "It's easy for him to make such promises; he has just been to the market and bought potatoes!" grins another. "See for yourself, sir, how he still has the skins in his beard!" "Filthy dog," the first screams back, "I suppose you eat of a roast to-night! Did I not see you myself bearing home a dead dog from the riverside!" Their poor English leaves them in the lurch. They drop back into their native Arabic, and I can pursue their quarrels no further. Suddenly one of them spits in the other's eyes, and is answered by his adversary in the same coin, and when this harmless ammunition had been used up, they turned to fistic blows and kicks. I took my advantage, disappeared into a side street and turned at every corner, in order that they might not be able to follow my trail. I had not gone far when the one-eyed fellow overtook me; his nose was bleeding; he looked like a fugitive but he snatched my bag and it came to pass, this time, that the vanquished won the spoils, a form of justice which is as reasonable as it is rare in history. Hadji abd Islam—for such was the name of my one-eyed conqueror—delivered me to the hotel keeper with much ceremony and commended himself to me as a guide. I used him so for two weeks; and though at first he seemed to me a bandit, he turned out to be an excellent fellow. He would go about with me all day long, from morning to night, asking but little in return, never sparing himself, never making any attempt to cheat me, and never permitting any one else to cheat me either. May Allah reward him for his kindness and preserve him from cholera and from the yellow snakes of the swamps.

I had an unusual feeling of delight as I stepped out on my balcony after Hadji had left me. The hotel was built in the Spanish style with balcony windows. Around it lay the Arab city, white-stuccoed, windowless, with flat roofs on which white-veiled women walked up and down.

It was evening; bay and street were silent; far off lay Spain and Gibraltar, like a distant wall of clouds. The moon cast a magical brightness over the white city before me with its deep shadows in the background, and the green air floating over it. Minarets and towers of azulejos seemed to come nearer in this nocturnal light. From my veranda, I could look down over the roofs into Moorish courtyards; under the pillared loggia in one of the courts an Arab sat on the stone flags, his legs drawn up under him, saying his evening prayers by the light of the red lamp. I could hear his assiduous mumbling. Then he ceased, prostrated his brow, which he struck thrice against the stones, and went on mumbling again. Later, as I sat bent over a letter to my native land, I could hear the Muezzin summoning the faithful to midnight prayers, in a soft but powerful voice, which came down from the slender minaret and bathed all the houses in its melody: God is great and all-powerful! Come to prayer! God the Lord Calls!

In the night I was awakened by loud calls, guttural voices and hasty steps in the alley. I jumped out of bed and dashed out on the balcony, whence I could see two white-clad policemen running along the railing of the bluff, pointing with the long barrels of their carbines in the direction of the beach. They disappeared in the misty light; I heard a shot. Then everything was still, I went back to bed, and lay, wide awake, listening for more.

The night was marked by the familiar sing-song hum that is characteristic of a still night at all times and in all places—it is silence audible. This silence was suddenly broken for a second time by the deep-chested call to prayers which came from the mouth of the Muezzin like a calm but strong swell of the sea. It was two o'clock. When I was about to sleep again, I heard loud but undistinguishable conversation going on under my balcony, and a shower of pebbles was cast into my room. Again I got up, and below on the railing, now covered by shadows, sat the two guards, staring at my windows. When they caught sight of me, they broke out in Arabic and made signs with their hands. I understood nothing. But began to feel quite nervous. I thought of everything: the street fight I had seen in the afternoon—no doubt they would arrest me—and I had not filed my papers yet—they would probably kick me out of the place—one of them suddenly called out to me in English: "Mind your pockets!" It suddenly dawned on me that the guard was merely giving me a general warning to beware of thieves. I answered him again in English, hoping to find out what he meant, but the sentence he had spoken must have contained all the English words he knew, and he kept on calling, "Mind your pockets, mind your pockets!" I took hold of the doors of my balcony to close them, at which the guards laughed loudly and clapped their hands with joy at being understood. Next day I told Hadji what had happened. He consoled me by saying there was nothing to be afraid of, still I had better lock my balcony doors and look under my bed at night.

I slept until long past the hour I had set for my next excursion. When I woke up Hadji abd Islam was sitting on a chair at the end of the room, legs crossed under him, his head at an angle, staring at me with his single eye, like an inquisitive hen. When I rose from bed, he removed—contrary to the custom of all good Moroccans—the red fez from his head, revealing a cranium that was entirely smooth-shaven, excepting a little patch at the crown, no bigger than a penny piece, from which grew a clump of long hairs. His skull, shining like polished bone, was covered with a crisscross of old scars extending all the way from hair patch to forehead. "Souvenirs of old brawls," I thought, but later I found the explanation. I saw the same isolated bundles of hair frequently during the following days among members of a Berber tribe, tall slender marauders wearing sandals of vine-wood and a *gehab* of camel's or goat's hair, hoods thrown over the back. In place of turbans, they often had rope strands or fibers of bast wound about their foreheads, which made them look very bold as they stood in large groups about the streets, haggling for carbines which they carelessly discharged at the white walls, so that plaster and lead fell in showers. They are said to come from the hills of Oran, and they believe that when they die Allah will draw them up into Paradise by the single strand of hair on their crowns.

After telling this yarn, Hadji sets forth to show me all the things which he likes to see himself, and this he does day after day. If the sun is not too high in the heavens and the *sirocco* not too hot, I am as zealous as he is, although my admiration is not always as undisguised as his. Hadji knows what is worth seeing, for he has traveled much. Once he went on a pilgrimage to Mecca, where he had the attack of smallpox which cost him an eye and spotted his skin. He has crossed the straits often to the Rock of Gibraltar, and once he took the train as far as Granada, where from the battlements of the Alhambra he gazed over the Vega, promised land from which his people had once been driven forth and to which Allah will again lead back his faithful ones. In the Alhambra, he tells me, the halls are larger and the vaulting more beautiful—in short all things are lovelier—than even in Mecca; it is the most fruitful land of the whole world, for the Heaven of the Faithful is arched over it. . . . He becomes so interested that he stops short in his tracks, crouching on the ground before me, and demands whether I too have seen Granada. For now the Spaniards hold it and they are the people who stick out their tongues at all nations that are different from themselves.

Hadji hates the Spaniards—did they not even try to get Morocco too? Fortunately Allah did not permit them to gain their end—Hadji clenches his fists and waves his hands wildly—as he tells of the bloody predatory campaign waged by Spain in 1859 and 1860. He himself as a child saw the men of his tribe dash westward over the desert in the direction of Tetuan, in order to drive out the great enemy; he saw them rushing back faster than they had come—broken and in despair.

At times, he forgets himself and me and his murder of the English language and relapses into incomprehensible Maghreb, his own speech. His English is poor in words but his narrations are rich in illustrative gesture. As he tells me of the Moroccan heroes Akhmed and Abbas and the cruel Spanish General Prim, he leads me out over the sun-dried, sandy, desolate heights and venomous swamps, which he loves so much.

On these hills are tall dry grasses which no animal will eat; there are rows of aloe, whose fibers are worked into textiles, as well as a few lone palms; and you enjoy wide panoramas of curved roads that lead through sand and nothing but sand. Down below in the swamps, there are dense jungles with poisonous snakes and acrid stagnant water that supply drink and pestilence to the city, and herds of little short-haired buffaloes that are served as food to the garrison at Gibraltar across the straits. The Moroccan himself eats no meat.

The dense under-growth of these jungles is the place of refuge for slaves that have fled from the hinterland. Tangiers has become a free city for them—the only such city in the whole country—although the city is subject to the same laws as the rest of the country.

For, the ambassadors of the powers to Tangiers do not live in the capital, but in Tangiers itself—there are times when it is a pleasant feeling to know you are as near Europe as possible—and the ambassadors have strongly fortified villas, which lie close together, as well as a numerous retinue of servants, most of them negroes.

These negroes are in many cases run-away slaves; the ambassadors take them under their protection and have made the slave trade impossible in Tandja—"the city protected by God"—owing to their energetic intervention.

There are probably great numbers of slaves still in the city, but these slaves are practically on the footing of servants, and the conditions of their lives are so favorable that they seem to have no desire to run away and expose themselves to the competition of free men.

In this respect at least, therefore, a few European settlers have inculcated the rudiments of European civilization—by reason of their superior authority— in this outpost of the Moroccan sultanate.

Tangiers is quite as taboo to European civilization as is all the rest of Morocco. Southern Europe is not particularly eager for conquest, and the current of water that flows through the narrow Straits of Gibraltar has too vehement a flow. On this southern side of the Straits, the number of wives a man keeps is in direct proportion to his money. A Pasha has only eight wives; he cannot afford to support more; and if there are so many men who have to get along with only one wife and some with none at all, Hadji says this is due entirely to the hard times. Hadji himself is not married and has not the slightest intention to marry until he can keep two wives. In fact, he would be in a position to do this now if there were more English women visiting the town, for the English women pay their guides very well. But since the bridge-head was finished down by the beach, enabling boats to moor instead of anchoring out in the bay, which obliged passengers to ride ashore on the backs of naked negroes except at high tide, the English women do not cross the Straits as much as they used to. For this reason, Hadji does not want to get married; it would be too boring to have to get along with one wife only; only "these niggers" could do such a thing.

Again and again he reverts to the subject of Pasha's harem, telling me all sorts of improbable things concerning the edifice and its inmates. But he has no hair-raising tales of romantic incidents, of faithless women of the harem stuck into bags and sunk in the Straits by night where the current is strongest. Pasha's women are proud of their station, which they have chosen of their own free will, says Hadji, and do not wish to go in for silly adventures. However, there are guards with long spears and plenty of eunuchs around the harem so that things hardly give the appearance of a Pasha as sure of his women as Hadji says he is. Men are not permitted to enter. But one day as I was going by, I caught a glimpse of a thick-skirted eunuch who was opening the door for an English woman to pass out. This woman told me that all the women inside sat in a beautiful apartment in semi-darkness stitching little objects intended for sale. Pasha's favorite wife, who distinguished herself from the others by doing nothing, had kissed the English lady's hand as she left and begged her for a franc for coffee.

These creatures so low in the social scale that each one of them is entitled only to a small fraction of the favor of the great Mussulman are of course considered objects unworthy of his glances at any moment at which he himself does not voluntarily come to visit them. Therefore they are not permitted to show themselves in the streets except when clad in a very plain white bag, their faces completely veiled; they may not enter the main street, but are required to keep to the small narrow alleys and, wherever there are large congregations of men, to make a wide detour around such groups. They remind you of perambulating flour-bags clinging as close to the walls as possible, and the constant repetition of veiled women and nothing but veiled women has the effect of an enigma, finally leading one into fabulous imaginings, not imaginings of wondrous beauties, but visions of old women of such unusual ugliness that they do not dare appear in the streets except with their faces covered.

However much these women may be crushed, they yet have something of the innate fearlessness of their sex. If you meet them in remote spots with no Mohammedan anywhere around, they will push aside their veils and smile at you, revealing features that are quite presentable. And you feel a desire to attempt the impossible, namely, to speak to these outcast creatures face to face and ask them whether they believe in Allah—although they have no souls of their own—and whether they do not feel it a deprivation to be forbidden to pray to him in the mosque. Or whether they do not know, perchance, that it will be possible for them to attain the Paradise of the faithful if their husbands are willing to dispense with a few of their celestial spouses to the advantage of their terrestrial brides? Perhaps they know all this and are nevertheless confident of securing admission to Heaven, because they are women, and because, being women, they have faith in men. Could it be any particular hardship for Pasha, for example, if he should renounce eight out of the seventy-two beauties which are destined for him after death, in order by this generous act to secure admission to Paradise for his eight wives on earth? Even if he should have had more than enough of them here below and should be no longer capable of tolerating the sight of them he might nevertheless take so generous a step, for he would still have sixty-four new wives. Yet, it is hard to say what Pasha will do about it. And besides, do women set any great store on getting into Heaven, anyway?

Not much has been done in the way of instruction in the school-room in Morocco, but there are a few schools. One I found in Tangiers in one of the narrowest little streets of the city. Here were eight or ten little mites from the most wealthy Moorish families crouching on the stone floor, rattling off their Koran. They are dressed like grown-ups, in a red fez, white burnous, and yellow slippers. Their slight limbs seem to be drowning in their voluminous garments as they babble away at the sacred verses, their eyes closed, their bodies swaying to and fro. The school-room is without any windows, and reminds you of nothing so much as an empty wagon-shed. There are no torn maps and charts on the walls, no school benches and desks for the boys to carve their names on, no ink-wells to be upset for the general amusement. In fact, there is no trace of any of the paraphernalia of teaching; there is nothing but an old white-bearded Moor, who sits in front of the boys holding a lash in his hand and playing schoolmaster, with an open Koran on his knees. He smiles and nods and I smile and nod; he politely invites me to have a seat and I seat myself on the soiled floor and make an effort to stow my feet Arab-fashion under my body. I now have an opportunity to hear the littlest one of the boys rattle off, without any interruption, a whole chapter out of the Koran, apparently without making the slightest mistake. A conversation ensues between the two of us, with Hadji serving as an interpreter—although the schoolmaster can speak "all the languages on earth"— and I compliment him dutifully on his pupils. Then I make a few attempts to test his prowess, but he is too clever for me and I am obliged to content myself with the knowledge that he is at least able to read. I rise, brush the dirt from the seat of my trousers, attracting as little attention as possible in the process, in order not to give offense, and take my leave. Hadji winks at me with his big eye from the doorway; I grasp the significance of the signal at once and give the old white-bearded "professor" a one-franc coin for coffee.

It cannot be said that the machinery of government

is very complicated. Twice a week Pasha sits on his heels outside the great gate of his splendid palace and administers justice according to the good Old Testament method. The adversaries in litigation approach, each from his own side of the road, and depart side by side, conciliated, along the center of the thoroughfare. If the case is particularly complicated, Pasha will angrily pull his long white beard, "and then the question is always cleared up."

If you are willing to pay a small gratuity for the guard, you may secure permission to view, from the outside, the treasure-chamber of the province, a massive stone structure with a solid door guarded by seven great padlocks. The seven keys to these seven locks are held by seven different men of excellent reputation in the city, and thus it is possible to feel secure from any theft of public funds. Not even Pasha himself may hold these keys, for his monthly salary amounts to barely more than twenty-five dollars.

One day Hadji and I undertook to visit all the public institutions, one after the other, on which occasion we also had a view of the municipal hospital and the prison. The former is in a narrow street with houses built over it, running along the rear wall of the mosque. After going for some distance along this street, Hadji himself poked open a door and we entered a dark space from which I was driven out forthwith by a stifling stench. But I had seen enough. It was a long apartment, one side of which was divided into sections resembling stable stalls. In each stall there was a bundle of straw or of ragged matting—it was too dark to distinguish which—and lying on this heap I could make out the shapes of naked human bodies writhing

and moaning. From one a pair of yellowish-gray legs
stuck out; a naked child with scales all over its body
was crawling out of another. The old woman who
had charge of the place swept the child back into its
section with the aid of her cane, and with a countenance
as angry as if she herself were a neat chambermaid and
the little one a toad that had crawled over the threshold. The principal duty of the old woman is to see to
it that the patients do not run away and that each dies
in his own section. There is no doubt that they will
all die—what other reason could have induced them
to resort to the hospital? They receive no food but
what is brought them by their relatives; and it is also
obvious that once one has brought one's dear ones to
this institution and thus made it possible for them to
die in its conventional surroundings, there is no particular reason for supplying them with too much food.
Such a procedure would be equivalent to throwing
Allah's gifts out of the window. They will have things
enough to eat in the place they are going to, at least
so Hadji says. But suppose they are slow in going?
"Then they send for the medicine man, and he helps
them to die," is Hadji's simple answer. Perhaps this
is the reason why I never saw a single cripple (and
cripples are the curse of southern European countries)
—anywhere in Tangiers.

The prison is based on like principles. It is situated
far above the city, next to Kasbah—the fort—and reminds you of a church built in the rotunda form. It
has no windows and no doors; light is admitted from
above through the rickety roof, and when new prisoners arrive to be incarcerated, a hole is made in the
wall, which is bricked up again after they are inside.

There is no chance of the prisoner's ever getting out unless a certain sum is paid for his dismissal, but this sum has to be raised very quickly, since no one could live very long in this place. Nor are such liberations frequent. There is a little extension built on by the side of the circular wall; in this lodge the guards sleep on stone benches, surrounded by rifles and spears.

The sentinel opens the peep-hole, about one foot square, and you may look into the prison. If the stench in the hospital was intolerable, it is ten times worse here; you hold your nose and draw back your head every moment to get a breath of air. The floor inside is a morass of manure and reeds; some of the prisoners are lying down, others crouch; others slink about in a circular orbit dictated by the length of their chains. They are chained either to the circular wall or to the pillar that supports the roof.

As soon as they discover me at the peep-hole, they move slowly in my direction, as far as their chains will permit them. Lean scraggy necks and long thin trembling arms stretch out toward me; their eyes, their open mouths, seem to voice a consuming demand. They take hold of each other as a means of crawling forward themselves, forgetting that it is the chain that is holding them back. Matted beards and shaggy hair, naked backs covered with a thick crust of human excrement mingled with straw, a few rags swinging about their loins loose and wet and slapping over their naked legs whenever they tug at their chains to get closer to me.

They are never allowed to go out in the open air; they receive no water to wash with and obtain food only when their relatives and friends bring them some.

Or, when they are able to earn some for themselves! Necessity has made them inventive and stimulated their energies. Although they may never have followed a calling while they were at liberty—here they sit surrounded by dirt and filth, engaged in turning out the neatest little baskets and purses of gayly colored reeds and Moroccan leather, which they sell to the tourists who come to see and enjoy this wretched spectacle. And the inhuman treatment they receive has made them more humane to each other; what other consideration could impel those who stand nearer to us and who are themselves offering objects they are eager to sell at any price, to pass on the output of the prisoners who stand behind them and offer them for sale together with their own? They would hardly do as much if they were trading under free conditions; in fact, society does not even deal so well by them, for society has locked them up here and exposed them to the certain fate of death by starvation and filth. Nor would any human society treat them much better.

This society, whose practice accords with the prescriptions of the Mosaic Code, and which dooms to destruction its diseased or demoralized members, by no means consists of barbarians who would find it a difficult task to acquire civilization step by step. In numbers, the Moors embrace but one-third of the population of Morocco, but they constitute the entire upper class, the official stratum—from the sultan down to the night watchman—as well as the merchant class and the higher artisans; they make up practically the entire population of the city. And they are the descendants of a race of high culture, remnants of which they still retain in the interior splendor of their buildings, in the gorgeousness of their raiment, and in the dazzling cleanliness of their outer garments, in their outward behavior and in their aristocratic bearing. You will look in vain in the streets of Tangiers for that "animal-like simplicity" and that frank and open conversation that is so characteristic of the cities of southern Europe; a lady can walk alone through these streets without hearing rude observations spoken behind her back or witnessing any sight that might cause her to blush. The Moors are well acquainted with the forms of good breeding, and observe them furthermore; for the rest, however, they have got far beyond these forms. They have freed themselves from the contents and requirements of these forms, because they had become a burden; and their feeling them a burden was due to the fact that they themselves had become degenerated and fatigued.

In their manners and their deeds they remind one vividly of a late scion of some great family. They are extremely blasé and incapable of feeling interest or compassion; in fact, of being carried away by any emotion. In southern Europe, the presence of a stranger may be the cause of a riot, yet, though strangers are far less frequent in Morocco than in some other regions, the Moor does not dignify him with even a fraction of a glance.

As for nerves, the Moor seems to have none; nor has he any evident desire for life and activity. He does as little as possible, hates to talk to you, prefers to walk by himself; he will stand leaning against a wall for hours, staring absent-mindedly in front of him without budging and without permitting any sound to awaken him; he will sit with his feet resting in the

gutter, with his chin on his hands, day-dreaming, trying
to fixate the tip of his own nose with his eyes. If you
talk to the most wretched of these philosophers and
ask him the way, or express some kindly polite thought,
or offer him a profitable errand to run—you can interpret his expression and his inapt answers as meaning only one thing: his desire for repose.

That is what he has: repose. Excepting the Jewish
quarter, the whole city is as dreamily silent as the
castle of the Sleeping Beauty, except when the Berbers
come to town. Life glides along with mechanical uni-
formity, with a sort of somnambulistic lethargy. The
Moor sits by the gate of his little shop, at shop after
shop, one right next to the other, and he reads in his
Koran or ponders, indifferent as to whether purchasers
come or not. He has made things comfortable for
himself, has drawn his legs up under him completely,
and his posture is such as to enable him to reach with
his hands any object in the shop, as well as to take
your money, without being obliged to rise. He has by
his side everything he needs: a jug of water and a
piece of bread. He can barely make the effort of
speech when the black water-carrier comes by and he
needs to have his jug refilled.

If there is a customer, the shopkeeper will hand
him the required article silently and without raising his
eyes, whereupon he slips the money into another jug
and continues reading or idling. He will not consent
to engage in haggling, nor will he take the pains to
submit a number of articles, so that the purchaser may
select what he wants. After the customer has received
his article and finds that it is too large or too small,
or at any rate not the right thing, and asks for another

instead, the shopkeeper will silently put it back in its place, return the man's money, and drop back into metaphysical speculations. This done, no amount of entreaty or beseeching can induce him to continue to serve the customer.

There are some signs of life only in the market place above the city wall; but the traders here are for the most part Jews, and the half-savage charcoal-burners from the mountains. Food will cook all by itself in this heat, and there is not much demand for their charcoal. They stretch themselves out in the sunlight, converse or amble down to the inns under the half-roofs and drink green tea with a honey-bread that is black with flies. Whenever one of them lifts his bread to his mouth, the flies disperse, with a sound like the rustling of reeds in a jungle. After a piece has been bitten off, the swarm again gathers on the bread. It is for the fly to take care that it does not become part of his meal; he does not care; he leaves that to them.

Under the awning sits the teller of fairy tales. He has no listeners at this moment, but he continues reciting his tales, for all that, swaying to and fro the while —it sounds like the ceaseless croaking of frogs on a summer evening. Now and again a passer-by throws a shilling into his jug. The snake charmer sitting near him attracts more attention. Two ugly negresses— slaves—and a few gypsy children are his whole audience and for their edification he takes out snake after snake from his leather pouch, with the utmost seriousness, and permits them to twine about his neck and arms to the accompaniment of a most diverting musical melody. When he is through and has consigned the snakes to his pouch again, the onlookers depart without making any payment; he does not care.

From the market-place I can view through the horse-shoe of the city gate the main street in all its length straight down toward the white beach-walls and a patch of blue ocean. It reminds you of a river bed that has run dry, in fact, in the rainy season it really is a river bed; you can see the marks left by the water along the wall and in the middle of its course great bowlders and sandy furrows bear witness to the latest rain. In all the shops all the way down the street salesmen sit in immutable postures, like the puppets of a marionette theater when the play is over. At the end of the street the ocean has a bluish shimmer. The houses gleam white on either side; petrified human forms, their legs crossed under them, lean against the walls; muscular artisans sleep under their tents, naked legs sticking out from under the canvas. A Moor in precious garments is sitting on the naked ground, his face pressed close to the wall; he is eating grapes, as silent and dream-lorn as a child.

For a moment there is life in the street. Three ragged men walk along singing and screaming. They strike a rattling instrument, causing it to sound, and wriggle about to the accompaniment of their howling melody, and there is delirious frenzy in their eyes and faces. These religious fanatics wander about with their host of admirers; they go and the street is again silent.

One hot August afternoon I was strolling in the market-place. The salesmen had disappeared, so had the teller of fairy tales, the snake charmer too; well-dressed Moors were standing in the sunny space, looking toward the city gate, expectantly. At the uppermost end of the market-place was a house whose flat roof was crowded with people, European settlers most of them. There was to be a parade I was told and accordingly purchased a ticket of admission to the grand stand on the roof.

An orange yellow banner came out from under the market gate. I could see the crowd milling in the gateway and hear a confused and distant racket. The market-place rises to the point which we occupied; the gate is about a thousand feet away.

The sun burned hotly and the heat of the flat asphalt roof seered your feet through the soles of your shoes; an hour had passed and I was beginning to think of going home. Suddenly the music emerged more distinctly—it was a deep boom! boom! which pounded away with a dense pertinacity as a clarinet shrilly embroidered it with a long irritating wail that rose and faintly fell, with no pauses for breath. It drilled its way into your ear monotonously and ceaselessly like the zoom of an importunate gnat.

The noise became more distinct; it seemed to me there was dancing with savage gestures and that I could see the onlookers being dispersed on one side or the other, retreating with yells.

The crowd would advance, then halt, then dance for a long time. Now and again I could see something dart forth and gleam in the air as a naked, smooth-shaven cranium rose high above the swarm and disappeared again.

Again an advance and again a stop. An ivory yellow skull rose in the air, disappeared; a gleaming flash had darted across it as the skull was at its highest point in the air. My eyes saw something red, like blood, a faint purple glow seemed to hover above the spot where the head had been.

I was speechless with astonishment, my blood was banging away in my veins. Explanations swarmed through my brain.

The bloody speck had just disappeared from my eyes when I beheld the great crowd parting on one side of the street while a fanatical figure in crouching posture, like that of the traditional American Indian, darted out of the circle with an ax in its hand. A veiled Moorish woman was fleeing from this creature in great panic. The woman became entangled in her long head-cloth and fell to the ground with a scream. Two men armed with heavy canes seized her pursuer just as he was raising his ax over her head; they took away his ax and pushed him back into the crowd. He permitted himself to be led by them without opposition and walked along as stiffly and inanimately as a sleep-walker. His close-shorn head hung down over his breast and bobbed up and down with each step he took, as if it was but loosely attached to his body; he was covered with dark red patches: coagulated blood.

Two hours have already passed since this crowd began flowing in through the market gate, so slow is its advance; now the crowd is directly in front of the house on which I stand, and I can see every detail of it. At the head of the multitude there dance a few savage figures with open wounds on their heads, their faces covered with blood, and blood also is on their chests and garments. They have thin-bladed axes in their hands, which they clash together over their heads with the beat of the music. A few sedate—almost indifferent-looking—men with long beards, holding great armfuls of axes, walk behind the dancers.

Then there follows a great circular train—perhaps half a hundred—who, holding each other by the hand and darting up and down like Cartesian divers, keep step with the leader of the dance, a gigantic negro who occupies the center of the circle.

At the very end comes the band of music, the instruments of which consist of a few sounding-boards covered with membranes stretched over them, and the cursed clarinet, which still wails out its lamentation like an endless thread. The whole procession is in motion, dancing either as it halts, or as it moves slowly forward, and the dance has not ceased now for two hours. Even those who prostrate themselves and beat their brows upon the ground do not cease their measured swayings for a single moment—the rhythm of the music has hypnotized them.

The procession moves through thousands of onlookers—men and children; and above, on the high banks under the aloe hedges, there are rows of sitting women, resembling white sea-birds in their curious costumes. At times a dancing fanatic will make for them with his ax raised, whereupon they will dart to their feet with screams and escape into the jungle-like brush-wood of the swamps.

As I stand there and look on, Hadji joins me; I ask him what this thing means.

"They are religious fanatics who are dancing in honor of Sedi Ali," he says. "They are genuine idiots who hop around and disfigure themselves." He assumes the expression of one who would say he is superior to all supernatural phenomena, but I recall the scars on his polished skull and am now able to guess their origin.

Fatigue seems to be making itself felt—after two hours of uninterrupted dancing uphill and two hours of ceaseless music. The dancer seems to be moving with effort, the music has lost its vigor; so have the fakirs; their axes are dropping, the men look as if they are about to collapse in their own blood.

Then come the sacred loaves from Fez. The leader of the dance lays a loaf on the flat of his head and resorts to a new rhythm as he leaps high in the air. The whole circle acquires new energy. The spirit suddenly moves one of the dancers; he leaves the circle, which closes again behind him. As he dances, he kisses the bread borne by the leader of the dance. Then he jumps over the joined hands of the circle, seizes an ax and attaches himself, still dancing, to the other fakirs—a new fakir. He dances alone, like them, swinging his ax in a challenging manner, then he stops and jumps high into the air, as the edge of the ax cuts its way into his shorn pate. Three bounds executed to the musical accompaniment, and three blows of the ax—one at each leap; and the blood comes pouring down from three open cuts. The man collapses, but leaps to his feet again and continues to dance—he has not broken the rhythm of the performance. And the effect of his act is incendiary; each fakir, swinging his ax, leaps in the air and strikes the ax into his skull three times.

The slow procession has passed the house. I leave my place on the roof and follow it, crawling along the slopes, repeatedly warned by good-natured Moors not to get too near the fakirs. The monotonous music no longer tires me; it stimulates me; my enervation has been succeeded by excitement, my excitement passes into delirium. Some of the fakirs are completely bathed in blood, and the two men who distribute the axes have had to take them away from the fakirs. Some of them have not one ax only, but three axes tied in a bundle, which clashes in the air and strikes three wounds at once. The axes have very thin blades and are very light; they do not fall with great impact; but they are sharp and can leave an ugly wound. Occa-sionally a fakir will fall and find it difficult to rise again. The sacred loaf is placed over his head, and he at once gets to his feet; then he prostrates himself, beating his forehead against the ground.

The cursed wail of the clarinet continues to pierce my brain incessantly; I have the sensation of being about to perform some insane act in order to liberate myself from this sound. These mad wretches with their naked torsos, sullied with blood, sweat and dust, and their bald heads covered with a profusion of red wounds, are no longer repulsive to me, not even the wretch who delicately caresses his own cheek with three ax edges, cutting triple scars. The color of blood is no longer the color of blood, but simply a fiery red, vo-luptuously splendid in the sunlight.

I am unable to tear myself away; I cannot do other-wise than follow the procession through the outer gate and on over the flat hills of the road toward Fez. The crowd is left behind, and returns to the city; the axes are taken from the wild fakirs, one after the other; the spectacle draws to an end. The last thing I see is the figure of a man who will not give up his ax. He strug-gles with the other men and kisses the edge of his weapon; the blood spurts from his lips. He even embraces their knees, imploring them to leave him his ax. And the host passes out in the desert. To-morrow morning they will be in Fez, where—according to Hadji—Sedi Ali's sacred grave is situated, which works such great wonders that a single prayer pronounced at that spot will cure all the fakir's wounds.

The sun is setting, pouring its purple glow over the lowlands and crowning the heights with gold.

Out of the Straits of Gibraltar float the blue smoky trails of hundreds of steamers. But Tangiers is not concerned with steamers; they steam eastward, westward, to the Orient and to America, with their cargoes. But inland, across the flat hills of the desert, a caravan emerges, and slowly glides toward the market-place. The caravan brings grain from the fruitful country around Fez. Each animal carries on its back five or six big bags. They stagger awkwardly under their burdens, their small malignant heads perched on their long necks, moving up and down with a sinuous snake-like motion which reminds me of the groping progress of the gondolas on the canals of Venice. This is the commercial fleet of Tangiers. And as the darkness falls from a verdigris sky I hear the drivers struggling furiously with their camels, as they command them to lie down for unloading. The cries of pain emitted by the camels who bend down with their loads and whose knees strike hard against the ground, are mingled with the soft, all-embracing cry of the Muezzin: "God is great! Come to prayer! God the Lord calls!"

VII

SUNLIGHT

THE sky is always blue above the clouds—so runs a proverb in the north as a consolation for our gloomy weather and our every-day cares. And from such ancient sayings we draw strength to meet more gray weather and more cares.

The Andalusian would fall sick and die if he had to accept such consolation—he lacks our highly developed sense of the abstract. But he fares very well without it, for the sun rises every day for months and sets again without a fleck of cloud. And the heaven's arch is so deep and warmly blue that we should fail to recognize it even on our loveliest summer days. The Moors had every reason to call Andalusia the earthly Paradise. In January, the mountain-tops are white with snow, but *el Sol criador*—the creating sun—rises every morning and warms the snow, sends it flowing down in crystal streams along the mountain slopes and bedecking its path with flowers: with blue irises, daisies, and bright-eyed marguerites. "See! There is the Creator! Behold God," say the people, their eyes shining, when the sun rises over the hills. And while the peasant is gathering his olive-crop, the orange-groves still glow with their golden fruits and the almond-trees are white with blossoms. Autumn and spring join hands across the threshold of the new year!

According to meteorological observations made in the province of Malaga, the rain fell in the province

262 times in nine years, twenty-nine times a year; precipitation enough.   In the same nine years there were three storms.   Some persons go so far in their theory of our natural need of obstacles, as to maintain that even the grain must have wind, since the stalk could not otherwise grow strong enough to support the ears; but in this country the loveliest cereals grow without ever having had an opportunity to sway in the wind. The beneficent peace that spreads within us and around us in northern countries on a quiet summer evening— when everything is so silent and motionless that we can see the blades of grass resume their upright positions as if a softly moving cat had trod them down, and so noiseless that individual calls may be heard from village to village—such peace prevails in this region all day long and for months and months without any interruption.   Nothing stirs the solemn cypress pointing heavenward in petrified repose; high up in the air the mighty crown of the pine-tree seems to be resting upon air; smoke rising from the fires of the shepherds ascends vertically to heaven.   The landscape seems as if enchanted in a sparkling sun-slumber, and over it hangs the pall of the monotonous sound given out by the bells of grazing beasts and caravans of donkeys. So silent is the foliage, that you start up in fright when a bird disturbs it; the air is so motionless that if you should put down a feather on a rock, you would find it a month later on the same spot.

Not without reason that the people who live here call the sun God and Creator; they are light-hearted children of the sun.   They do not at all possess the superiority of the northerner to matters of climate and temperature.   On rainy days they are attacked by discouragement, they sit around in a state of collapse, shivering, with an expression of such hopelessness on their faces as if their lives had suffered ship-wreck. But let even the tiniest rent appear in the clouds, and it will be reflected in their eyes, and as soon as the sun shines forth again the whole sad business is forgotten —not to be treasured, like *our* misfortunes, in one of the obscure corners of the spirit—but forgotten, wiped out. They hum and joke, work like beasts of burden for a day, in order to lie about idly in the sunlight on the following day; they drink from every brook and spring they encounter; they gnaw a bit of bark for food, and are happy, care-free—mindless of the day that is to come.

It appears that the sun, which destroys so many bacteria, destroys care. In the innermost spirit of the Andalusian there are no lightless corners where bitter experiences accumulate a sort of mold—but as well they have no recesses in which such unhappiness and bitter experience may precipitate and solidify into some sort of useful guide for the future. If you should tell an Andalusian that ugly experiences make a man harder and develop his character, he would look at you open-mouthed; such conceptions as personality and character, in our sense of the word, are to his mind— if he ever encounters them—merely expressions of a disturbed digestion. The thought of living his life in accordance with some collective idea, and setting himself a goal and patiently striving for this goal in spite of distress and self-denial—perhaps even risking the probability that the goal will never be realized before death comes and bars all doors—such a thought would be monstrously funny to him. He is a child of the moment and the present hour is for him the only true value; he does not like to give up any of to-day's possessions in favor of an already quite uncertain morrow, and he certainly is still less interested in remote future prospects.

As the Andalusian's crops flourish excellently without any wind, so his own development proceeds successfully without any obstacles to overcome. He is like an orange-tree that fills the valleys with fragrance, spreading its foliage harmoniously and uniformly, because no wind has stunted its growth and bent its crown. The golden fruits blaze jubilantly in the sun; and if a gust of wind should come along, they would all fall, for the tree has not been tempered by adversity.

Like a sun-flower, the Andalusian lets his being flow toward the sun and all the wrinkles that deposit themselves prematurely in his brow come from the sun; they radiate like crow's-feet from his blinking eyes, living witnesses of the sun's strength and favor—tokens of happiness, they have nothing to do with suffering. What matters it to him what the sun is made of? It shines! And the celestial spaces, the terrestrial globe, the customs and practices of other lands—why should he rack his brains over these? Here he is; he exists; that is the essential—the whole thing! And what other reason is there for living if not to enjoy himself, to consume the fruits of life, and to slip as adroitly as possible through all difficulties!

To live and let live, to enjoy, to be happy!—is the refrain of his life; he is an Epicurean. But he is an Epicurean of a peculiar type, making as few demands on life as did old Diogenes himself.

The Anglo-Teuton nations have developed hardship as a doctrine of life, and yet their care for self-preservation has resulted in more suicides than those due to any other cause, even including unrequited love. These solicitudes for self-preservation have, furthermore, very rarely any direct connection with starvation; you shoot yourself because you do not possess the necessary number of one-thousand-dollar bonds to enable you to live according to your station. The Andalusian, on the other hand, will cast a ragged bag about his shoulders with as much pride and decency as he would put on a velvet-lined mantle; he is no lower in his own eyes or in the eyes of others because he is obliged to eat hard bread and drink water; his sense of status does not depend on external things, and his feeling of hardship is not aroused until hunger gnaws at his vitals. But even in this case he will not take his own life; he will let hunger do the job. And if hunger does not accomplish the task, well then—obviously the matter could not have been so serious after all.

He is not an ascetic. If you serve him a tasty meal, he will partake of it gladly—but he will not go out of his way to obtain it; such things do not move his ambition. The mode of cooking that results from this attitude is more or less haphazard. After breakfast has been taken from the stove at eleven o'clock in the morning, dinner is put on, because it saves you the trouble of making a new fire later, and the food will go on boiling and frying until six o'clock, regardless of recipe. It is only in the boiling of eggs that some attention is paid to time; for in this process the kitchen girl will recite the Credo at a greater or less speed, depending on whether the eggs are to be boiled soft or hard. Food is rather uniform in the various classes of society, and it may at first disturb strangers somewhat, on their first visit to the home of Lawyer So and So, or Editor So and So, to find him lunching on a mixture of chunks of bacon and vegetables, of which he will amiably invite the visitor to partake. No one ever thinks of issuing a formal invitation for dinner or supper, since dining is not considered one of the great enjoyments, and no one ever thinks of offering you anything between meals. Furthermore, very little taste is displayed at such meals; to be perfectly frank, the Spaniard eats like a pig. When you pay a visit, you will sit opposite your host or hostess over a carafe of water or a bottle of wine and sugar-bread. Even in higher circles, which consider it their duty to live in the French style, the question of arranging a large number of courses is easily disposed of. First they have soup, then the vegetables that were boiled in the soup, then the pieces of meat and bacon whose broth imparted strength to the soup. The fourth course is usually a salad, cold water being drunk with it, and the fifth course some fruit or goat-cheese. There are fresh plates for each course and the requirements of social decency are thus fully complied with.

In our country it would be an offense to a plain man to offer him water as a beverage—because it costs nothing. But in this country, whenever the train stops at a small station, you may often see the wine peddlers out-distanced by the water peddlers, although their wares are of exactly the same price—about a cent a glass. For his world-famous wine the Andalusian has only the words "quite drinkable," but when he speaks

of water, his tongue revels in the use of all the rich
and tender adjectives of his language. But he dwells
above all on the circumstance that water has no price
but gushes forth freely and extravagantly from the
ground—a gift of God for the poorest. On one of our
mountain tours in the environs of Granada I had occasion to talk to a cottager, who, when we told him of
our voyages, burst out with the exclamation: "It must
be glorious to see so much of the world, and to taste
all the waters of the various places"; and a woman
from Granada who had gone to visit the mountain city
of Loja in order to be cured of a stomach trouble and
had drunk from *los veinticinco canos* (a spring whose
waters are made to flow from twenty-five tubes), assured me that she could taste a distinct difference between the waters of the various pipes. At first she felt
bloated and her entrails were mortified, but after this
water had won the victory over the local waters, she
began to feel uncommonly well, and finally, after she
had drunk from all the pipes, it seemed to her as if
she had a slight intoxication as from wine. This
legendary delight in water has about it something that
is not so much native to this part of the country and
may have arisen rather in conditions in the Sahara, or
in Arabia.

This happy superiority to circumstances puts the
lower class on practically the same basis as the possessing class, imparting to the former, in its relations
to its betters, a feeling of self-dignity which one seeks
in vain elsewhere. In this "aristocratic" country, it is
the most natural thing in the world for a proletarian
to stop a cabinet member or a nobleman and ask him
for a light—and get it. If a market-woman happens

to upset her pushcart, it is a perfectly natural thing for any one who happens to be about, even if it be the King himself, to help her pick up her wares. The King will not be mentioned in the newspapers for this uncommon act of kindly condescension—but he might get into the papers if he neglected to perform it.

The Andalusian, who maintains his joy in life under conditions we would suffer under or even succumb to, remains a human being under circumstances in which we should cease to be human. Hundreds of beggars, hundreds of unemployed looking for jobs, I encountered; but I have never met any one in Spain with the soul of a lackey. Dog-like servility and its complement—snobbish aloofness are both unknown in this country. It would never occur to the poor people living in back alleys to sneak in a wide circle around a policeman standing at the corner; they do not tremble even when they stand before a royal officer. And the result is the authorities and the official class bear the stamp of this feeling on the part of the lower classes.

The same virtues which are displayed by the Andalusian under favorable circumstances are also shown as a rule when things go not so well. If he is charitably disposed, poverty will not kill his charity. He always has the possibility of denying himself some new necessity. In Granada I often saw the more successful beggars playing the part of alms-givers to the less favored. And if they have nothing to give, they can always offer the services of their own persons. The practical northern European, whose entire life is dominated by considerations of a commercial nature, is sometimes amazed at the outrageous prices asked by the Andalusian; but he is just as frequently disturbed by the unselfish spirit in which a poor man will accompany him for a distance of five or ten miles to show him the way through the mountains, and then disappear at once as soon as his debtor moves his hand to his pocket. It is not an infrequent thing for a poor woman to come to the market-place in Granada and to say to a baggage-carrier: "I have a box that I should like to have taken to the station, but I have no money; God will reward you for it." And her box will be brought to the station.

In Copenhagen we say: "The poorer the man, the higher the price." The most impoverished persons, whose purchases amount to two or three farthings each, pay as high as one hundred per cent more than persons of better station. It pays to do business with poverty. In Andalusia, no reduction is made for large purchases. Any one who suggested such a thing to a merchant would encounter the reply, as a rule: "It would be a sin against the poor!" And what is more, when you make purchases on a very small scale you are not subjected to the treacherous reduction in quantity which seems to have become the rule in Denmark and which limits the poor to half their proper nourishment.

"It isn't so very bad to be poor," said a poor widow of Granada to me. "At seven o'clock in the morning the milk goats go by. I buy two farthings' worth of milk then, and that means a glass filled to the brim. It would cost any one else five farthings, but they can see that I am poor. At eight o'clock God comes out in all his glory and shines right into my room; so rich, so rich, that I do not need to kindle my brazier. I can hear my blood boil, so warm is the sun and—tra, la—

sometimes I dance. But in the evenings the sun goes down behind the high houses and it becomes cold down here. Then I simply go over the street to the coal-dealer and beg him for five farthings' worth of wood-coal; and because I am poor he gives me twice as much as he would give others. It is the same way at the grocer's."

And what she said was true! I was once in a shop and observed that the brown-clad beggar by my side paid only half as much for his eggs as I did.

"Oho!" I said to myself, "they are trying to do me because I am a foreigner"; and indignantly I demanded my rights in a voice trembling with the Nordic sense of justice.

"But those are the regular prices for the poor, sir!" said the tradesman, seriously.

"Then I demand that I be charged the same prices as the poor," I said with determination, not wishing to be cheated under any circumstances.

The shopkeeper shrugged his shoulders and let me have my way; and I gathered up my things, faintly triumphant over my success. The only thing that irritated me was the fact that the shopkeeper showed not the slightest embarrassment at being thus caught in the act in the presence of all his customers; and the latter looked at me as though I were a criminal. I hesitated in my defiance. Then I saw a poorly dressed man hand the storekeeper a few coins and exchange a glance with him, whereupon he left the store. And when I myself turned to go, the merchant came up to me, handed back my money to me and said:

"Please, sir, the eggs shall cost you nothing." I

looked at him in astonishment. "The gentleman who just went away begged to be allowed to pay for you," he said seriously.

Were these words spoken in contempt? I looked around me at the others. They did not turn an eyelid, but nodded in earnest approval of the stranger's act.

"But—I cannot accept this," I protested.

"Poverty is an honorable thing, my man," said the merchant, as he slipped the money good-naturedly into my pocket.

"*Eso es,*" the others said with straight faces—"it is a true word."

They appeared ultimately to have arrived at the conclusion that I must be wretchedly poor, for they could not otherwise explain my behavior, and they looked at me with glances of compassion.

"No! here in Spain—thank God!—it is not a disgrace to be poor," said a customer confidently as I was going. In fact, it would not be a disgrace in northern Europe either, if there were only some profit in it. If this shopkeeper, for instance, retaining the same principles of business, should settle down in Copenhagen, he would probably encounter very few persons who would not gladly call themselves poor for the privilege of taking advantage of the prices fixed for the poor. We owe this to ourselves though the poor should lose their privileges.

Trade and industry are not extensively developed in Andalusia. Even their counterfeit money must be obtained from England if it is to gain any currency. And yet these persons are in many ways quite capable of softening the discomforts of existence, for themselves as well as for others, by means of their frugality and their humanity.

But there are visitations from which none can escape: disease and death! The Andalusian cannot bear the thought of death. I suppose we cannot bear it either, but death does not impress us as a great piece of the madness of life. Our whole existence has been too far tinged by death to make this possible. From early childhood we are on speaking terms with death, accepting it as a natural final link in the chain of all our other unpleasant experiences. Whatever we cannot fully dispose of in this way is taken care of by our religion. But death strikes the Andalusian as an obstruction in his path, an overwhelming contrast to life. The two cannot be reconciled in his mind, and he shuts his eyes to everything that might remind him of the existence of death. But if death penetrates his life in any way, he is not capable of accepting it as an abstract conception. His abhorrence takes the form of a certain coldness toward whoever brought death into his world, toward the dear deceased.

The northerner is unpleasantly impressed by the indifference with which the Andalusian treats the earthly remains of his relatives. In former days, corpses were always taken out of the city at night. Now, in the gully behind the Alhambra you may meet the corpse-bearers every day, six ragged drunken creatures who bear the dead of Granada out to the cemeteries in the hills. Four of them carry the coffin, a plain white box, rough and unpainted, made of thin pine wood, with spaces an inch wide between the planks, for the purpose of economizing lumber in the construction of the box. Two of them are carrying the coffin and stand ready to relieve the others. When they change bearers the coffin is set down on the bare soil, right in the filth of the shadowy pathway, and the corpse lies there uncovered, staring coldly at the sky. People gaze at it as they pass by and indulge in careless observations, and the mud kicked up by their donkeys' hoofs is splashed into the dead man's face. The hot sun makes his cold skin steam. Again the procession ascends, a jerky, dilapidated funeral procession of filthy wretches, with their loud yells, their breath stinking of alcohol and garlic. When they arrive at the churchyard the corpse is again set down on the ground to wait—often for hours—for the few relatives whose presence is to lend solemnity to the occasion. Surely the dead man will have time now. He never hurried very much when he was alive.

One day, as we passed by the cemetery, a coffin was standing in the middle path. From a distance it looked like a box filled with flowers. It gave us something of a chill to find the flowers transformed into a small child-like corpse, its eyes half opened and its cheeks tinged red, neatly dressed as if for a festival. And it was alone! There were no other persons present than the merry youngsters who had borne the child up hill and were now playing tag and amusing themselves with the coffin-lid.

In front of the cemetery gate we met two black-clad ladies, the eyes of one of them red with weeping. Farther down hill on the road, near a closed carriage, a gentleman was walking up and down restlessly reading a newspaper. His grief-stricken appearance, in the situation, indicated that it was the father who was here pacing up and down, for distraction, for forgetfulness, running away from reality.

At home in our country, we take our dead with us, if we have the means, or at least we stay in their proximity. Here the living remain as far away as they can from the city in which their children or loved ones have died. I am acquainted with two ladies of good family. They are sisters. All their relatives are dead. They are attached to each other with the eager affection of deserted little birds. The fact that they have no mother has gotten into their blood and made them quite motherly in their solicitude for each other. One of them refused an excellent match in order that the other might not stand alone in the world. And they say, whenever any reference is made to the beautiful cemetery of the town: "Yes, it is beautiful, and formerly we often went there. But since mother died fifteen years ago, we have never been to the place." Never in all that time! They do not even know where their mother lies!

These people have a capacity for love and a solicitude for the living that is as great as any in the world. They cannot be accused of heartlessness. Nor can it be said that they are faithless to the memory of their deceased. I have never seen any persons revert more readily to the thought of their departed loved ones than these. But it must be remembered that their association with their loved ones was an association not of common suffering and trials, but an association in common pleasure. Their reminiscences of the dead, in order to be precious to them, must be reminiscences of happy hours shared together; and their paths do not move heavily over graves, but build lightly and swiftly a rainbow bridge, of each smile, and of each stanza of a song, of each dancing step that meets them on their path. "That's the way my little Carlos laughs!" says the boy's mother. "That is just how my loved one dances!" is the young man's exclamation. Please note: they do not say, "He laughed—she danced." They do not use the past tense, although they are speaking of the dead; for no shadow must be allowed to fall upon their memory, least of all the heaviest of shadows, the shadow of death.

And how wonderful is their ability to forget! Time and time again you may be sitting opposite a mother, hearing her delighted account of her child's miraculous gifts, until some little external circumstance suddenly causes you to doubt whether the child still lives. And if you then proceed to ask the mother this question, she will burst into irrepressible tears. She has actually forgotten the hard fact.

This obliviousness, this capacity for escape, is the only bulwark to protect these children of the sun from care and misfortune. They are incapable of acquiring strength from tribulations, of obtaining a profound view of life by reason of misfortune. But they can shake off the whole business and simply forget it, as the bird forgets and bursts into a flood of jubilant song when the showers of rain have passed and the sun shines once more.

The Andalusian is so happy as not to possess a soul. He is not subject to the cleavage involved in this dualistic system. His nature is purely material. It never is developed in the form of a protest against his environment. It always unites with the environment. The spirit which radiates from him has neither assumed a special form by reason of a partial warfare on the body, nor does it demand any separate existence by the side of the body or transcending the body. This soul is only the mirror of the body's equilibrium and flows out to meet us as a pæan of praise for a life resting rhythmically on its own foundations.

Perhaps you will not encounter so many beautiful faces and seductive eyes in Andalusia as you may expect from the tales you have heard, but you will encounter much rhythm. Rhythm hovers over this people as their soul. It lies latent in the structure of their bodies and finds a faint reflection in the aristocracy and dignity of their bearing, qualities displayed even by the beggars and the decrepit old men. An indescribable charm is a natural birthright of the poorest girl of the lower class. This pleasing rhythm is not interrupted even in the most careless posture or in the most violent mental commotion. It cannot be superseded, for it is a law in the body, obeyed inviolably by every one of its parts. I once saw a bull-fighter depending impaled from the horn of a bull liberate himself, jump to the floor of the arena with the neatest little bound, holding his hand over his pierced breast, take a few steps and then fall down—all as beautifully rhythmical as if the whole incident were an episode in a ballet and not a bloody reality.

It is a joy to behold infants not more than ten months old suckling at their mothers' breasts and assuming postures that make an impression of a mature and carefully calculated coquettishness. Or, you will observe children at play who give evidence of the same irresistible impulse to dance that may be found in our country only among lovesick adolescents. In the midst of their play a gesture will suddenly break through the feeble barriers and expand into a passionate swing of the dance, which reveals that even at this early age both the required tension and the required harmony are already present.

It is in the dance that the exuberant life of Andalusia attains its highest expression, and rhythm blossoms so luxuriantly in this country that it perishes of its own excess, like the *agave* of the mountains. Beyond the hot whirling maelstrom of passion, embodied in the dance, lies animal nature; but the joy of life plays in leaping tongues of fire about the trembling edge of the whirlpool, and at the bottom of its crater quakes the lust of life, burning, breathing purple, like the deep tint in the calyx of the cactus-blossom. Andalusian dances cannot be described; they must be seen, and not on the stage, in foreign parts, but here in their home, preferably in the poorer quarters, as they are danced by a girl of the common people who knows no bonds that can be imposed upon her young vigor.

You may find happy creatures among these people, but no philosophers. When they are alone, you have the impression that their mental life proceeds in a vegetating manner like that of children, fluttering from impression to impression. They talk aloud to themselves, or with the flowers, animals and stones—leading a life of communication with these objects. In the villages of Alpujarra, the people practice sericulture, and on rainy days the women will approach the silkworm and strike their castanets for its amusement, so that the worm may feel more gay and show a better appetite. They make direct inferences from their own case as to the life of nature, so great is their feeling of oneness with nature.

They are not disposed to think out a serious situation of their own volition; but if you propose a problem to them they will instantly improvise a conception that often is characterized by genius, always radical in its thoroughness, but whose ultimate conclusion is essentially a matter of indifference to them. Being incapable of thinking in league-long chains of thought, they are not pedagogues and are therefore not encumbered by preconceptions. Enclosed by the four cold walls, with no other society but that of the naked problem, any Andalusian intelligence would collapse like a pricked bubble. But the slightest blaze of an idea in the glance of another person will be reflected in his own, and under the influence of this external mental pressure he rises to higher and higher heights, alternately fructified and fructifying, until the mental exchange has ceased. Then he again relapses into the material world about him.

How this all-pervading material attitude influences the Andalusian's religious conceptions in general, I shall show in another chapter, but now let us return to Death.

It is obvious that the Andalusian can have no desire to cleave his nature in twain, into soul and body, and to pursue the soul in its flight from the body. In spite of the influence of the Church, the Andalusian is incapable of making this mental experiment, which has become as wide-spread among northerners as the association of foot and sock. Confronted with the question of what is to become of him beyond the grave, the Andalusian can reply only with a shrug of his shoulders or at best with some maxim learned in the years of childhood, but never from personal reflection. He is certain of the existence of the body, he delights in its beauty; the body for him means jubilation. But the soul he does not understand; however assiduous his attendance at church, it never becomes a living element in his consciousness. Under these circumstances, Death is an absolute thing. Death destroys the body and consigns it to dissolution. Death is the end of all things.

Since the Andalusian is incapable of pursuing his own destiny beyond the portals of Death, how could he show greater interest in the destinies of others? The churchyard does not attract him. The churchyard is the great refuse-heap of life, on which life stealthily discards its offal, immediately turning its back on this heap of garbage. Perhaps the Andalusian did visit the churchyard once, ten years ago, when he watched his father's coffin being shoved into one of the numerous pigeon-holes in the cemetery wall. Perhaps he stands again in the same spot to-day, watching the grave-diggers remove the plate and slide his mother's coffin into its narrow orifice like a drawer in its frame. Perhaps his father's half-consumed remains are crushed against the interior walls as the new coffin moves in. There is a grinding sound as the old remains are pounded together, as they emerge from the coffin through the cracks under both sides of the lid. All around our Andalusian friend lie the mounds of graves, desolate and neglected, often devastated by wild dogs who dig up the remains of those of the deceased, whose poverty prevented their acquiring a sufficiently protected refuge under the ground. What feelings of piety the Andalusian may have do not lie in this quarter.

Even if he did have feelings in this connection, he might do no better than did Beppa. Since the last time I had seen her, life had dealt so hardly with her that she had attempted to seek consolation by her husband's grave—"but one ought never to do that." For although she had paid her good money for the grave at the time, it transpired when she revisited it that the parish had meantime sold it to another family and thrown her husband's remains into the boneyard. "And there was I kneeling and singing my song of lamentation, to a strange man, thinking it was my husband," was her smiling conclusion.

The Andalusian has no predilection for a cult of the dead or of graves; but he is much concerned with his cult of life. As far as the eye can see, there is a golden flutter of butterflies' wings playing carefree up to the wall of the cemetery, and occasionally even entering its grounds. The child of the sun does not always shun the habitations of the dead. At times he will gather his relatives and they will trudge along to the cemetery with their wine, their lunch-baskets, and their castanets, to celebrate a little bacchanale on the graves of their loved ones. In several localities the authorities were obliged to issue stringent prohibitions of such a use of the cemeteries. It was therefore quite reasonable for the young girl whom Beppa had to array for her last journey to be given dancing slippers, powder and castanets—all attributes of the joy of life —to take to the grave with her.

How strong we northerners are in the presence of Death! Most of us have defeated him by our certainty of an eternal life. Others have at least removed his sting by their feeling that man will continue to live from generation to generation through his deeds. But few of us are so poor as to be obliged to encounter him empty-handed.

The Andalusian is poor in comparison, but to make up for this he is infinitely rich toward life itself! Even the most penniless proletarian can say: "I have lived," and he can point to his joy in nature, his humanity, the personal superiority with which he regards the petty stings of life. You can approach hundreds of persons of the common people and exchange comments with them on the beauties of the surrounding natural scene, and each one of them will express his delight in rich picturesque terms and phrases. No human enjoyment remains strange to them, for they are poor.

Hence the fullness of human kindness in their spirits! And, not having wasted their own lives in training themselves to be the surly slaves of an insurmountable aggregation of petty needs, they cannot be deprived of their happiness even by Death's sudden intervention. They have taken their happiness day by day.

It may be partly for this reason that Death is not so intimate a concern of theirs as he is of ours. They do not feel the need of a solution. Nevertheless their victory over Death is an easy one. They remain carefree and happy. They have the incomparable faculty of forgetting.

It was Dumas who said that Africa begins at the Pyrenees. This is quite right, but it would be just as reasonable to say that Spain begins at the Straits of Gibraltar. Anglo-Teuton civilization has undertaken to conquer southern Europe, so rich in natural resources and such an excellent field of endeavor for usurious capital. Although Anglo-Teuton civilization has as yet done little for its own masses, it is being welcomed as it advances toward the south. It is astonishing to observe how much of the characteristically southern tone has been obliged to give way within the past few decades to the bias of European industrialism; astonishing to watch this civilization, rooted in mist and cold, its essence in a thousand substitutes for sunlight and warmth, as it takes up the combat with the sun in the sun's own land.

Industrialism will come out on top. It scatters its seductive products along its path among the masses, slowly but surely enmeshes them in its countless little needs and habits of luxury; imprisons them and fixes them in the yoke, as it has imprisoned its own people at home and harnessed them in the traces by perpetually increasing their external needs.

For us, it has become an unalloyed bliss to see the number of factory chimneys grow. The nations that suffer from a fever of overproduction are accepted in our eyes as the foremost in the world. To them belongs progress and therefore the future. Have we not been so thoroughly imbued with the doctrines of capital that we all, without exception, are doing its bidding? Is the Dane or the German, who dutifully puts in his ten hours daily year in and year out, tending his machine, is this man essentially more valuable than the Andalusian who does nothing and yet has plenty to eat? More valuable in the eyes of capital no doubt! Your Dane or your German probably has a nice parlor at home full of bric-a-brac, but never time to spend in it. He has a stovepipe hat and two pairs of Sunday shoes, but he falls into mental stupor as soon as he leaves his machine. His routine labor has consumed his intelligence. He has become a part of his machine. When his machine knocks off, his own intellectual clockwork also ceases to operate. The Andalusian may have poor clothes and Spartan repasts; he has little or nothing inside his four walls; but all the world around him is his. He has his intelligence, his unspoiled senses to seize and enjoy his surroundings. Who is better off? Who is happier?

The answer does not matter, since facts cannot be changed. Machine civilization with its uniform tread, its goose-step, its modern form of slavery, advances on and on. Out of each million of everyday men, each with a soul of his own, it will create one great man, turning the rest of them into more or less well-fed beasts of labor. Italy has already been conquered as far south as Naples. Its inhabitants have already had their ambitions awakened, though at present there appears to be no prospect of satisfying these ambitions. You are fed here with the ungratifying spectacle of half a million persons dashing about madly in an unsated utilitarian bustle and a fever of acquisition, half determined to provide themselves with a neat little yoke in which they may harness themselves while they pray for the greater yoke to come. Northern Spain, particularly Catalonia, including Barcelona, has been entirely Europeanized. Here there are great industrial centers and trade is carried on along modern lines. But there is already a predilection for cheap goods, and farther to the south the only industry is a sort of bogus industry favored by the climate.

In the manufacture and sale of spurious and adulterated foods and other articles, no other city can outstrip Madrid. This city, lying in the midst of a great bare plateau, is a capital only in name and has been obliged to put on all the European shams in order to satisfy all the cosmopolitan demands. Those of its one million inhabitants who do not draw their sustenance from the court or from the bureaucratic administration, make a living by manufacturing foodstuffs of chalk, erecting splendid apartment houses of holes in the air surrounded by pasteboard, and preparing lovely articles of *papier-mâché* which are exhibited in the luxury shops with much gilding and electric illumination and window-dressing.

The Andalusian too has plenty of sham in his commercial shops. Still he does not manufacture the bogus stuff himself. He is too inexperienced, both as a merchant and as a consumer, to detect the difference. It is difficult to conquer him for the new culture. He is protected from it by all his qualities, good as well as bad.

When a Nordic importer has received a consignment of wine from an Andalusian exporter, he may to his profit quite easily take advantage of the Andalusian's inexperience in the tricks of the trade. He may send a cable immediately, announcing that the wine is not up to the quality agreed on, and the Andalusian, without making any preliminary investigation, will take the man's word and send a new consignment to make up for the defect of the old. If he discovers that he has been deceived, he will make no protest and will not go to court. He will show his scorn for the customer by letting him get away with it this once; but he will then draw back into his shell, perhaps refusing any further orders for abroad.

There are very presentable shops in Seville, in which they will not wrap up your purchases unless you request it. Other shops, better acquainted with the amenities of business, will furnish wrapping paper, but it will be second-hand paper, already once used. There are splendid modern department stores here, with fine dressing-rooms and comfortable arm-chairs for customers. If you should require cheviot for a suit of clothes it may be your lot to have the shopkeeper offer you a lady's jacket, because it happens to be more accessible, or because he has made up his mind he must get rid of it. He cannot comprehend the fanatical obstinacy with which you revert again and again to this silly cheviot. His cheviot happens to be in the rear room of the shop, or perhaps is as far away as the first story. He assures you that he sold the last lot yesterday and can barely conceal his joy when he accompanies you across the street to the shop of his competitor. These shopkeepers even ask with a slight bow whether you do not wish to have the package delivered. But the package will remain in their shops until you call for it.

The Andalusian merchant is no more concerned with the sale of his goods than the merchant of Morocco. Often you must take him away from a conversation in some neighboring house. He will promise to come at once, but goes on with his conversation. Or you will find him seated in his shop engaged in eating. You must wait until he gets through. Perhaps he is buried in his newspaper. Have patience! If you show any irritation, he will become brusque—there is no one to prevent your leaving the shop. If the fancy takes him, he will shut up shop and take a walk.

German factory owners in Seville have informed me that it is almost impossible to operate a factory with Andalusian workingmen, since they are too independent, too obstinate to allow definite hours of work to be assigned to them. They are not lazy. Sometimes they are ready to work day and night; but the factor that determines their energy is never the urgency of the work to be done, but their own caprice. If they happen to feel disposed, they will celebrate a Blue Monday and it is impossible to tempt them to work by any offer of money.

The beginnings of a change are no doubt already observable. Not so very long ago, Andalusia was obliged to obtain all its servants from northern Spain; now even Andalusians of the lower classes are beginning to be applicants for such posts. However they always bring their ideas of independence with them and a staff of servants consisting of Andalusians is a very interesting one.

If a servant-girl's mistress tells the maid, "You must look after the house and the children to-day; we are going out this afternoon," it is not unusual for her to receive the answer: "But I was going out myself to-day!" There are even cases where a servant-girl will leave her cooking pots and take a walk in broad daylight.

Nor would it avail to go to court about it. Isn't the servant-girl as good as any one else, though the others may have more money? And has not their dear Lord created the bright daylight so that people may enjoy it? A simple order would not settle the question, for the Andalusian recognizes no one above himself and will not even submit to obligations which he has voluntarily assumed. Punishments merely make him obstinate. The servant-girl will simply go out. If there is any objection on the part of her mistress, the girl will leave so exacting a post. But if you accept her whims, you are considered a kind employer and the demands made on you for pay and food are very small.

There are quite a number of old noble families in Andalusia who have not a penny to call their own. Yet they keep male servants and maid servants who remain with them for many years, though they never see a month's wages and are obliged to beg their own food from neighboring families. They even go so far as to make advances of money to their employers out of their own small savings. They seek to obtain credit for their employers, and in their interests will lie, beg, and cheat. Under all circumstances they will look after their masters, but in return, they demand that all their human dignity be respected, and this human dignity may at times be a considerable item.

The servant-girl becomes initiated into all the secrets of the house as soon as she takes up her position; but she will never gossip them about unless her employers try snobbishly to keep them hidden from her. She sings anywhere in the house, whenever she likes; joins in the conversation when there are visitors; anticipates the mistress' vigorous onslaughts on the master of the house, and gives him a piece of her mind. In affairs of the heart, she is always the eldest daughter's ally against her parents, and in the secret liaisons which are almost the rule in upper-class marriages, she is the confidante of the wife. She calls for her mistress' letters at the post-office, and if she is able to read she will open them on the way home, so zealous is her interest in the affairs of her employers.

As the servant-girl is the woman's confidante, so is the male servant the master's confidant. He looks after the master's interests in the same way. The male servant also takes his liberties. He smokes a cigarette while serving meals; he swears in the drawing room; he lies like a lizard in his master's window and spits through the window on the sidewalk.

The servants who faithfully share their master's poverty also demand their part in the master's wealth, and a normal employer makes no objection in such cases. As an example of the tolerance with which the upper classes regard their servants, it may be mentioned that Andalusian servants have the reputation, as compared with all the other servants in Spain, of being as true as gold in matters of money. But their fidelity turns out on closer inspection to consist in their not cheating their master for their own advantage, but only in the interests of their own parents, or of a child, or of a lover, or of all three at once. Since all persons have some one who is near and dear to them, this form of mulcting is almost a certainty and may become quite costly. Andalusia resembles Greenland in one respect at least: as soon as any member of the family has found some means of a livelihood, all the rest of the family will retire from active life to sponge upon him.

The native-born employer accepts these conditions with that incomprehensible charity which always imparts to the Andalusian's countenance, even where his pocketbook is intimately involved, an expression of comprehending sympathy, and which never permits him to drive a beggar from his door with hard words, though it may happen that a hundred beggars knock at the door on one day. A foreigner finds it harder to adapt himself. Particularly if the foreigner is a housekeeper, she may wage a desperate struggle against all these relatives of her servants who loll about in her kitchen all day long, consuming her food and wearing her clothes. But in the long run she will yield, after which these light-moraled creatures will serve her devotedly, will read her every wish from her eyes, will weep loudly when they see her downcast and sing when she smiles; invoke upon her head all the kind gifts of heaven and earth, and be ready to do everything for her. Yet even without permission, they will take in advance their own share of all this plenty, and their new kindliness of to-day often makes them forget to translate into actions their goodwill of yesterday. This difficulty however is only a formal one, and exists only when viewed from a northern European point of view.

The Andalusian is an excellent worker in the open air. The soil of his country affords abundant evidence of this. Give him a bare steep slope of rock and he will hew steps into it and carry up the dirt on his own back and then plant his crops. He will conduct the thin mountain stream from its source over a distance of many miles; will pipe it in primitive but ingeniously constructed canals across the mountains in order to irrigate his mite of artificial ground. Like a China-man, he will carefully collect excrements in the road. His technique is primitive; his tools and methods often remind us of the Old Testament; his plow is a pointed stick; his wine is trodden by his own heels. But his tireless diligence and the vigilance of his hands lure wealth out of the ground. In the rare cases in which the land belongs to the state, the crown takes its yield, otherwise the proceeds will flow into the hands of the lord of the manor. And yet, the Andalusian keeps on working none the less. He loves the soil.

The only work for which he is not suited is the work in which he must be incarcerated in a factory and made a cog in the machinery. He would be an obstinate fellow to deal with and would merely be in the way. He lacks the discipline that is imparted by misfortune and rough weather; and he hates discipline and submission. He is glad to give up his seat to the most wretched of his fellow-mortals. He never makes use of his position to set his heel on another's neck. He raises his children by kissing and fondling them; nothing but caresses and kisses. It is a self-willed and unreliable method of training; but they turn out to be essentially good men, like himself.

VIII

WITH THE COTTAGERS IN THE MOUNTAINS

DAY after day, from early in the morning until late at night, we have been stationed on the highest pinnacles surrounding the lovely mountain city of Loja, gazing all about us, in every direction, with eagles circling over distant mountain regions. We have reveled in the sun-sparkling air and in the mountain stillness which is further sweetened by the soft lullaby of the cattle-bells, and deepened by the distant seething of the water-falls in the "Two Infernos." The mountain battlements have a hard ringing sound of their own when the sun breaks through the cold of night; and in the peaceful valley beneath us an occasional railway-train dashes like a devil insane into the gloomy recesses of the tunnel. A sudden nervous tremor shoots through the stillness, grazes us momentarily like a distant wail of complaint—for we are sitting here so idly—and disappears again in the sunny haze. We try to work up a little of our national pride, because this railroad was invented by our own Nordics, and we look down with condescension on these people who have invented nothing, not even a bit of religious puritanism. But once we are brought face to face with one of these mountain shepherds, the entire edifice of our racial conceit collapses. We cannot help loving this people, and in fact envying them; our concern is that they appear to have no envy of us. We are a

155

matter of complete indifference to them, though they conceal this indifference under a boundless amiability, for we are their guests in Spain.

We are now making a tour to Granada on foot. Directly below us rises the great Vega, thirty miles across, entirely surrounded by mountains, and on the other side of the plain lies Granada, a gray speck on the mountain slope. We follow the curve of the mountain chain, keeping the plain on our right. Everywhere there is a bustle of activity, although the sun has not yet risen. On the northern slope of the hills, men are going about with long sticks, beating the late olives from the trees while women and children are lying on the ground ready to gather them up. Along the southern slopes there is wheat under the olive-trees, and men bend low cutting it and binding it in sheaves. On the diminutive farms, the entire family is on its knees delving in the sod; but on the great estates, the farm-workers advance in long rows, each row followed by an overseer who walks with the aid of a heavy stick. If we like, we may leave the mountain road and follow the railway tracks, which show traces of much traffic. They will lead us through short tunnels and across a deep valley with a torrent foaming along its bottom. At the end of the valley we can see the stream break over the rocks like disheveled silver hair.

All around us water gushes from the soil, sometimes in bubbling springs as large as a big round table. These are *los Nacimientos,* the famous springs of Loja. Some of them spew forth hot water, and many women of the plain people stand naked in the springs up to their hips, engaged in washing clothes. We cross other water courses, the waters of which come from the opposite side of the mountains, from artificial canals or broad river beds. The streams are carried by means of a delicately distributed network of veins over the mountain-tops till water reaches every single fruit tree. Then it is gathered up again to run on and expand like a mirror over a leveled cornfield, after which it floods another field at a slightly lower level, and then again another—a great staircase of horizontal plane mirrors, one after the other. At the very bottom, the waste waters are again collected to drive a stamp-mill, with another water-mill below it, and after this it flows all around the mountain into a lower valley still to begin its work over again. And wherever this water flows, wealth springs from the ground. The wealth flows into the pockets of the great real estate owners who live in the cities. The people here on the soil stay poor forever.

Almost all the land is in the hands of people who spend their lives in the palaces of Madrid, Seville, or Granada, often not even aware of where their property lies or how it looks. Sometimes the soil is worked with the aid of stewards and day-laborers, along modern lines; but for the most part it has been parceled out as farms and houses which are rented to tenants for a term of years. Many of these tenants have never seen their landlords, only the land-agents. The Andalusian absentee landlord, it is said, makes more trips to Paris than to his estates.

The high rents, the oppressive taxes and the city duties that are added to the cost of production, make it impossible for these farm workers, in spite of all their diligence, ever to rise—except in the rarest cases—out of the stratum of the poor. Those workers who have not hired farms of their own are even poorer. They live in wretched tumble-down villages with from ten to thirty thousand inhabitants, and keep fhe wolf from the door only with the aid of a miserable daily wage. Every morning the steward of the estate will appear in the market-place of the village. The job hunters are drawn up to meet him and he makes his selection for the day. The day's pay amounts to about fifteen or thirty cents and a *gaspacho:* a refreshing mixture of water, vinegar, oil, salt and pepper stirred and cold. This *gaspacho,* which is distributed at noon, with the bread the workers have brought with them, is their entire meal. Before the laborer has gone to the labor market he has eaten a plate of bean-soup; and in the evening, when he gets home, he will again eat a plate of bean-soup.

A stony path crosses under the railway tracks. In reality it is a dry river bed. As we pass over the bridge, a big dog bounds from the dark tunnel in front of us and inside we can see tall dark figures of men around a bonfire. Robbers, I thought suddenly. We turned aside and tried to descend into the river bed to avoid them. But with eager shouts they prevent us from going down, and force us to come into the tunnel with them. They are hunters about to broil a hare for breakfast. They delve inside to find his heart, cut it into pieces and offer it to us from the tip of a great Andalusian Jack-the-Ripper knife. We eat the heart and it really makes us more courageous. After we have drunk from the mouth of their great wine-pouch, we are permitted to go. They are happy to have been able to invite us to their meal, and guide us back through the dark tunnel with the most amiable assurances of their good wishes.

Once more we are out on the foot-path which runs between the edge of the abyss and the far-flung olive-groves; or we move over a road of chalk-dust, with two-wheeled ox-carts rumbling and swaying over it, roofed by a circular barrel-vault of canvas. The oxen mind their own course while the driver, singing love-songs, lies on the floor of the wagon, which fairly slides along the ground. At every inn the oxen stop of their own accord while the driver crawls out of his Pullman-compartment with the greatest amazement, looking inquiringly at his animals and at the strange universe around him. Then he enters the inn and calls for a penny glass of something.

We have seated ourselves in front of a decrepit lit-tle house by the edge of the road in order to rest. At once an old woman comes trudging out with a couple of chairs; but when a younger woman comes out and sees what she has done, she rebukes her. What a peculiar thing to invite people to sit out on the bare road! Won't you please come in? The house has one room only. One half of it contains the open hearth and the living room; the other half is sleep-ing quarters and the stable for one goat and one donkey. As we talk to the younger woman, the old woman does not turn her eyes away from us, and she moves her lips.

"You come from far away I suppose?" she finally asks.

"Oh, yes, it isn't so near."

"Then you must have seen the ocean—you must have sailed on it? It must be a curious thing, the ocean? Is it true that it runs all around the globe and that it can rise like a steer on its hind legs and knock over ships? Pedro, the donkey-driver, was up on the peak of the Sierra Nevada and saw the ocean; but he is a liar. He says it is liquid gold and that the sun comes right up over it. But I say he is a liar; I say, 'You are a liar, little Pedrico, for gold is hard, and the sea is water and you can bathe in it and drown in it. And the sun would be extinguished if it went down into it.' "

She once had a daughter, we learn, who was drowned in the sea on the northern coast of Spain. That is why her thoughts are so much concerned with the sea. But there is no one in these mountains who can talk to her about the sea except Pedro the donkey-driver, who has seen it from the top of the Sierra Nevada, and he is a liar. We have actually sailed over it and bathed in it, like her daughter, that time when she was drowned; and we have no reason to lie to her. She drinks in every word and makes the motions when I tell her what swimming is like. Suddenly she interrupts with a vehement statement: "Indeed, if I could only see it or even stick my hand into it—that couldn't harm me, could it? Sometimes when there is a storm and I cannot sleep I look up to the thunder-clouds and imagine that the sea must be like that too, and then I weep for my daughter who is faring so ill. But when the sky is calm and blue again, then I think that the sea must be like that too, and this makes me so glad, so glad for her sake." She nods to herself confidently, and we set out again on our journey.

Like all travelers, we have our little passport difficulties. Under ordinary circumstances a passport is a stupid thing. It costs you money and diminishes the excitement of traveling, by annihilating every possibility of an unusual adventure; for if you have a passport, all the boring police officials on earth are your protectors. I, therefore, ignored all passports when we set forth, taking with me instead two vaccination certificates which remained to us from the days of our childhood. I thought it would be interesting to learn what such a scrap of paper really was worth in a pinch, and I must admit that my certificates stood the test very well. Although smallpox was in the virulent stage at most of the towns of Andalusia at which we stopped, we remained quite immune from it.

Since we planned to travel on foot a passport would be indispensable for us, so every one told us, including a consul in one of the seaport towns; but this consul had no authority to issue a passport. I wrote home to a friend to go to the passport office for me, where he obtained the sage answer that it would be necessary for me to go back home myself and present my person to the high authorities.

All in all, these high authorities are really quite superfluous—like all things that exist by the grace of God. I went aboard the Danish ship that lay in the port of Cádiz and borrowed some Russian clearance papers from the captain. These papers identified me as a bark with a tonnage of 530 tons register, bearing the name "Marianne," and sailing in ballast from Riga to San Fernando to call for a cargo of salt. Whenever we meet a gendarme, I begin to unbutton my coat long before we reach him, and since they never show any inclination to demand our papers, I force these clearance documents on his attention. Thereupon he sets his lips in motion as if he were reading these Russian hieroglyphics and returns our papers to us with a protective nod. Always this performance is a lot of fun.

It is now afternoon. We have probably covered half of our journey, and are going down the other side of the hills to the edge of the Vega in order to finish the trip to Granada by train. At the station we meet an acquaintance from Seville: Don Louis, one of the leaders of the South Spanish Revolutionary Party, handsome, a little too well-groomed. He dazzles the eye with his gold and his diamonds and his neat manicuring. He is taking a trip to the poor people of the mountains to carry on subversive agitation. He proposes that we accompany him to the village of X., where a local branch of the Federation is to be established.

He is met at the station by a two-wheeled cart and we trundle up hill again with him, drawn by a skeleton which the driver maintains is a mule. Five minutes later the animal confirms the statement by an attack of rage and obstinacy. It suddenly stands still on a steep ascent, walks backward, and almost plunges us into the depths. We save ourselves, as well as the beast, by getting out of the cart and holding fast to the spokes of the wheels. These mountain-dwellers are accustomed to such interruptions, and in a moment the driver and his companion are again on their seat, inviting us once more to get in.

Shortly before we reach the village, two cottagers come out to meet us, typical Andalusian mountain peasants, lean and smooth-shaven, light of foot, wearing broad-brimmed hats, scarfs, and laced shoes. The name of the elder is Pedro R. He is head of the agricultural workers' organization of the village. He is fifty-five years old, tall and sinewy, with a large face and immutably peaceful features. He reminds us of a West Jutland farmer. The other, Alfonso M., is the chairman of the revolutionary agitation committee. He is twenty-six years old, feeble in appearance, with a gait that is more of a dance than a walk, and a child-like insular face with dreamy enthusiastic eyes. His wan temples and cheeks suggest a doctrinal mania, and Don Louis whispers to me that he is a fanatical anarchist.

There is also a third, a smiling old man whose body, either from hard work or poverty, is bent double, horizontal, from the hips upward. But he is able to walk very well and goes about through the hills with us all morning, smilingly repeating, like a big baby, all the words we say. He has become childish, but the others show much consideration for him. On our arrival, he peeks into the bottom of the cart and looks at us, one after the other, questioningly: "And where are the Mauser rifles?" he says.

Don Louis replies: "Do you know that it is just thirty years ago to-day that you proclaimed the republic, José?"

The old man nods admission to himself: "Do you think I could forget it; wasn't I one of the chief leaders in these mountains?"

"So you were," says Alfonso the anarchist, as he executes a little step, "and you came near losing your head in the job, too. They had set him up against a wall of rock to shoot him; but he was out of luck and came off with his life."

"Yes, that was it; I got away and hopped about the

mountains for years and years, without ever having a roof to sleep under, until the amnesty was pronounced. That's where I get this trouble from," and he lays his hands over his loins.

"Well, now tell me, have you gotten to the point where you can afford to drive around in broad daylight with a wagon load of Mauser rifles?" asks Don Louis with a wink.

"No, we did not go about it that way. We weren't as stupid as all that," the old man answered, offended.

"Neither are we, so have patience!"

"All right, Don Louis, it is all very well to have patience, but you are not eighty years old! For some fine day I tell you, man——" He moves his hands as to indicate a body somersaulting down hill toward the churchyard below. These cottagers bear the mark of the soil, as our cottagers do at home in Denmark—the peace and solidity of the soil, but not its heaviness. There is no heavy weight dragging from their soles as they walk about talking to Don Louis, a man of university education, concerning the conditions of this place. There is only an external difference between him and them. They are just as much at ease, speak the same rich figurative language, without a trace of dialect, and without any fumbling for the proper expression.

We, the strangers, are enveloped from the very start with a benevolence, a delicate consideration that might be the result of many generations of inherited gentility. They change the conversation to our interests, so that we may not be bored; pluck flowers for my wife; pick out the best spots in the road for us to walk on. They insist we must certainly take some refreshment before we get to the village; and one of them must run on ahead and get it for us. We exchange a few words concerning the beautiful appearance of a blossoming almond tree that makes a fine contrast with the blue sky, and Alfonso climbs up and brings down a branch for us.

The village of X. is half way up the southern slope of the mountain. Its huts appear to be glued to the slope. It has twenty-five thousand inhabitants, five priests, and no school-teachers. Like most of the larger villages in Andalusia it has electric street lights, the power being generated by the water in the streams. This progressive fact is really the outcome of an excessive conservatism, for one liter of petroleum costs, because of the immense taxes on all articles of consumption, four times as much as in Denmark. Electricity has not penetrated the houses. Inside they sit about or grope in the light of an oil-wick which has been ignited with great toil with the aid of flint and tinder, because the state insists on collecting a million dollars annually in taxes on matches alone. It is a strange sight to watch a fellow work for a quarter of an hour banging steel against flint in order to light a cigarette, when he is standing right under an incandescent electric light bulb.

There is no middle class in this village, and yet its population is as large as that of a fair-sized provincial city. The whole population lives on the soil, most are day laborers. But there is a class here not found elsewhere in Andalusia, landowning cottagers. We have already made the acquaintance of three of them and others are waiting for us up in the village. They conduct us to the inn where a dinner is served for us: pork in tomato-sauce, fried eggs and bacon-sausage.

At dinner, the cottagers talk to us. One of them tells how he fared before he tilled his own soil. He was working for a rather wealthy tenant-farmer down in the Vega, at a daily wage of about fifteen cents, on which he was supposed to support his wife and six children. After the day's work was over, he would walk every day the seven miles or so to Granada to beg until midnight on a street-corner of the Corso. In this way he would acquire some fifteen cents more, and this sufficed to nourish his family. But he had not much time left over for sleep, and his nocturnal walk of fifteen miles went into his legs. One night he found his place taken by another beggar, who had a woolen blanket wrapped around his head as a protection from the cold. In his anger he went for the man and tore the blanket from his head, to discover it was his own brother who had heard tidings of the fifteen cents a night and had tried to cheat him out of them. He never went to Granada again, in order that he might run no risk of encountering his employer; but he lost his job all the same.

"Things like this make people revolutionary," said Don Louis fiercely, gesticulating with his white ring-encircled fingers. "I was in Madrid last week. What an accumulation of wealth is found there, concentrated in a few hands; and what a boundless poverty among the great masses of the people! Society cannot but collapse under this monstrous injustice that cries to heaven. We shall soon have the revolution."

He looked reassuringly at each one in turn and they

all nodded gloomily and hopefully. It must soon come! Then his face brightens.

"It was an expensive trip, I tell you," he says, as he looks about with a childlike sense of his own importance. "It cost me more than five thousand francs, and it only lasted one week, and I did not touch a bed on a single night. I can still feel it in my bones." And he yawns immoderately like a boastful young school boy.

"Five thousand francs!" they repeat to each other, marveling as he corroborates his previous statement with a modest smile and nod. "I have never seen so much money at once!" And they laugh and shake their heads at such extravagance.

The repast is over. Don Louis pours out a glass of wine and hands it to one of the men with a single slice of bacon sausage. The man drinks a little out of the glass, whereupon it is filled again and passed to the next man with a new slice of sausage. He also takes a little sip and it is again filled and so on all around the table, until it comes back to Don Louis, who drains his cup to the dregs without turning an eyelid. I pull myself together and perform the same heroic deed. But when my glass returns to me with its very unappetizing contents, my nearest neighbor, with a most tactful consideration, passes the vessel not to me but to my wife. She sends me an imploring glance; but the success of our trip depends entirely on whether she will prove herself equal to the situation. I nod inexorably. She empties the vessel and hastily manufactures a pretext for leaving the room.

Nothing can be more justified than the pride with which the cottagers took us into the hills and showed us all that they had done. Some twenty years ago, the heirs of a landed proprietor had sold these naked mountain slopes and retained for themselves only the fruitful Vega down below in the vale. The parish had bought these rocks and parceled them out into little areas to assign to the poor people of the village for a small annual fee. Many persons applied for such land for the sake of the unusual experience of feeling that they were landed proprietors, but they soon relinquished it again. But some hundreds, however, took the thing more seriously and began to slave over their rocky freeholds. Wherever there was only a little humus, they planted something. They blasted away the surface of the rock, pounded it to pieces with hammers and mixed the fragments with the faint traces of humus that had been formed by the mosses and brushwood in the course of ages. Or with the aid of dams they gathered up weatherworn substances which the rain water had washed down from the steep rocks, and mixed them with the dirt they hauled from distant places on the backs of donkeys. Now you have field after field hanging between earth and sky at five thousand feet above sea level, framed in sharp bluish-red rocks. Half-grown fig trees, olive trees, almond trees dot the hills and appear at many points to be sucking their nutrition out of the bare rock.

"You see it is quite an expensive thing even to-day to be a land-owning cottager in Spain," said Don Louis. "But once our party has won the victory, things will change, and we shall introduce a law making all those who really till the soil owners. I tell you at present my tenants have a much better time than you do."

It comes out that he has inherited from his father a great estate near Murcia and that since he came into the property, his tenants hand over heavier shares to him; what they formerly paid was not enough for him! But this peculiar circumstance appears not to cast doubt on the integrity of his theories in any way, nor even to concern his fellow revolutionaries at all. You see, they are Andalusians.

However, there is a distinct line of cleavage between these cottagers and the other villagers, who believe that the cottagers have muskets concealed in the caves in the rocks. It is they who are the consciously revolutionary element, and they stick firmly together. The spirit of companionship in which they associate with each other, and the long cold glances with which the other inhabitants treat them as they walk in groups down the street, indicate very clearly that they are a distinct caste within this little society. They are regarded partly with envy, and partly with fear which leads people to keep away from them to avoid any difficulties. They have even established an evening school in which their children as well as the adolescent young men may learn to read and write, while the rest of the inhabitants must content themselves with the oral religious instruction imparted by the priests. Most of the grown-ups also have taught themselves to read. They have formed a newspaper circle which receives anarchist and socialist periodicals, have more or less severed their relations with the church, and a few of them, such as Alfonso M., openly oppose the church. This peaceful man flies into a rage whenever he even thinks of a clergyman. All the injustices that have been committed by the priests who keep down the

Spanish people seem to have been deposited at the bottom of his soul as a hatred that is so strong as to drive him even to be consistent. He does not pronounce the usual Spanish salutation: *Vaya con Dios!* but says instead: *Vaya en salud!;* and when he encounters a priest accompanied by the monstrance, he would rather be fined for his transgression than bare his head in greeting.

When our path leads us by a wooden crucifix that has been erected by the priests on a rock above the village, he kicks it over with his foot. Don Louis approves his act and praises it, but the older man, the cautious Pedro, the chairman of the agricultural laborers' organization, sets up the cross again and rebukes him seriously.

"You must not forget that you are a marked man already," he says. "The slightest little fuss and you will find yourself looking into the muzzle of a gendarme's rifle. And we can't get along without you," he adds quietly.

Alfonso indulges in an excessively boisterous step. He has red specks on his temples. But suddenly he becomes more restrained.

"Forgive me—I can't help it," he says downcast, as he embraces Pedro.

How simple they are, these people! How thoughtless and inexperienced! They count on being able to arouse fifty thousand men in the province of Granada, and perhaps they are not altogether wrong. But they imagine that they could conquer the province with two thousand rifles. For this purpose they are assiduously collecting weapons, and Don Louis recounts with a mien of secrecy that he already has gained possession of five hundred Mauser rifles which are kept in an old cabin in Granada. On the day that has been set for the insurrection—when things get that far—he will invite all the officers of the garrison of Granada for supper, will lock the doors at the hour agreed on, and will say to them:

"Gentlemen! the country is in the hands of the revolutionists. You are my prisoners." The cottagers follow his words with flashing eyes. They do not see through his phrases. Perhaps he himself believes them. And though they have never seen me before this day, they point out to me the numerous caves in the mountains behind the village, which contain their weapons and which are to be their asylum if they should suffer defeat.

They speak of these things as lightly as if the whole business were child's play; but they are in dead earnest. Spain is not a stranger to revolutions. It has had more than any other country in Europe. The nation has grown up with remembering this; revolutions match its temperament. They prefer sudden upheavals to a painful evolution which is beyond their grasp. Particularly the Andalusian is lacking in the "forward-looking" quality that would endow him with a steady perseverance. He does not grasp the utility of carrying on a work of agitation, of casting his vote, and of waiting for the remote day at which the party may have a majority in the government. He merely feels the desperate situation of the present moment and wishes to put a stop to it as quickly as possible. The urge to revolution is in his blood like a permanent fever. Every day there are little uprisings here or there. A few men are shot down, perhaps a few women and children, too; a gendarme is wounded or killed. You may live in a city without suspecting that anything is going on until you read the telegrams in the Madrid papers on the day after. Uprisings are such an every-day matter. It is only because of the difficulty of organization that such uprisings do not take place simultaneously in all parts of the country.

But there have been cases, and there may again be cases, in which the people's powers of organization will be sufficient for a general upheaval. In that event, they will be found lacking only in all the things that assure successful revolutions: resources, weapons, reliable leaders. Don Louis and the others—for the most part well-to-do men of the world who need something to keep them amused—will drop the whole business when things reach that stage. The most practical among them will sell out to the government; and the people will permit themselves to be shot down like sheep, with that peculiar contempt for death which is characteristic of Spain. The survivors will then begin to hatch a new revolution, without having gained the slightest lesson from experience.

Each cottager has been told to bring a farm-laborer with him, and two or three hundred men are thus gathered in the evening in the Worker's Home, a great bare interior, the attic chamber of which harbors the evening school. Alfonso M. delivers the introductory speech, a short but impressive account of the Wolf (Capital), with a bone lodged in his throat, and the Stork (Labor), which pulls the bone out for him. The Wolf's answer to the Stork when the Stork asks for his reward:

"Did I not have your head between my teeth? and

did I bite it off? and don't you owe me your life, therefore?" runs through the audience like wildfire.

"Damned thief! He should be made shorter by a head!" they cry out; and a confused mutter runs from man to man. They offer their assistance to the speaker as he interprets his story, help him out with vigorous interpolations and encourage him by interjecting spirited remarks.

Then a seventeen-year-old shop-clerk jumps to his feet. A year ago he was taken prisoner down in Jerez as the ringleader of an insurrection. He was maltreated by the gendarmes and taken to the prison of Río Frío, where he was kept for several months. Now he is actively at work again. He attacks the priests, declaring them to be piggish, stupid, ignorant, hostile to culture, and demonstrates in forceful periods that all great men have been pagans. He has the soft undeveloped form and features of a child, and his face beams with infantile pleasure as the audience clap their hands in stormy applause. The sonorous gift of Spanish eloquence seems to have been given to him in his cradle, for all the most incendiary slogans in his language trip lightly over this child's tongue. You feel somehow that he is a sort of middleman who acts as mouthpiece for those whose thoughts he does not understand.

Don Louis pitches into the state savagely: "Capital, Church, State—what a lovely Trinity!" cries Alfonso, as he holds three fingers of his hands in the air. In the street outside the crowd buzzes with excitement, imagining the thing is to come off to-night. On the next corner the uniforms of a few gendarmes flash in the moonlight. In the packed meeting hall the men's shoulders touch, the smoke of their pipes ascends in thick clouds. Every one is smoking now, even the speaker, who stops while launching a particularly savage attack, to mind his cigarette. From time to time a great jug of water is brought in, and passes from mouth to mouth. Occasionally, vehement cries shoot through the air.

Northern countries know little more of freedom of speech or freedom of the press than their names; but both these things are realities in Spain. In our country, where the introduction of republican ideas into the form of government may not even be discussed by the most advanced parties, what would people say of a meeting, attended by poor cottagers, which resolves, after hearing a free and unadorned criticism of the existing order, to overthrow the dynasty and establish a republic with all the means at their disposal?

When they proceed to organize the new local section, there is a scene that would seem strange to the eyes of any northern European. Alfonso M. asks all those who cannot write their names themselves to call them out. They shout their names from all sides— old men and very young men, poor devils and others who have made their pile and appear to be living in comfort. In a list of one hundred and twenty-three signatures, I subsequently count fifty-seven whose names were not written by themselves, and these include men from the most radical elements. These men do not need to acquire a radical mode of thought by laboriously poring over books and newspapers. They instinctively possess it from the start.

There are humorous incidents.

"Won't you sign, Antonio López?" they shout to an old man.

"But I can't aim a rifle any more, or ride after the gendarmes in the mountains," is the discouraged reply.

"But you can stay home and defend our wives and children!"

"Yes, indeed, that I can," he proudly answers, as he signs.

A few have withdrawn into the corner of the room in order to avoid setting down their names. They are forced out into the open with great merriment and are introduced to the assembly as the vanguard of the revolution.

The women of the village did not attend the assembly, but after it was over, a delegation of cottagers' wives visited us in order to salute my wife and beg us to choose something in the village that we should like to take back home with us. In this act these simple women felt themselves to be the representatives of the whole nation. They expressed their hope that no one might have given us any cause for annoyance in the course of our journey, that we might take home with us a favorable impression of Spain and that our little trip to the village of X. might not be any exception in this general favorable impression.

Don Louis took the night train to Granada; but we intended to go back on foot the following morning, for a view of the Vega and so we took lodgings for the night in the inn. We had to pass through another room in order to reach ours. There was no door between them, only a curtain in the doorway. We had just retired for the night when a commercial traveler entered the anteroom, his, it appeared, and prepared to go to bed. As he undressed he occasionally lifted the curtain a little and peeked through the darkness in our direction. The inn had electric lights, but as if to counterbalance this excessive modernism, the windows of all the rooms—and this was the case also in all the other houses of the village—did not have any glass panes, but merely wooden shutters. On the wall of our room hung a curious tablet which transported us to the South Sea Islands. It was an enumeration of the hotel linen. The front side of the tablet bore little pieces of wood that were carved to represent the outlines of the various types of laundry, and following these images there was a series of holes running straight across the board. From some of these holes little sticks of wood projected in each row, obviously corresponding to the number of pieces of linen of each type.

When we had walked back through the commercial traveler's room the next morning, our shoes in our hands, we found Alfonso in the waiting room together with Pedro, the chairman of the agricultural laborers' association, and a few poor cottagers who were waiting for us. They insisted that we should not pay for our stay at the inn and since the host was obviously on their side, we could do nothing about it. While we were having our breakfast, which consisted of goat's milk warm from the udder, Alfonso was making a little plan. He had to go on an errand to Granada, he said, and if we had no objection, he would like us to accompany him and use one of his two donkeys. I suspected that it was again a case of excessive hospitality. I did not wish to have this man sacrifice a whole day's labor for our convenience. So, giving my reasons for hesitancy, I furtively inquired among the others to discover whether he really had anything to do in Granada. They all looked very thoughtful, discussed the matter at great length among themselves, mentioned the long and poor road, and finally unanimously agreed that there was no doubt he had something to do in Pinos-Puente, a village that was about half the way to Granada. It was at the time of the most important spring farming and they wished to do justice both to him and to us in equal measure.

So we took our leave and set out upon our return trip. Alfonso had his little eight-year-old boy sitting in state before him on the donkey. My wife and I preferred to walk on foot through the steep village. It was early morning and there were great numbers of workers in the market-place, while a few men in cloaks were going about inspecting them.

"That is the slave-market," muttered Alfonso. "You see, they feel of them with their hands, almost as if they were beasts."

For quite a time he was silent, uncommunicative; then the sun came out above the Sierra and he once more became animated. He did not wish to ride, but walked by the side of my donkey, leaning on my cane, speaking of the time when there should be no masters and no wage-laborers of any kind, no poverty and no capitalists. His cheeks assumed their red roses of yesterday. He took a soiled book out of his pocket.

"I have this thing with me when I work in the fields and when I travel on foot, always," he said. "It sets the fire burning in you when you begin to be lukewarm." It was the anarchist almanac, which contained pictures of Tolstoi, Kropotkin, and of all the assassins of kings and presidents of recent years, together with brief and vigorous reading matter which accorded well with its agitational purpose.

My cane seemed quite heavy to him and he asked whether it was a sword-cane.

"No," I answered; "but the head is of lead. You can give a good whack with it." He looked at me very seriously.

"I have never been in a position where I had to defend myself against my fellow-men, or vice versa—"

"But aren't you engaged in warfare on society?" I interposed.

"Yes, I am making war on those in authority, that is true; but not on my fellow-men. They are not doing me any harm, and I believe I should rather die than inflict any injury on any one of them. All persons are good, after all, unless they have too much power. I know the men in the mountains and I know they are good. Don Louis, who comes from way off near the Mediterranean is good too; and here are you coming from way up north and you are like a brother to me."

The fact that he had had to borrow a second donkey in addition to his own in order to take us back to Granada and that he was walking the whole distance himself in order to permit us to ride; in short, the fact that he could not think of things enough to do for us, these things meant for him that I was like a brother to him. When I got off and tried to oblige him to take my place on the animal, he declared he was freezing with the cold, and that his physician had ordered him to do as much walking as possible. He invented a lot of other such statements—merely in order to compel me to take my seat again.

"Why, I can ride back all the way from Pinos-Puente," he declared, "and you will have to walk, you know." But when we reached Pinos-Puente, he found that he must go with us to the other side of the town; and once we were there, he insisted on accompanying us still farther.

Finally he stopped, about three miles outside of the town. We had a little meal in an inn and he took his leave.

"No, it is too ridiculous," he declared at the last moment, as he turned his animals' heads around. "You must take your seat again, my friends. It is a long way to Granada, much too far for you to walk, and I have an aunt there to whom I really must pay a visit!"

I reminded him of his work at home and of the fact that he would have to travel home by night and could not work on the following day. So he yielded, pronounced a last farewell and moved off on his way home. He sat up with a sudden jolt.

"The boy shall decide the question!" he said as he turned around. "Where would you rather go, home or to your aunt?"

"To auntie's," the little one replied seriously, and Alfonso smiled a smile of triumph. "So we shall stay there to-night and go back home to-morrow," he announced with decision.

We rode on. I repeatedly observed in him a quality that is rare in Spain—kindness to animals. And it was even more remarkable to observe that he did not smoke.

"I do not wish to become a slave in any way," he said, "and we Spaniards cannot smoke without becoming slaves to tobacco." But his spirit of self-denial was for himself only.

"Will you take it?" he asked his boy, when I offered a cigarette to the father. The little one shook his head with comical seriousness. The two treated each other as if both were grown-ups.

We followed the edge of the mountains without interruption, for we had been told that the roads out on the Vega were flooded. It was almost evening when we approached Granada, where high up behind the city lies the Alhambra, golden against the setting sun. We took leave of Alfonso, whose journey led him toward the other end of the town, and ascended through the steep section of Albaicin. When we turned around after reaching the topmost terrace and looked back over the luxurious Vega and the violet-tinted silhouette of Sierra Elvira surrounded by the flaming sunset, we discovered Alfonso and his little boy far beneath us on the road, riding at a brisk trot back to the hills. They were trying to get home before morning. His little fields at home could not do without him for one more day.

This anarchist Alfonso! To do a kindness to us he ignored all his own personal needs; and now he was riding back home to his farm, happy in his deed, conversing affectionately with his little boy, with whom he associated as with a brother—at peace with all men. And when one day the tocsin sounds for the great upheaval, he will leap to his feet with enthusiastic joy, ready to give his life for the new era of human happiness, and will fall pierced by a gendarme's bullet while the old era trots on gayly over his corpse. Such will be his fate.

And yet! whenever I search in my mind for a prototype of a man whom it would be well to emulate or at least to envy, I always think of the anarchist Alfonso.

IX

A MORNING'S JOURNEY

EVERY morning, at the first faint glow of dawn, I was awakened by a deafening twitter. It burst forth outside our bedroom window as unexpectedly as the twittering of sparrows in the trees in Denmark, and it was just as purposelessly boisterous; but it came up from down below, not from the trees above. The bottom of our little alley and the fronts of the house would begin to bustle with life. Women and girls and boys hung over the balconies or out of little observation windows or crawled along under the milk goats and under the leather-clad shepherds. They emitted strange sounds in the air, with no other purpose than sheer joy in the use of their lungs. And from the swarming level of the street, which reminded one with its dirt, its semi-darkness, and its stench, of a great sewer, there ascended something like a natural hymn to the rising sun.

I shall tell you now of my customary morning walk. It extended through the city and passed over the Vega in a great curve to the foothills: then up the mountains until I was far above the city on the other side, and then again downward toward the city, through Alhambra or Albaicin. The whole trip could be taken in three or four hours. I probably walked over this course a hundred times and knew every step. I knew precisely at what point I should meet this beggar or that. I knew on what walls hung the most lizards. I knew where the aqueduct was in ruins and where each little peep-hole was situated. I knew the street gamins. I knew exactly what each one would shout after me. I knew all the serving women in Albaicin and I knew which would nod to me and which would not. The whole stretch was so bewitchingly full of life that I walked over it again and again and every day I met something new.

When the dawn crept up and Don Pedro in the next room shouted *"Beppa!"* I jumped out of my bed. First I immersed myself in *el pilar,* the fountain in the courtyard, and then I mounted the little turret in order to decide what sort of weather the day would bring. From our little turret I could see the millennial red walls of Alhambra. I could count the domes of thirty churches, and hear their cheap bells tinkling. The snowy summits of Sierra Nevada glowed far above me and off in the opposite direction I could see Sierra Elvira encircling the Vega. Don Bonifazio entered the church and went about his work while his wife directed his activities from her bed. As I would pass her open door, she would halt a sharp and vehement stream of abuse. Then I nodded to the merry old *"facio"* and was out in the street!

Scarcely was I out of the house when I was obliged to take a long step to evade a big dead dog—(there had been another dead dog on this spot yesterday)— before I ambled up the street. In a short side-street there was a great heap of refuse with two unkempt dogs and a beggar delving in its entrails for edible remnants. As I gazed up along the house-fronts, there were white shreds of mist between the many-colored balconies. The morning sun shone along the length of the narrow alley, filling it with a rosy light and inky shadows, while the balconies cast long streaks of shade obliquely down the house-fronts.

The ground floors of the houses had no balconies with their flowers and green lattice work. Here and there were portals leading into the yard or to the upper stories, and between these were several doors which passed directly from the street into the one-room dwellings that received all their light from the doorway, or perhaps from a small latticed window also. These were the dwellings of the poor. With the first rays of the sun they came crawling out like adders on the south side of a dike to warm their limbs that were damp and cold. Furniture was carried out of the houses; the children hopped forth in fragmentary shirt-tails almost black with dirt, and dressed themselves in the open air. The men hung sideways out of a chair, rolling a cigarette or allowing themselves a last remnant of morning slumber. Women swimming in their own fat, wearing only petticoat and skirt, combed and searched each other's hair. As I walked by, I looked into the houses. The impression was gloomy; you smelled the stench from oppressively close bedroom air. In some of the rooms, the beds were arranged in tiers, one over the other. In others, there were no beds at all; the people slept on the floors. In these sections, several families often shared the same room. It was customary in such cases to suspend a string across the room as a symbol of a partition.

In the wider streets only the better classes live. Here none but the servants were stirring early. They were cleaning up for the day, opening the glass doors, one after another. You could hear them sweeping the floors in the first and second stories. They did not sweep the dust into a dust-pan, but simply propelled it over the edge of the balcony so that it landed on the heads of those passing below on the sidewalk. But only a foreigner would think of walking on the sidewalk, so it did not matter. They threw out even more questionable substances from the windows and balconies at this time of day, and a wise man soon learned to keep to the center of the street. Furthermore, you were never without reasonable warning. Persons about to empty certain secular vessels into the open air never neglected to pronounce the blessed words: *"Jesús, María y José!"* before they did so.

In the sunlight on the market place there were groups of idle Spaniards standing around—slender, draped in their cloaks, smoking—chewing the political cud of the latest events. These discussions were as long as a sun's ray and as frail as a rotten egg. The beggars were already on the job—Granada's hundreds of beggars. They had spent the night under staircases, in obscure corners, under wagons, any place which offered some protection. There were some whose rags were a mere crust of blue loam and mire. They had slept by night along the subterranean course of the Darro. Now they emerged from their secret hiding-place and hobbled above, pale with the cold, performing their morning toilet by the fountain or begging for alms to pay for breakfast.

Cattle-bells were heard from up the market-place and a herd of goats turned into the street, driven by a shepherd clad from top to toe in sheepskin, with the woolly surface outside. Women and servant-girls came with glasses and pots and the shepherd took a goat by her hind leg, folded his hands about her udder, and squeezed out the required quantity of milk. Then the goat was released until the next customer came on the scene, and this went on until all the goats had been emptied. This is the milk supply of Granada—milk on draught. The system is much better than any sanitary inspection of milk anywhere in the world.

I made my way out of the city and crossed the bridge where the city customs officers stood on guard. All along the road peasants were halting with their laden donkeys, waiting for the officers to attend to them; one farthing for an egg, one shilling for a turkey. The officials walked around with smooth steel spears in their hands, jabbing into the donkeys' burdens, and smelling them to determine whether there was any contraband. The peasants were in their national costume; short jackets, knee-breeches with red sashes; white woolen stockings and laced sandals.

And there lies the Vega before me in the transparent morning air!

The mountain slopes were white and red with blossoming fruit trees. But down where the gardens were suspended like terraces one above the other, blossomtime was already past. We were in the middle of March. The fruit trees were quite green and the grape vines twined upward about their stakes, sprouting green antennæ into the air and holding out tender pale leaves in the sunlight like children's little hands spread out in the rain. Even the old elms in Alhambra's grove were seriously engaged in putting forth blossoms. At their feet the celestial blue China aster of the *borago* peered forth, and the "Tear of the

Virgin Mary" dazzling white on its long stems, nodded over the running water on both sides of the footpath.

The flat Vega lay before me shining in the sunlight. Over the Vega there extended the thousand-branched system of canals, so that it might rain whether the Lord willed it or not, as the merry peasant put it.

"But God's rain is better than the river's rain," his wife added by way of gentle correction.

The floor of the Vega was a green surrounded by green, broken only by the many whitewashed huts which flecked the great space like white sails. And then the snow-line! How it crept upward, rising higher each day. First the snow ran all the way down, down to the backs of the nearest hillocks, and one night there were even traces of it way down in the valley. But the sun touched it with a magic wand and the snow dissolved, filling the clefts with cascades and making the stream tumble head over heels into its subterranean bed. The stream boils and babbles under the city streets. On the other side, when it comes out again, it suffers a blood-letting at the hands of the peasants, which makes it quite weak and pale. Its waters are drawn off to the east and to the west.

The wheat stood knee-high and bushy, as thick as grass and without any weeds. One day in the fall the peasant went out and delved in the side with his pointed prong, to which his two mules were hitched. Then he walked over the same plot, sowing.

"For God, for the birds, and for me," he would say as he cast out a handful of seed at each step. The frivolous birds ate their share on the spot, but the good God and the peasant permitted theirs to grow. All winter long, sheep and goats grazed on the wheat.

As a result the wheat became thicker and thicker, and one fine day many men came with hoes and thinned it out, leaving only a little clump standing on each square foot. After that, it grew so vigorously that you were astonished to think the Vega had men enough to mow it.

At harvest time, every one able to walk and with a thumb on his hand went out into the fields and pitched into the work. The reaper seized a clump of wheat with his left hand while his right wielded the sickle. The sheaf was laid aside and another sheaf attacked. Then came a day when the wheat was to be threshed. Here and there in the fields there were paved circles, so that viewed from the hills above, the Vega appeared covered with scars. To these spots the sheaves were gathered and the oxen made to plod about, stamping the grain from the ears with their hoofs. The greedy peasant muzzled their mouths despite the adage: "Thou shalt not muzzle the ox when he treadeth out the corn!"

In some places, a great roller was dragged over the paved ring. The roller was provided with iron pegs that pressed the grain out of the ears. This was called machine-threshing. Then, on a windy day, the wheat was winnowed. It was thrown into the air and the superfluous portions flew away "like chaff in the wind." The ancients harvested in this manner in the days of Homer. The Moors harvested so eight centuries ago; and the peasants of the Vega still harvest so to-day.

The broad highway lay straight before me, but it was dusty and monotonous and there were green alluring donkey-paths leading off in every direction to the houses of the Vega. You could choose any path you liked and go as far as you liked in any direction, for there are no *"verboten"* signs in the south of Spain.

On one side of me there was a *sequia* (an aqueduct), probably built by the Arabs seven or eight centuries ago. The aqueduct was provided on each side with little weirs leading into troughs that extended into the distance, so that each field could be inundated by itself, while occasionally one of the troughs operated an olive-mill. On the other side, the path was hedged with blackberries. Black pigs burrowed under the clinging vines; fiery red suckling pigs scurried about devouring the grass. The air was cool and spiced with the fragrance of blossoming fields of lupine.

Laden donkeys trotted by, with peasants sitting on their cargoes, as well as neatly arrayed peasant women who were heading for the city to salute their saint there. There were very few wagons; every one rode. Long-eared gray mules were cantering to town, bearing burdens of straw or wood—burdens so large that you could not understand how they kept their equilibrium. Fruits were carried to town on the donkey's back and fertilizer was brought home in the same basket. Goods and men rode over the mountain from time to time.

But these caravans of mules bearing cargoes of goods through wild *sierras* and desert *llanos* were even then becoming more and more infrequent. The railroads were already beginning to dispose of them as they have already disposed of so many other things. However, I often met such caravans on my tours in the *sierra*. Long trains of mules wound down along the mountain-path, each animal laden with two casks of wine, the mule at the head of the procession being provided with a piece of iron pipe in which a tongue produced a ringing sound. His caparison was adorned with colored tassels. The thick-voiced bell had a modest and comfortable sound. In one place a donkey had left the line, in another a mule, in order to eat the flowers growing by the way. A well-aimed stone soon restored them to their places. At the end of the caravan came the *arrieros,* the drivers, sitting comfortably on their donkeys' backs and droning their monotonous *coplas* of unrequited love.

This donkey-path was joined by two others and the triangular plot at their intersection was crowned by a crucifix bearing the crucified. Right next to it was a saloon, in which the peasant might rest on his outward journey as well as on his return. The crucifix practically obliged him to dismount, and he obeyed this obvious command from heaven and took a little refreshment. He paid three cents a glass for the same wine that he would not drink at home. In fact, he had sold this wine to mine host, for half the price.

I usually took my breakfast here: ham and eggs, last year's grapes, and a very good wine. The whole meal cost a few cents. The table was set under the bright green vine-leaves outside the house, and a Madonna of a girl served me. In fact, if she could have recovered her two front teeth and acquired some cleanliness, she would have been quite heavenly. I took my seat and minded my p's and q's, for I was now in a land that had a very definite sense of form, and among people who didn't like foreigners anyway. I invited every man that halted at the place to have a cup of wine or share my meal with me. It was a delight to note their astonishment at this foreigner who could be as polite as a Spaniard, and their faces relaxed a little. They called me now by the title of *Excelencia,* now by that of *Compañero* (comrade), and talked to me on every possible subject. They asked whether it was possible that I was from Old Castile, which is a very cold country far to the north, and shook their heads when I told them I came from a country that was even colder than that. They politely declined to empty a glass with me; but when I insisted, they put their lips to my glass and wished me good health. It is a sacred duty to pronounce such invitations, but it is bad form to accept them, particularly from a stranger.

Not one of them had heard of Denmark, not even by name. A few of them had heard of a country called France, and one of them mentioned Arabia, "where the sun does not go down for half a year." He glanced in my direction, for corroboration, and I nodded, because to contradict them would mean to lose all the favor you had gained among these people, who have the habit of saying anything that comes into their minds. They pointed to one of their number, who had visited Murciar, a city on the Mediterranean coast, and this man, turning to me, told me there was nothing he would so much like to do as to travel and become familiar with the world and its peoples. He said, "the whole world!" How Spanish this is! How well it accords with their childlike, even their grandiloquent conceptions. To see another city is equivalent to seeing "the whole world." If a thing occurs to you twice, it has happened all over the world. Spain is the best country in the whole world, the coldest country in the whole world, the hottest country in the whole

world.   Everything Spanish is superlative.   And
Andalusia in turn is the first province in all of Spain,
and the Vega the backbone of all Andalusia.   In the
privacy of his own mind each of the fellows I talked to
regarded himself as the foremost man in the whole
country.   "If I wanted to——" is a universal Spanish
expression, always accompanied by large gestures.
They are children, magniloquent braggarts; but they
are also splendid——a peculiar mixture of the Cid and
Don Quixote.

Small wooden bridges led over the aqueduct.   At the
end of each bridge there was a gate with a niche and
in the niche stood an oil-lamp with a Madonna.   Over
the gate was the name of the farmyard to which it
led: "The Farm of the Immaculate Conception," "The
Farm of the Annunciation," "The Farm of the Passion and Death of Christ."   The white farm-houses
were two stories high and had no windows.   The
upper story consisted of a roof only, resting on white
pillars.   The deep blue sky shone on the other side of
the second story, and ears of maize as well as Spanish peppers were hanging out to dry in great sheaves.
It was the yellowest yellow and the reddest red!   The
colors were further intensified by the powerful sunlight that imparted a bluish tint to the whitewashed
walls.

The path was crossed by a stream.   I took off shoes
and stockings and waded to the other side.   A band
of men and women approached me from the village, on
their way to early mass in the cathedral.   As I was
again putting on my shoes and stockings, they reached
the water.   The men walked into the water, one by
one, took their places under the low bank and bended

their backs forward. The women got on the men's backs, took hold of their necks, and were thus borne to the other side. The scattered houses were succeeded by close-built villages and the hills that limit the Vega on one side became more distinct. Donkeypaths could be distinguished, winding like white bands over their slopes. On one of them a black streak was crawling upward—possibly a caravan.

A man was walking in the fields, engaged in shooting song-birds on their way to the north. I shouted to him: "God greet you, my friend!", and he came toward me, taking a crumpled pocket-handkerchief from the pocket of his trousers and disentangling it. In it was a little half-stifled song-bird which he had captured in his noose. In fact, the string was still around the bird's legs. Did I want to buy it? I paid him ten cents, cut the string, and cast the bird far up into the air. The bird flew away as it burst into song.

"What are you doing that for?" I was asked.

"Perhaps he will fly to my home and sing to the people there!" was my answer.

"Well, well!" he answered laughing, "he is not a canary." And he made an attempt to catch the bird again. Perhaps he would be able to make another sale when I returned home by the same path.

A row of pollard willows, with hundreds of crows bickering and racketing in their branches, indicated the point where the river emerged from its subterranean course. With its bed more than half a mile wide, along one side of which the current had bitten a deeper course, this river created a desert in the midst of the flowering Vega.

All objects that are in the way in the city are simply

dropped through a trap door into the river, which washes them in this direction, creating a huge slough of despond. A stench of carrion meets your nostrils. At other points the river spurts and bubbles about the skeleton of a horse or an ass; the denuded ribs stick out like the ribs of a stranded ship. Dead dogs and cats, surrounded by a gay mass of branches and reeds, are stalled at points where a projecting stone prevented them from floating away. Half-fallen willow-trees hang down over the river, which reflects their wretched wooden skeletons when it is calm and peaceful enough to reflect any image at all. Ravens and wild dogs fight over the fresh bleeding carcass of a horse.

But you had to arrive even earlier if you wanted to see the beginning of the fun. Long before the first beam of morning had kindled the glaciered top of Sierra Nevada, announcing to the Vega that the sun had risen over the Mediterranean Sea more than two hundred miles away, the peasants had taken their decrepit beasts down to the river, put bullets through their heads and walked off. The ravens in the tops of the trees were already alert, and the dogs came slinking down from town, their flanks flapping loosely over their empty bellies. But they were driven away by the flayer who darted forth from the bushes, peered about in every direction, and dropped down the bank. In two shakes of a lamb's tail, he had finished any job that was undone, putting the unhappy beasts out of their misery, and then rolled the dead trunks from side to side as he pulled off the steaming skins, while hundreds of hungry eyes watched him from the bushes and the tops of the trees. A final liberating incision, and he threw the hide over his shoulder, gave the carcass a parting kick and disappeared. At once there was a furious swoop from out of the air and over the ground. In an instant the carcass was covered with hungry dogs and greedy ravens. But an old gypsy woman was walking down the river. She threw stones to drive away the animals and then proceeded to cut away the juiciest slices from chest and thighs of the carcass. She cut the meat into thinner slices, concealed the slices over her naked skin, and then adjusted her clothing over the slices. This is the conventional method of smuggling meat through the excise gates. Afterward it is an easy matter to sell it in the market-place as beef or pot-roast. Finally the dogs and ravens could start their breakfast. When the sun appeared over the peaks of the Sierra, only the skeletons remained.

After this incident, the dogs ran about half sated, sniffing with curiosity at the blue luster of the inflated bodies of their fellow-dogs who lay dead in the water, with their snouts submerged and the corners of their jaws reversed. Perhaps they would be in the same position themselves the next morning, in the same spot, and in the same state of decay.

There was a tremendous number of masterless dogs who had been going to seed for several generations in Granada, a plague indeed to the city and its environs. It was a difficult matter to overcome the natural inertia and the dogs were left to themselves, until the hot weather came. It had already come, in March, and hydrophobia had resulted in mortal injuries. On one day six persons were bitten by mad dogs. Finally the city administration deigned to intervene and ordered poisoned meat to be laid in the gutters at

street corners. You could see large dogs walking
down the street with blunted senses, suddenly fall, stick
up their legs and die. As you walked through the
streets in the evening, you stumbled over their bodies,
and you found more at each street corner on the morning after. They were ultimately dropped into the
river through the trap door on the promenade and
floated out to the carrion-pit. Many of them ran out
of town and lay down in the ditches by the sides of the
promenades to die. There they remained, filling the
air with their stench. The rain and the waters of the
river finally disintegrated their corpses and fed fountains and wells with the venom. When the cholera
came from the south across the Straits of Gibraltar, it
found a very favorable soil.

I continued up the river until the hills stepped into
the foreground, intercepted the Vega and transformed
it into a narrow gulley through which the river flowed!
Here in these foot-hills in old deserted river beds were
the dwellings of poor adventurers who were washing
gold. These men who would show the utmost re-
luctance to undertake any definite task yielding a sure
income were ready to work here eighteen hours a day,
the sweat pouring off them all day long. They were
taking a chance, and the chance was always pretty
uncertain. The work yielded but little profit each day;
yet there had been cases several times in the last
twenty years when a gold washer obtained fifty dollars' worth of gold in a single taking from the sand.
Such an incident furnished sufficient stimulus for a
whole generation.

On the bank of the river waved the high Spanish
reeds, and over the slopes of the mountain ascended

the broad-leaved fig-cactus, carrying its flowers like a torch-light procession over the cliff. Hundreds of holes might be seen in every direction, above, below, and in groups; each hole was the entrance to a sub-terranean cave. Here lived the filthy, ugly, thievish gypsies, who had formed a society of their own, which, though it was under the jurisdiction of Granada, continued to exist only by virtue of the dubious moral practices of this curious race.

I was on the soil of the Alhambra!

Put your ear to the ground! In every direction you hear a gurgling, laughing sound as cold iridescent streams shoot forth and disappear again. Over a steep, moss-green hole that looks like an ancient cliff under its covering foliage, the water dashes down in mighty cascades, breaking up in rainbow mists of spray. Birds fly merrily and noisily in and out of the crystal rain. Two ragged boys try to walk between the descending water and the wall behind it. They stick their heads through the thin sheet of the fall and scream in wild delight. A gypsy woman places her black pock-marked face under the sparkling rain of spray, at the very point where it holds suspended the fragment of a rainbow.

"Jesus, how lovely!" she shouts, shaking her sides with joy.

Far out in the sunlight, between the tree-trunks, the water drives on like a cloud of diamond dust; and under a mighty remnant of ruined walls, which creeping plants have transformed into moist dark grottoes, there is a ceaseless tinkling and trickling of drops descending on trembling maidenhair fern. The water is singing its oriental song. And the walls of Alhambra rise before me mighty in their mass as the walls of Babylon.

I walk around the projecting bit of wall—Charles V here glued a pasticceria fountain against the stout masonry—and I turn in under the horseshoe vault to enter a pompous four-cornered tower, the Tower of Justice. To this tower the King would descend twice a week from his castle to adjust the litigations of the Granadinos—like the kings of the Orient in the Bible. And here, over the vault, is a counterfeit of the hand mentioned in Deuteronomy (VI, 8), the symbol given to the Jews by Moses that they might be mindful of the doctrine: "God is one only!" On the capitals that support the vault the same tenet is repeated in Arabic characters: "There is one God, Allah, and Mohammed is his Prophet!" How modest old Moses was compared with his Mohammedan rival!

The Old Testament and the Koran! Moses and Mohammed! And up on the battlements, high above everything else, stood two freckle-faced American gentlemen discussing quotations of shares in the Río Tinto copper-mines!

The hill of the Alhambra opened at this elevation on to a perfect plateau, framed on all sides by massive walls with solid turrets. Down in the bowels of the mountain lay the vaulted cistern fed by miles and miles of canals from the glaciers of Sierra Nevada. A deep shaft led down to the water, which is as cold as ice even in the hottest summer.

Even at this height water was gurgling in every hole, singing and trickling forth from little pipes, and dancing gayly in the air, rising and falling like a juggler's balls. And way down in the Vega I could

see a far-ramified network of channeled veins that
once made this great plain into a garden of Paradise
sung by all the singers of the Moors.

This mountain of the Alhambra, which affords a
matchless view, is surrounded by a halo of legends
rich and varied. Every turret is woven about with
tales of magicians and warriors, wondrously beautiful
women and imprisoned sons of monarchs. Here love
blazed forth in deeds of blood, a bloody deed for every
poppy which now burns on the steep walls of the mountain; and hatred ate its way through every crevice of
Alhambra.

The Orient sowed the seeds of its culture to this
far-western limit; intrigues of the harem, revolutions
of the palace, mass murders, hatred as venomous as
verdigris, all-consuming love. The Zegri and the
Abencerrages murdered one another openly or in
secret. Each dynasty was eager for the blood of the
other; and on one day we encounter in the tales a
youth from one of the two families concerned in the
feud, and a young girl from the other. Their hearts
found each other in spite of the barriers of hatred and
blood-revenge, and they met by night in one of the
little gardens full of flowers which still hang perched
in spots between the walls, like swallows' nests over
the abyss. Their young love bore both white flowers
and red berries. One night he found her murdered in
the garden, lifted her radiant body in his hands
lamenting, and attached it to the sky as a new constellation.

Zelinda and Zorayda, Adalifa and Lindaraja still
dot the nocturnal sky in this zone as radiant bodies, so
powerful has been the effect of Moorish romance.

How firmly the hearts of the Moors were attached to this place! They called the Vega "the Garden of Paradise" and imagined the Heaven of the Faithful lay directly above it. Any one who died here could not help going to heaven; hither the warrior felt compelled to return in order to die blessed. And the Moors wept—wept like women, says the romance—when they were driven from this place by Isabella the Catholic. Many regions about the Mediterranean still retain shining traces of this highly gifted, gently judging people. But it is at this place that the Moors attained their greatest achievements—in architecture and poetry, in agriculture and engineering: in civilization. So greatly did they love Granada.

Granada was founded by ancient Iberians and is mentioned in history as early as about 500 B.C. But the city attained no importance until twelve centuries later, in 711 A.D., when the Moors, aided by Tarek the One-Eyed, ventured across the "Straits" and conquered southern Spain. Granada was taken the same year. The era of its blossoming followed, and it continued to expand in glory for eight centuries and then suddenly it collapsed.

The penetration of the Moors into Europe was like a flood of light piercing our dismal medieval darkness. The migration proceeded by way of Africa; but most of the persons that made it up came from remoter parts of the Orient, from the vicinity of Mecca and Medina, Damascus and Bagdad.

The settlers from Damascus chose Granada as their place of sojourn, because this city with its hills behind it and the broad Vega in front reminded them strongly

of the city in their homeland at the foot of the Anti-
Lebanon, with the large and beautiful level plain of
El Ghuta. In fact, the name "the Earthly Paradise"
had originally been used for Damascus and El Ghuta,
but was now transferred to the new home. And together with the name went all the solicitude, all the
pride and all the affectionate care which the inhabitants
of large cities felt for their home in antiquity and in
the Middle Ages. Just as the Barada in their old home
had irrigated the plain of El Ghuta, so the Genil and
the Darro had to be conducted over the Vega; for
water is the blood of the earth, and as the blood
washes every cell in the body, so the water must trickle
about each plant.

Seville was the city of commerce, Córdoba the city
of science. But Granada, which did not lie on the
great arteries of traffic, attracted all persons of delicacy and nobility, by reason of its beauty and its bewitching climate, as well as its great idle riches. Sixty
thousand knights were in the service of Granada in its
most flourishing period, one braver than the other.
By day they wore the colors of their lady before men's
eyes in the lofty plumes of their helmets, which flut-
tered with ribbons, and they engaged in tournaments
to win a smile from her. On the spacious Vivarrambla,
where the Inquisition later kindled its pyres, they
fought the bull, mounted on horseback and armed only
with a lance. All the chivalry of Europe may be traced
from them; and here also was laid the corner-stone for
Don Quixote.

These were the days when the Alhambra came into
being. Everywhere in the city splendid buildings rose

to the sky, each one richer than its predecessor, until one day there stood the Alhambra, more radiant than all the others, more lovely than any other structure erected by the Moors in Spain. Generalife, the summer palace, put up at about the same time, surmounts another hill, even higher than the Alhambra, but the horizontal distance between them is so short that you can throw stones on Alhambra's turrets from Generalife. When there were palace revolutions in Alhambra, the kings sought asylum higher up; and here they spent their honeymoons each time they took a new wife.

You may walk about for a long time within the strong walls of Alhambra without coming upon the palace. There is an entire city here reaching in every direction, with wine-rooms, churches, slums, photographers and bunco-steerers. Suddenly you stand at the edge of a sharp declivity, from which a path leads downward into something that looks like a collection of cabinets with roofs of glass. This is the palace viewed from above. A rickety door is opened and you find yourself in a long gloomy courtyard in which the custodians sit over braziers, nodding. One of them opens a door and—

Who will describe these magic apartments with their vaulting, their columns and their basins? The wonderful stucco, the symbols, the delicate lines and tense forms, the great green surfaces of water disturbed by the leap of gold-fish and framed by tablets of marble, hedges of metal, luxurious orange-trees! Here you have all the forms that describe life and well-being and the symbols of Islam; all the colors that are elevating or stimulating in their effect, or that relieve a sense of tension; bright perspectives, tall apartments, a sense of the whole and an enjoyment of petty minor parts. Everything that begets and maintains life in the world outside is found counterfeited in this place.

No, it is not counterfeited! It is organically present! It has been made into a new concentrated world. Here the mystery of the vegetable world has been dissolved into its secret curving lines and interwoven with the structure of the earth and the vault of heaven to restore the old unity of the universe. Behind the most ingenious network of tracery pulsates the purple hue of blood. It strikes the eye from a thousand angles, issuing from many points, merely as an indication, as a symbol, as something on the surface of a rich unseen undercurrent. Here are the mysterious aspirations of life, aspirations for that which is above and beyond, in the most glorious lines and in the purest blue—the blue of the mid-day sky—that rises forth from the dark pool of blood. There is a deep indigo of the night, woven in lines and forms that make the eye of man gentle and his hands caress. Gold is there in all its importunate glitter; and high over one of the apartments there is a dome-like cupola, a vault of heaven dotted with stars, whose ingenious mosaic reflects the profoundest of all follies, man's abstract thought.

All that the earth holds of brightness and exultation is to be found in this magic castle which has so mystic and bewitching a power to attach the onlooker to the great world outside, to make him feel that he is a creature of the universe, the center of its glory. The

Alhambra is like a world freed from its elements of slag and dross, a world in which you stand face to face with the great and eternal things of life.

So rich is this castle, so rich is the civilization in which the castle has its roots, it is impossible to describe it.

X

SAN ANTONIO

O F course we again took lodgings with Beppa. She was now more than sixty years old, but as buxom and voluminous as when I left her roof seven years before, after more than eighteen months of sojourn under it. She was just as poor as then; in fact, she was much poorer. She had lost her exuberant good spirits. She no longer had any hopes of her husband's pension. He was a captain in the army. She was crushed; and to a certain extent it is my fault.

The fact was that she had regarded my stay with her as an omen of great prosperity to come, and when I left she gave up her responsible position as an intermediator between the nobility of Granada and the public pawnshop, and established a boarding-house with thirteen rooms and electric light. Most of her boarders were students, and Spanish students have the unfortunate habit of discontinuing their stay in a boarding house once they have been given notice to pay up. The business ended with her giving up the whole thing after a four months' experiment. She could say at least that she had had nothing to lose.

But she had lost something; for she never thought of returning to her former occupation as an intermediator. Instead she tried to starve her way along, and it was in this condition that we found her.

She lived in a narrow street, in a nice little two-story tenement which served as the bottom of the street, cutting off one of its ends. The whole house consisted of an upstairs room and a kitchen downstairs, with a dark little cubicle behind the kitchen. We rented the upper room and did our own housekeeping.

On the day of our arrival, she was completely penniless and it was apparent that she had not had much to eat during the week before. But the first thing she did the day after we came was to go out and hire a servant—a little old woman of seventy—who was to take care of the rough work of the house, in return for board and lodging. During the day, while Beppa was noising about in the kitchen, the other old wretch, who barely hung together at the joints, would sit in a reed-chair bending over the brazier. She spent the nights in a hallway somewhere in the neighborhood. She permitted Beppa to call her *tú* but called her *Señora Beppa* in return, and this was a sufficient regulation of their social relation for them. So, from the first day, we had two mouths to feed, sometimes even more. Fortunately we did not feel it very perceptibly, for Beppa did the shopping; though, in general, we found her prices pretty high.

Beppa's peculiar love-story was known by every one. If it was not, it certainly was not my fault. She was still Don Pedro's beloved, although it had turned out that he was ten years older than we had all thought on our previous visit. At that time they lived together, and Don Pedro would eat at his own house, where four daughters and one son-in-law parasited on his meager income. Now he had not even that home, but spent his time with his daughters at Albaicin, and had a chest complaint furthermore. He could no longer look after the duties of his position in Alhambra; but if the sun shone very warmly, he would get up and hobble down to see us. Then Beppa would bang at the ceiling of her kitchen and shout: "Don Martin, little Pedrico is here!", and I ran downstairs. He sat crouched and coughing over the brazier, holding an extinguished cigarette butt in one of the corners of his mouth. But this was only for the sake of appearances, for Pedro could no longer afford to smoke. He had become faded and decrepit. His clothes were dirty and neglected; yet there was a certain nobility about him. He fixed his dull eyes affectionately on me and again and again spoke of the miraculous disposition of Providence that had enabled us to meet again. Sometimes he addressed me as *tú*, with the effect of a caress.

Suddenly he would become animated:

"How did you succeed in sending me a letter from Seville to my new address? Nobody knows Pedro Rebollo so far away from here." He likes to repeat this question, and I answer, half as a joke:

"Of course they know you in Seville. Aren't you an employee of the King? The idea!"

"No, certainly not!" he would say as his furrowed face twinkled with delight. "I am nothing but an overseer, that's all. No doubt I was once a goldsmith and had a big business of my own; but that was many years ago and no one knows of that. No, I simply cannot understand how you got my address."

"What, I simply looked into the Granada Directory in a public library!"

"But only well-known people have their names in that book, don't I know that?"

"Of course, Don Pedro!"

"I don't understand it, I don't!" he would repeat,

shaking his head; but his eyes continued to have their delighted look. Then, unable to sit up any more he crawled back into the little cubicle behind the staircase, Beppa's bedroom, and went to bed. Not long after, we heard them muttering to each other, just as in the old times.

But the quarrel seemed to increase. Beppa was scolding and calling names. Pedro painfully coughed out his words. A few hours later Beppa banged the door and was off on an errand to town. Then I heard Pedro calling me very softly, and I went down to speak to him.

"What was that book of which you spoke before?" he asked in a whisper. He was freezing; his teeth were chattering in his mouth.

"The Granada Directory."

"And was my name really in the book?"

"Yes, and the name of the street, and the number, and everything."

"It is remarkable that they should know all this— you surely aren't making fun of me, my boy?"

This damp hole had no windows, but there was a little oil-wick with a flame as big as the head of a match stick, burning in front of San Antonio's image. I could barely distinguish Pedro's shadowy outlines.

"Oh, I am freezing," he lisped. "There must be a lot of snow in the hills. But now go up to your little wife. What do you think she thinks of old Pedro? Has she said anything? She surely considers me ill-bred; but you have known me of old and you know that I am sick. If I had been in good health, I— Tell her that I find her charming and that I kiss her feet! Tell her that Pedro is not a tactless idiot, but that he would

hate you for jealousy if he were younger. And that—
ka, ka—*preciosa*—ka—every virtue—*adoración*—"
His gentle and gallant heart inspired him to say even
more things, but these were consumed by his cough. I
put fresh embers into the brazier and put the brazier
into his bed before I went.

Next morning Beppa came into the kitchen and engaged in a loud conversation with San Antonio and the
Holy Virgin, alternately lamenting and scolding.
There was something wrong again. At noon she came
pounding up the stairs:

"Now just think of it, Don Martin, there he is out
walking again and he can hardly stand on his legs for
illness. Jesús, María, what wretchedness!" I looked
out into the street and there was Don Pedro hobbling
along.

"And he didn't even say good-by, not even to you!
He hasn't said a word to me all day; simply lay in bed
and turned his back to me. And do you know why?
Just because I would not lie in bed with him. That is
the only time he doesn't freeze. I breathed on his
back all night to keep it warm; and all morning I
heated bricks for him and put hot water into his bed-
warmer and embers into his brazier, and my bed-sheets
are all charred with them. But it's all no use. What
misery, what misery!

"Since we discovered last year that he was not
seventy-one years old but eighty-one, he has been going down hill fast. But just for his sake I cannot lie in
bed with him all day if there is nothing wrong with *me*,
can I? What would become of you and the house?
He began the business even yesterday as soon as he
got to bed. 'Beppa,' he said, 'little one, aren't you

coming soon? I am freezing!' But it is little one this and little one that; Beppa upstairs and Beppa downstairs. They are all howling and screaming for Beppa every minute, now for this thing, now for that thing; and in addition I am expected to lie in bed with them all day long in broad daylight." She was quite indignant.

"Just look at the old fool!" she suddenly burst out in malicious laughter. "He is stumbling over his own legs, so offended he is." Suddenly she weeps: "And yet he loves me, wicked woman! Oh, Madonna, Mother of Pain, how he does love me! Alas!"

Pedro did not return for a whole week and Beppa walked about engaged in loud conversation with Saint Anthony. She discussed with him all the affairs of the house; but her general solicitations were confided to the Madonna. Often I sat on the stairs and listened stealthily, thus gradually attaining some understanding of the multitudinous duties of San Antonio.

In the afternoon, and more particularly in the evening, the women of the quarter gathered in Beppa's kitchen. At times some old man joined them, and their conversation flowed on at a great rate, the subjects being the lottery, the miracles of the Saints, love, million-dollar bequests from South America, dragons and evil juices.

One of the women had nearly been taken sick the night before, for having drunk water without first shaking it to wake it up. For by night water sleeps like a human being and if it wakes up and finds itself in strange surroundings, it often attempts to go back to the place it came from. For this reason no one should take any medicine at any other time of day than midnight, the threshold between day and night, for then all nature has a turning point. But the most important turning point is at the new year, and then things can be changed easily—of course if you know how. It is by no means simple.

If you wished to play the lottery, you must first go out on the road and watch the figures lashed in the sand by the *lagarto* (a large lizard) with his tail; for that would be the number of the winning ticket.

"Ridiculous!" was the interruption heard from an old working-man in the gas-works. "Silly stuff! The controlling element is the natural force, that's the thing! It is just as with the gold on the sand-banks of the Genil above Granada! Why does it float on the surface, being so heavy? Simply because the sun draws it! There is a relation between the sun and gold as anybody can see from their brightness. Natural forces are the whole thing. All this talk about lizards' tails is silly stuff." And he looked to me for corroboration.

"You always set such great store by your gas and your natural forces, José, that one has to hold one's nose shut with her fingers," said a corpulent woman, every one laughing with her. "And what about snakes? It is perhaps untrue also that snakes exist? Everybody knows well enough that in the big tower behind the Alhambra they found a snake not so many years ago which was five or six yards long. She never appeared, but occasionally you could tell that she was alive because she would throw a young one more than a yard long down into the yard.

"One fine day, when some men who had the devil in them ascended the tower, she had disappeared, no man

knew whither. My own son was one of them; so nobody can say I am lying. And many of her brood are
still living in Granada. We never see them any larger,
for a snake takes a thousand years before she is full
grown. Since their mother is dead, they are always
looking for milk, and by night they creep into the beds
of women nursing their children, lay themselves over
their breasts and push the child aside. Then, to prevent the child from crying, they stick their tails into its
mouth as a nipple, for they have some sense; and if the
child cries anyway, they make themselves scarce. They
remain in hiding all day long, but you can always tell
that they have been around because the child has a
black mark around the mouth next morning and will
not grow properly."

They continued talking about snakes and adders, but
persistently avoided using the Spanish word for snake,
culebra. They said, "the animal," or "the large insect." I knew that there are certain words that may
not be mentioned because they will bring on some
dreadful event; perhaps this is one of them.

"I have never seen a *culebra* in Granada," I said
quite innocently. The women stared at me with terrified eyes and open mouths and began to scream. Beppa
addressed me with wails and reproaches and rushed
upstairs to San Antonio.

"Turn it away, turn it away!" she cried, lamenting,
and hastily began to repeat the charm, in which she
was joined by the voices of the other women: "*Lagarto, lagarto—vete á comer esparto*" (lizard, lizard, go eat esparto grass). This was said to be an
excellent device for exorcising these monsters; but the
old gas-works operator completely lost control of him-

self. He banged his knuckles on the table and roared at me, saying that if I ever repeated that word again he would not be responsible for his actions.

"If you must speak of this animal, then be so kind as to say *el bicho largo* (the large insect). That's what I have been saying ever since I crept out of my mother's womb!"

I was not very popular in the company that evening and hastened to retire. Beppa told me next morning that San Antonio had fallen down during the night.

I wondered whether any other religion than Catholicism would be suitable for these people? I doubt it; and the foreign creeds which make an effort to establish themselves here lead a pitiable existence without exception. In spite of all his arbitrary use of the imagination and the reasoning powers, the Andalusian does not like to think of matters which are not accessible to his senses. He will not protest if you maintain that you can see a fly crawling on the surface of the church-steeple a mile away, or hear her buzzing; but if you discuss with him a being that is invisible, and omnipresent, and enduring from eternity to eternity—in other words, God—he will shrug his shoulders, if he does not go so far as to indulge in blasphemous language. He has no use for expressions that hang loosely in the air, and long ago he found a use to which he put divine properties—as devices for indicating the superlative degree. The word "invisible" to him means something very small, let us say a dwarf. "Omnipresent" he would use for a swift, active creature. "Omnipotent," "omniscient," "all-wise," these words are for himself. He can subscribe to the Doctrine of the Infallibility of the Pope without a single scruple, for he begins with his own infallibility. And the Church does not create a chasm between itself and him by persistently forcing the conception of God upon him. The Church is diligently engaged in the same task of depriving God of his properties and applying them to extremely mundane things—to images of the Pope and the Saints, to old rags and bones.

The case with Christ is a little easier. At least Christ was a man on earth and the story of his passion can be made quite vivid with the use of wax figures or living human beings. But the significance of Christ is not overestimated either by the Church or by the people. It is taken quite naturally. On Christmas eve we visited the great Cathedral at Seville, believing that we would find some celebration to mark the birth of Christ. Up at the main altar a few men were working on a scaffolding that would be needed during the following week on a certain Saint's day. It was late in the evening, but they were working overtime to finish their job. Their hammer-blows reëchoed through the dark vaults. On the pavement, a servant was carrying two big pails of water, from which he was filling the fonts of holy water. Any portion of the fluid that overflowed was dried off with a dirty rag. I turned to a priest who was walking through the church.

"Birth of Christ? No, we have nothing to do with that," he answered absent-mindedly. "You will have to go to such and such a church."

The people themselves of course were not so indifferent to the Nativity.

"Hello, it's Christmas to-day. Everybody is going to get a jag on to-day!" was what my acquaintances shouted to me in the street; and when night came we were convinced of it by the evidences of our own eyes. The streets were full of drunken men who drifted about in groups until late next morning, screaming and howling, beating their tambourines and singing hymns, all of which seemed to end with the refrain "brandy."

In Granada there was even a worse racket on Christmas eve in the year 1895. On the Alameda there was a fair-ground with jugglers' tents, carrousels and booths where gay objects of all kinds and noise-making instruments were on sale. In the evening, the whole population was up and doing, moving through the streets, a noisy crew of men, each one with his *zambomba* (a kind of rustic drum) or his *chicharra* (a sort of clapper). About midnight they gathered in the Cathedral to attend midnight mass, planning to continue a custom of former years, by banging all their *zambombas* on the floor at the stroke of twelve and cutting off each other's coat tails in the resulting confusion. But nothing came of this latter folly, since the new prefect of police had stationed about one hundred gendarmes in the church.

The Andalusian attaches great importance to noise. Noise will drown out his grief. He uses noise in the chamber of confinement to reduce the pains of travail and accelerate birth. There being no great distinction between a birth and the celebration of a birth, he has no difficulty in applying this custom on Christmas eve also.

Of course, noise is an outright necessity in any celebration of the Resurrection. During Easter Week all loud noises had been banished from Granada, but on Easter morning the inhabitants hastened to make up for lost time. They caught all the unclaimed dogs they could lay hands on, tied old iron junk to their tails, as well as tin-cans and the like. At six o'clock sharp, when all the church bells of the city began to ring at once, the dogs were released, dashing away with rattling noises, accompanied by their own howls. From all the balconies shots were fired, and a veritable pandemonium descended upon the city.

During the rest of the year, the Andalusian is more reserved. After all, there is too much solemnity, too much ceremony connected with the cult of the Son of God. One does not feel quite at ease in His vicinity. He would not take a joke. The Andalusian never turns to Christ in prayer, and his reason is not an excessive humility. The Son of God is not too high, but too remote for him.

If there is a burden on his heart, he turns to the Madonna, or, in minor matters, to some saint. His celestial hierarchy really begins with the Madonna, descending through the saints and through a great number of relics. Where the Mother of God is concerned, his religion becomes a relation of personal confidence. He adorns her with every manner of divine quality and surrenders himself confidently to her, for, after all, she is a human creature like himself; being a woman, she can understand his cares, and being an Andalusian she can take a coarse joke into the bargain.

But since the Madonna controls the whole world, fills all hearts, and affords aid for all suffering, she becomes too vague, too hazy for the Andalusian. He needs some more definite hold to cling to. The Madonna performs this miracle or that, but which Madonna is it? There are nearly thirty Madonnas.

"Is it the Madonna of the Grapes or perhaps the White Madonna?" (two goddesses of the vineyard), asks the peasant far off in the mountains.

"Is it the Madonna of Pain or the Old Madonna?" (the favorite Madonnas of Granada), ask Beppa and the others. "You shall see, it is the Madonna of Pain," adds Beppa with importance, for the Madonna of Pain is her special guardian saint.

"No, it is the Madonna del Pilar," say I, who have brought this bit of news.

"Bah, it is always Seville!" they say as they turn up their noses. "What great thing can she have done? I suppose she just walked about a bit. She cannot do anything else," some one adds contemptuously. It is not to be wondered at that Beppa at once ascends to my room, where the Madonna of Pain is hanging, and has a little discussion with her, ending with a good-natured bit of consolation:

"Well, well, don't be down-hearted over it; your turn will come next." She speaks just as if she were a father or a mother whose child had been worsted in some encounter with another child.

Needless to say, the Madonna of Pain can also reveal herself. The women told of many examples, and I myself remembered from my last stay in this town, that she revealed herself to an assembly of five thousand persons. It was late one spring evening, when Beppa came in and related that there must be something doing, for so many people were walking through the streets. I hastened down the street, following the crowd to a great square that was black with people. They were staring at the roof of a house on which the Madonna had revealed herself. On the roof was a white chimney, with the moon shining behind it. Quite possibly white clouds of vapor occasionally rose from the chimney, like a saint's halo. Next day this fact was reported in the papers.

But this was only the beginning; this was only the Madonna's way of arousing men's attention. Shortly thereafter she accomplished a positive miracle. It was at the time of the Cuban War, and there was a great service of celebration one day in the Church of the Madonna of Pain, which is the most frequented in Granada, for the benefit of certain volunteers who were to leave for Cuba on the following morning. There were many torches and candles and above the high altar sat enthroned the Madonna of Pain, adorned in her most precious mantle, which was embroidered with real jewels. On the following day it appeared that a large hole had been burnt in the back of the mantle. This was a great loss, but the priests at once explained that the damage could not possibly have been inflicted as a result of carelessness in the handling of a wax-candle, for such an event would have caused the mantle to burn from the bottom up and not straight across. Expressing a truly divine inspiration, one of the priests interpreted the phenomenon as due to the fact that the Madonna had been in Cuba during the night and had fought against the rebels there. The flames from the rebels' cannons or perhaps a bomb—God alone would know—must have burnt this hole in the back of her garment. Of course, the Madonna could have protected her mantle as well as herself, but she needed this hole as an evidence to unbelievers. More than ten thousand persons visited the church during the next few days. Gifts flowed in in great abundance and the Madonna was given a new cloak even more splendid than the old.

The various Madonnas have no connection with each other. Over a century ago, the adherents of the various Madonnas used to meet in savage street fights and to this day there is a very strong feeling between them. To change one's Madonna or one's saint is equivalent to an outright defection, and I have rarely seen Beppa so excited as when an old aunt from Seville attempted to persuade her to try her luck with San Esperitu, who has in Seville about the same position as San Antonio in Granada. It would have been just as reasonable to propose that she should become a convert to Mohammedanism.

But the Madonna of Pain has quite a number of churches besides the church in Granada. Everywhere around in the country there are altars with her wooden image, more or less richly dressed. And there is no relation between any of these either. The Madonna in Malaga was not in Cuba on the occasion above described, nor was the Madonna of Pain in Cádiz or the other one, in Cuba. As a matter of fact, the latter does not amount to very much anyway. It was the Madonna of Pain in Granada, the wooden image, cloak and all, that fought the rebels that night; and the peasants of the Vega, who have their own Madonnas of Pain standing in their villages, will come to town for the express purpose of worshiping this Madonna because she is the best of all. The process of concentration goes on apace. The wooden image becomes the actual incarnation of the divine properties. Back of it there are mists, at best a few vaguely floating outlines.

This condition is even more apparent in the case of the saints. There are plenty of saints in Andalusia; one saint for each complaint. They are one's refuge in times of need, in sickness, in times of poor crops, and earthquakes. On such occasions they are carried in a procession and the whole matter is placed in their hands. This results in considerable economy, in the matter of hospitals, disinfectants, doctors, street cleaning, in short, in all this modern and expensive hygienic mechanism. Way up in the steep streets of Albaicin I once met Latia Lorenza, Beppa's ninety-year-old aunt, who was painfully hobbling up the hill. She had inflicted a serious cut on her foot while paring her toe nails, and was now on her way to pray to San Nicolá, in order that he might cure her.

For you must understand that these saints are no mere quacks. They are not Jacks-of-all-trades who can cure anything. They have developed a high degree of specialization, in accordance with the modern evolution of the sciences. Thus, San Nicolá cures corns, callous spots and injuries to the legs; Santa Lucía specializes in eyes and breasts. Her altar is surrounded by many eyes and breasts of plaster of Paris or metal, which have been suspended as mementos of her cures. Many nursing women may be seen daily kneeling with great concern before her image. The Old Madonna has a mass of her own said every Saturday morning at eight o'clock, in the Cathedral. It is attended by pregnant women who pray for an easy or speedy confinement, or by friends who come to take their places. The birth-pains will last as long as the mass, and the priests therefore have every reason to dispose of the matter quickly. San José (Joseph, husband of Mary) has nothing to do with cures; but he can drive out bad tenants, tenants who do not pay their rent or have too many children. The police will do the same job for you, but their charge is twenty-five francs. San José will do it for a wax candle. San Medardus will ward off drought and Santa Barbara, the beautiful virgin of Nicomedia, will turn aside the lightnings and soften the roll of thunder. She is the patron saint of the artillery, and her day is celebrated with fireworks. But these are mere details; the whole year in Andalusia is one great All Saints' Day.

San Antonio plays a rather droll part. He is the special property of Granada and is a mixture of domestic god and jumping-jack. Every home has its Antonio of baked clay, holding a child in his arms. He is the object of a peculiar dual treatment. At times he is regarded with great respect, at other times he is made the butt of scorn and ridicule. All unpleasant domestic incidents are attributed to him. He must keep away rats and mice, ward off thieves, take care that his worshipers do not forget to lock their doors when they go out. If anything has gone wrong, he is promised a few cents' worth of oil for his lamp—*tres cuartos*—if he will afford a remedy. If he fails, he is punished. Easy-going people content themselves with setting him under the bed or in some dark corner, and I have often seen my friend La Concha's saint sitting in the dunce's corner behind the dark portal, when her kitchen supplies were furnished in too meager a measure. More determined persons go about the thing more viciously. They will tie a cord about his neck and lower him into a deep well; and there they let him hang, up to his neck in water, until he becomes more tractable.

The child which San Antonio bears in his arms has only a little peg to connect it with the saint's image; and it is indicative of the Andalusian's love for children as well as the serious spirit in which he administers this chastisement, that the child is always removed before the punishment is executed. The image is a living reality and consequently may feel pain. In fact, I was told that there were ladies in the best circles of Granada who would not give away photographs of themselves, believing that any harm that came to the picture would also be inflicted upon them.

One day I missed some papers. I asked Beppa about them, for she had just tidied my room. She did not even take the pains to look for them, but went for San Antonio, at once, treating him to a savage mouthful:

"San Antonio, we will have none of your tricks here! I will have you understand that you must treat our tenant well! You know what you look like? You look like a plain ordinary drunkard, nothing better than that!" She was very angry, and the papers were soon found. I had mislaid them myself and was obliged to beg the saint's pardon by sacrificing a *cuarto* of oil, "for otherwise he might not help us the next time."

It must be hard for a saint to be called a drunkard and other bad things, but San Antonio accepts these epithets with admirable humility. The fact is, if we may believe the unanimous report of all the women in this section of town, his own fingers are not always clean. His moral code seems more like that of plain men than that of the sublime saints, and occasionally, if there has not been oil in his lamp for a long time, he will hide some needed object in order that he may distinguish himself by causing it to be found again.

But San Antonio is not the only saint who is subjected to such denunciation and chastisement. The Andalusian assumes the existence of human weaknesses even in the gods. In the spring of 1896, the Virgin Mary was taken from Joseph's side on a certain occasion and placed by the side of San Cristobal up the hill back of Albaicin, in order to make Joseph jealous and thus oblige him to do his duty—at least that was the explanation offered by the common people.

On one side of Los Campos, a market-place of Granada, there was a hospital. On the market-place in front of the hospital stood a stone crucifix bearing the image of the Crucified. The hospital had been commended to his special attention and accordingly he had been placed so as to face the hospital, as was no more than reasonable. But in the cholera year of 1885 all the patients died, and as a punishment, because Christ had done his job so poorly, he was made to face the other way. He still has his back turned to the hospital.

The true value of San Antonio is not appreciated until some one steals him. Beppa's was stolen four years ago, and her boarding-house began to do badly at once; but the people that stole him now have lots of money. San Antonio suffered much on earth, and for this reason he was made a saint. He was always most kindly and generous toward those that had treated him very badly; so he brings most luck to those who steal him and treat him ill. La Incarnación, who stuck him in the stove and singed him, drew a winning number in the lottery. But Beppa could not find the heart to do such a thing; she would rather remain poor.

It is also good luck to obtain one's San Antonio as a present—from a man, in the case of a woman; and vice-versa. This is indicative of San Antonio's immense importance in the relations between the sexes. San Antonio has jurisdiction over the most important and difficult of all the phenomena of life, namely, love. In Andalusia, where the young women are so sharply segregated from the other sex, some sort of go-between must be resorted to, and the saint does yeoman service in this connection. He is a regular pander. In Granada he has a church of his own, in which mass is said at twelve o'clock noon, every Tuesday. He does not seem to mean much for men; at least they do not attend his mass. But in the end it does not matter, for the women are all the more assiduous in their attendance, women of all ages and stations. Here are aged widows who wish to find a husband to support them in their old age, as well as younger widows, who have no objections to assuming the discomforts of marriage for its own sake. Here are married women who beg the saint to make their husbands a little more faithful to them and who call down his anger upon their more fortunate rivals. The mass is also attended by young girls who have cast an eye from their balconies on this young man or that and who beg the saint to turn the young man's thoughts to them— simply to make him give them a little attention, for they will take care of the rest themselves. Then there are very young girls whose affections have not yet found an object, but who are about to join the great majority.

There stands San Antonio, more than life size, listening to their prayers, bearing his dear little symbol, the child, in his arms. The child wears genuine white linen and the sweet young things beg the priests to let them take home the child's linen to wash and iron it. They vie with each other to do the neatest job, for it is true of San Antonio as it is of others that the way to win the heart of grown-ups is through the children. You may visit San Antonio's church every Tuesday for weeks—although you are not a welcome attendant, I can assure you—and you will always find it full of praying women. You will hear unexpected outcries, little bursting sobs:

"San Antonio, hurry!" "Not so many children, San Antonio!" "Dear little San Antonio, my heart bleeds!" Or, you may hear a bride-to-be, whose lover has gone overseas, saying: "San Antonio, if there is a letter from Juán, please see to it that it is not lost on the way!" For the saint who assigns the number of children to be born to each married couple also serves as a *postillon d'amour* for parted lovers.

Once he is off on an errand, San Antonio might just as well take care of several things at once, so he is given charge of all the letters sent by women, regardless of whether they deal with love or not. But having so many irons in the fire, he necessarily fails to strike all of them when they are hot. Those who are disappointed or cheated revenge themselves by lowering him mercilessly into the well.

While San Antonio is the refuge and hope for legitimate affection, he is also the great protector of the women who live by the sale of their bodies. They do not like to visit his church, but each one of them has in her home a little altar with a lamp burning before his image day and night. On my former visit to Spain, Beppa had lived at the corner of a street of ill repute, and whenever we sat out on the balcony in the evening, we could see the women of the streets in the neighboring houses kneeling before their saint and addressing him sometimes in the following words: *"San Antonio, que vengan cabrones!"* (San Antonio, send along some bucks!). If by any chance a priest happened to slink along the wall and knock at one of the little doors, Beppa would clap her hands together and shout with a ring of true respect in her voice:

"There is a saint for you, this San Antonio! He even goes so far as to send a priest, a real priest!"

No one is better suited to run the errands of the church than her own servant; and besides, who would be so narrow-minded as to insist on his celibacy? Of all the hundreds of priests in Granada, the population does not know of one who has no children, but they do tell you of one that has nine. And the common people humorously make the priest utter the touching sigh:

Merciful God, thou who forgivest all things!
Why should my children call me uncle,
When everybody else says I am a father?

Gods, saints and priests are nothing but big children in the eyes of the Andalusian; and the Andalusian considers that like children they may at times be naughty, but they are essentially good. One should not demand too much of them but treat them with a certain degree of human consideration. Then they will continue to resemble the blessed children whom every one kisses in Andalusia, because they are the incarnation of the luxuriant joy of life of this people.

A pious Andalusian saved money for a number of years to go on a pilgrimage. He did not go as far as the Tomb of Our Lord, but only to the Church of Saint Lateran in Rome, to see the foreskin of Christ which is said to be preserved there. So gay and cheerful is the religion of the Andalusians!

These are merely illustrations. I might communicate many more. I might even stand on one leg and crow offensively and turn my eyes heavenward in moral indignation at these godless wretches. But it would be of no use—and besides I have no desire to.

Now Beppa bangs at her ceiling again, and Pedro has come back to ask me probably whether his name really was printed in the book.

Yes, he really does ask.

XI

THE GYPSIES

GRANADA is unique. Many circumstances contribute to make it so: the wonderful natural surroundings, the pure mountain air, the quite Moorish imprint still borne by the rising and falling sections of the city with their staircase thoroughfares, remnants of arches, bits of battlemented walls, and most marvelous of all the magic castle Alhambra which seems to the beholder as if light itself had crystallized into color and substance.

But it is the gypsies who make Granada unique. No one knows how many gypsies there are in Spain; there must be hundreds of thousands. They seem to congregate in Andalusia where the climate and the peculiar temperament of the inhabitants provide a more agreeable hunting-ground for these gay, light-moraled wretches than the cold and sober regions of northern Spain.

Everywhere you encounter these dry, agile folk with their cunning glances and greedy miens. In the broad current of pedestrians on the promenade you will find these children of fortune, happy in the sun, darting in and out bare-footed. The men have a long staff in their hands and a great pair of cattle-shears in the back of their sashes; the women carry a basket of flowers over their arms, a child tied to their backs in a scarf, while another child is hopping about their skirts, clad only in a frill. They wander hither and thither like bats in a swarm of dancing gnats. They beg; they tell fortunes; they haggle. They stick to the foreigner like tenacious street dogs and will not release their hold until something remains in their mouths.

They have their shearing-grounds in the small streets of the large cities as well as in every village, and there they clip donkeys and mules in the most marvelous patterns. The Andalusian considers this occupation unclean; but the gypsy has no delicate feelings and is quite content to be well paid for the job. He will go to the flayer's pit and will carry off the hides of dead beasts as well as the best parts of their meat. He will buy decrepit mares from peasants and sell them for bull-fights. In addition he is a basket-weaver, a tanner and often a fine copper-smith. He fashions keys, donkey-bells and ox-bells and sometimes rises to the height of manufacturing a wretched counterfeit money of tin. But he is just as fond of smuggling or begging; and most of all he loves to steal.

One night a great anchor weighing nearly four thousand pounds disappeared from the quay at Seville. Knowing their business, the police at once proceeded to the gypsy quarter of Triana, where they actually found the anchor, buried several yards under ground, at the place of a gypsy locksmith, who intended to make keys of it!

"How on earth did you manage to drag this heavy anchor all the way out here?" asked the policeman.

"Well, you see, Your Most Infallible Highness," answered the gypsy, "I was just taking a walk down by the shore looking at the moon, when suddenly something got stuck to the fringes of my pants, and when I got home and looked at it, it was the anchor."

Even in a crowd the gypsy will at once attract attention by the peculiar shape of his head and his swarthy complexion, which resembles that of the negro in not reflecting any light and at a glance registering only as a dark spot on the retina of the eye. His bold and somewhat peculiar manner assures him of attention, even if he is alone among hundreds. He appears to possess the same talent as the Jew for acquiring superficially the peculiarities of the people among whom he lives, retaining simultaneously at bottom his own racial traits. He is swift in his motions and knows no fatigue. He is frugal, proud, boisterously merry and full of bubbling humor. He represents all the prominent characteristics of the Andalusian in an exaggerated degree and is thus assured a prominent place in the consciousness of the population. The merriest tales are told of him. Puns and jokes often end with the words: "as the gypsy said."

In the case of the Andalusian, these qualities are innate; they seem in their natural place. But in the case of the gypsy they have been assumed for the purpose usual with uprooted races: getting hold of money. The gypsy can be carefree and unselfish. He can have just as clever notions as the Andalusian, but this is merely sand to be thrown in the eyes of gullible persons. He is frugal, but only in order to be able to set aside his savings, and because an appearance of poverty may call forth charity. The gypsies down on the Huelva go about naked the greater part of the year, with nothing but a cloth about their loins, although they are by no means poor and the climate is not exactly Eden's. Up at the Alhambra you may see a well-to-do beggar woman leading a perfectly naked child by the hand, sometimes when there is snow on the ground.

The gypsy does nothing for nothing. Whether he acts proudly as a Spaniard, or babbles away carelessly at a great rate, he always has his eye on the main chance. The Andalusians themselves say of him that he takes pay for every blink of his eye. Arch-impostor that he is, the gypsy knows the value of repartee when dealing with Andalusians. He does not scatter his wit but saves it for a flare in crises, and rakes in his shekels while the laugh goes round. The people know his technique but they pardon him for the sake of the joke and revenge themselves by regarding him as a rather contemptible but amusing parasite.

The Andalusians of former days appear not to have been so good-natured as those of ours. Since they too were usually worsted when doing business with the gypsy, they limited him, as they did the Jews, to certain quarters of the cities and restricted his freedom. Such a gypsy ghetto is to be found in the Sevillian suburb of Triana, and it is not so very long ago that a massacre of the Triana inhabitants was perpetrated by the population of Seville. Most of the gypsies of Seville still live in Triana.

In the flat southwest of Andalusia, the gypsy lives in houses like those of other men or builds a funny little cabin of old rags, rusty tin plates and leaves of cactus. But wherever he finds even a trace of a hillock, he prefers to dig himself in on its slope. By far the greater portion of the gypsies of Andalusia live in scattered caves, and near Granada there are cave-dwelling communities of several thousand persons.

Granada is held to be one of the loveliest places in the whole world. The city lies at the point where the Sierra Nevada puts forth its foothills, a bundle of rays extending toward the Vega like gigantic roots that have come up out of the ground. The new section of the city has spread placidly over the plain with its spacious horizontal streets and lines of elms (*alamedas*), or is wedged in between the hills, following the valleys and riverbeds, and terminating in thin lines extending far into the Sierra. The older part of the city has not been able to make itself so comfortable. These ancient quarters still bear the marks of having been built in insecure times, when the houses clung for protection to the steep mountain ridges. There they still stand, a densely packed mass, like a flock of frightened mountain goats. So have they stood for many peaceful centuries still spying out the enemy in a sort of petrified panic.

Steep staircase streets lead through the city, with traces of Moorish times meeting your eyes everywhere. Here, a great vaulted cistern covered with glazed tiling; there the ruins of a little mosque or an arched gate built to break the force of a hostile onslaught. In the city walls are fragments of stucco arches resting upon marble columns, and now and again your eye wanders into a still perfect Moorish courtyard.

In some places the slope becomes too sharp to be negotiated by staircases and the path is then obliged to assume a long zigzag rise. It has been impossible to build houses except on the inside of the zigzag, where they may use the mountain for a back. The outer edge of the path is a white railing and a file of slender cypresses topped by an ocean of blue. As you mount the path into an endless labyrinth of cabins and weather-beaten walls, fig trees peer forth from the ruins. There is indescribable filth. The streets are impassable for their mounds of offal and excrement. The women sit in the gutters doing their neglected laundry, and in the doorways of decrepit huts sit half-blind smallpox patients, picking their scabs and blinking. Their faces look as if they have been exposed to a rain of blood. In front of one house a small child lies on its back, wound in rags, staring into the sky with its single eye. The other has been eaten away; and dense clouds of flies have gathered in the suppurant crater.

You already find gypsies here.

The news of visiting strangers has quickly spread in the quarter. We are surrounded by a host of begging women and children. They have low brows, broad noses and searching malignant eyes which with their whisking motions and uncouth gestures make them look like monkeys. They beg and they scratch themselves and peer under their finger-nails, and the gray spots in their raven hair make plain what they are looking for. When we give a coin to one, the others become importunate, tug at our clothing and stick their hands into my pockets. Finally we give an old gypsy man some money to chase them away and deliver us from this wasps' nest.

We emerge on a terrace where an old church stands. From the platform we gaze into an abyss outlined by the city itself in its furious descent. You feel that you could jump down over all the rows of houses and land directly on the Promenade of the Poor by the River Darro. And on the other side of the valley, the city

again rises over the slope which carries the mighty
outworks of Alhambra in sharp rectangular strokes
against the white snow background of the Sierra.

We creep under the broad Moorish wall, cross a
sun-dried parched mountain top and are again on the
southern slope of the range. The steep declivity is
covered with Indian fig-cactus, which grips the cliffs
with its broad flat roots. Below us, the paths meander
downward like ribbons along the mountain-slope, and
over them irregular rows of smoking chimneys seem to
stick at right angles to the red mountain soil. We can
see the entrances to the caves from here; it is easy to
imagine that trolls and kobolds are cooking their early
breakfast in the heart of the rock. At certain points
the steep rocky wall changes to terraces where peach-
trees and almonds blossom; at other points the walls
are pitted by soft shots, sites of caves that have collapsed.

The side of the hill has been blasted away to make
room for the road. The outer edge is protected by a
row of aloes, to keep travelers from falling over the
precipice. Naked gypsy children crawl under the
aloes, on whose blue-green horns the washing waves in
screaming colors, while the children thrust hands and
legs over the abyss. In the mountain wall there are
doors, outside which scarlet pigs are tethered by the
hind legs. Above in the mouths of the caves, browsed
by the cactus, that grows out of the cliff twined with
blackberry and wild ivy, sit swarthy babbling women,
helping each other in their morning toilet. *"Ingleses!
Ingleses!"* they cry as soon as they catch sight of us.
They come dashing or crawling from above and below.
The whole slope begins to swarm with life, and in an

instant we are the center of a host of begging women and children. The women offer little brass souvenirs at fabulous prices, and beg to be allowed to tell our fortunes or dance for us. When nothing else avails them, they slap their bellies with their hands and whimper: "A little alms for the unborn child—how about it? It has no father!" and all the women in the crowd grin with delight. The children—little wretches that they are—dance about us and shout that we are the loveliest creatures they have ever seen. Some of the children bear wounds on their faces and reach out for our hands, which they press to their lips. An eight-year-old boy has a naked child about nine months old straddled over his shoulders. The little one, whose short black shirt has wrinkled up all the way to his neck, hangs like a withered weed over the boy's shoulders.

In one of the crevices of the mountain lie the caves, their entrances close together and rising in almost concentric curves like the seats of an amphitheater. Hanging paths, half supported by the powerful cactus, intersect the mountain and communicate with all the caves. Wrinkled old men and women, looking as if they were smoked and cured, are seated at the entrance weaving willow baskets. A twelve-year-old girl cowers on the threshold of a cave, nursing a baby. She looks after us with childlike curiosity. On a knoll sits a gypsy engaged in the task of imparting a lovely mouse-gray tone to an old speckled gray donkey.

A few copper coins rid us of the most impudent, but their places are taken again and again by new beggars. And those we have disposed of will crawl off along an upper path and come down to meet us a little further on with their: *"Mossiu,* Madame—a little gift, please! I am dying of hunger!" But we are already able to distinguish them in spite of their filth and pock-marks and we drive them away; and the others who have not succeeded in getting anything from us help us in this work.

Finally the whole crowd disappears one by one, uttering words of abuse and contumely over these "stranger dogs." A few fair-sized rocks roll down by our feet as their parting greeting.

We look through the cactus and follow the paths upward from level to level. Everywhere there is the odor of human excrement. The caves themselves are not so disorderly, some even show traces of prosperity, and the most poorly furnished contain collections of highly polished old copper and brass utensils to arouse the collector's envy. The poorest caves have a single room, ceilings and walls being formed by the rough conglomerate rock; but for the most part there are two rooms: a living-room, which obtains light from the entrance and—in particularly aristocratic cases—from two glassless windows one on each side of the entrance, and a bedroom behind the living-room, with an entrance through the rear wall of the latter. In this rear room the ceilings and walls are not without adornment and are painted white; sometimes there is even a bricked ceiling vault.

We choose a newly blazed trail which winds up the hill. Ahead of us walks an old gypsy woman with a great jug of water on her shoulder; these mountaineers have leg-muscles of steel and we admire the old woman who moves along so straight and easily under her burden, while we drag our weight uphill with so much toil. From our voices she can tell that we are strangers; she does not turn round, but simply collapses under her load, continues dragging along ahead of us like one mortally ill, moaning and lamenting: "Oh, I am dying! Jesus, Jesus, I am dying. Oh, Oh!" She closes her eyes, opens her mouth like a bird about to choke and puts out a trembling hand to us. A small copper coin allays her attack only long enough to permit her to open her eyes and observe the insignificance of the gift—whereupon she has an immediate relapse. But when she sees us going on our way, she suspends her death-agony and the next moment strides by us with vigorous steps, with a pardonable but ill-meant mutter on her lips.

Few men on God's green earth live in such lovely surroundings as these pariahs. The wide snow fields of the Sierra gleam like silver in the noon-day sun; you can see them thirty miles away, yet so near that you can distinguish the caravans winding over their surface. The snow that fell the night before may still be seen along the northern side of all the hills. The mountains round the Vega are like a white wreath crowning the luxurious ever-green plain. The city seems to run down the steep slope, break into a chasm and spread over the plain, inhabited by masses of foliage which roll in upon the houses like surging billows in an ocean of green. The Vega itself, though its circumference is more than a hundred miles, seems small; it is as flat as a lake and the houses speck it with white dots like sails. Already the fruit-trees turn green below us, and on all the southern slopes of the ranges and far into the deep riverbeds there is a warm flickering of blinding white and coral red, the colors of blossoming almond-trees,

apricot-, peach- and cherry-trees.   And the blue sunny
air warms us with fragrant breath.

The gypsies have been an inexhaustible source of
popular superstition and romance.   Their restless
vagabondage, which has scattered them from the Cau-
casus to the Atlantic Ocean, from the North Cape to
the southern boundary of Morocco, and their apparent
contempt for any mode of life that is associated with
fixed tenure of land or with fixed social forms, their
lack of respect for the property of others, their un-
trammeled existence and apparent contempt for comfort, which enables them to sleep in the snow and to
give birth to their children at the edge of an open
ditch, their mysterious appearances and disappear-
ances, their slick thievish exploits and their incomprehensible thievish jargon—all these conditions were
forced upon them in the Middle Ages.   In that era
they were driven from place to place and denied any
possibility of existence; but they remained a cause of
offense to the medieval man, securely ensconced in the
walls of his cities and customs.   How was it possible
for such careless birds to make a livelihood while
starvation harried the most orderly system of society?
How did they escape from robbery and violence when
all the others, gathered together under the protection
of fortified castles and city walls, could not maintain
themselves?   How could they survive nights spent in
the great forest, while other men in their secure al-
coves dared not draw a breath in their superstitious
awe of spirits?
Surely they must have allied themselves with the
powers of evil, always the only powers that grant vic-

tory to men. Europe's lower classes, weakly intimidated and ever fearful of spirits throughout, set the gypsies in their curious mythical cosmos peopled by devils, witches and evil wights. And with the instinctive hatred of the domesticated animal for his wild kindred they sought to wipe out the gypsies. Decrepit old gypsy women, hardly able to obtain a scant livelihood for themselves, were transformed into wonder-working fortune-tellers, and more frequently into bringers of evil, mixers of poisonous potions, vile witches, consorts of the devil who substituted wrong children for right ones and thus dictated the fortunes of empires. They were outlawed in the popular imagination and the ever-zealous Inquisition assigned them to the stake.

The tribe was thus spared the unpleasant task of eliminating the old wretches who were no longer capable of accompanying it in its endless wanderings; and it thus obtained one more advantage over ordinary mortals.

Hundreds of gypsy women graced the pyres of the Inquisition because these wretched creatures were believed to possess a diabolical power which the tribe as a whole considered to be to its advantage. The hoarse croaks of desperation emitted by these unhappy women when the flames licked their dirty wrinkled skin, resounded in the ears of the assembled populace like devilish curses and strange conjurings, which enhanced its fear of this marvelous race whose conceptions of good and evil were so completely upside down.

What the persecution of witches failed to do—and this persecution was not particularly fastidious—was later accomplished zealously by romanticism. The insignificant gypsy girls, whose lives are limited to the most rudimentary forms of animal existence, were transformed under the idealizing touch of poetry into cold, soulless but entrancing beauties who served as tools for government intrigues and whose embraces lured the secrets of diplomats from their breasts and made princes forget their duties. Amulets and the evil eye, love-potions—what things have gypsy women not been made capable of in the riotous Western imagination! Only the men—who are sometimes fairly decent—have played a subordinate part, either as the tools of their intriguing women, or concerned in sordid thievery.

This remarkable race, which without reason has so fed our imaginations, repels one at the very outset by its ugliness, which, particularly in the case of the women, is of rare proportions. Even on knowing them intimately, it is difficult to overcome a feeling of aversion. Ugliness may be accompanied by powers of introspection, of personality, which enable a northerner at least to regard it without disgust. We live on this "ennobled ugliness" in the north and it imparts a more soul-like quality to our ideals of beauty—we make a virtue of necessity. But the ugliness of the gypsy has too much of the animal element and much is the result of personal neglect. Thin hair, running eyes, purulent noses, skin diseases, are universal among them, and the aggregate impression of a gypsy face is a voracity hardly found in the beasts. In addition, most of the faces are pierced like sieves by the small-pox, which visits the caves every few years.

The gypsy woman in reality is very different from the literary image. When she is a little girl, it is quite customary to lend her to beggars, and as soon as she can stand on her legs, she is chased out to go begging for herself. She is a mother at the age of fifteen or sixteen, and until she reaches the age of thirty has constantly a little baby with her, for she adds one to the series each year. At thirty she becomes an old woman and continues to be an old woman until death at seventy or eighty. She cleans her black, shining, thin hair with her finger-nails; she is sloppy and neglected, crushed by the bearing of children; she has no carriage and is bow-legged. When a family is traveling and has only one donkey for the purpose, the man will ride and the wife will walk alongside with her youngest child tied to her back in a wide cloth, leading the other children by the hand. In the eyes of the men she is the female animal who must be subjected by force even to the tasks of love. She has no one to admire her and never tries to distinguish herself in any way. How different is the Andalusian woman, who, however low she may be in the social scale, is always an object of homage in her youth and wears a flower in her hair. She need never deny herself a bit of coquettishness.

You will find gypsies everywhere in Granada, singing and playing in the streets, haggling in the market-place, begging by the church-yard. They sit along the gutters of the Vivarrambla and offer honey for sale, singing bawdy songs to attract purchasers. They have a little junk-market of their own in front of the Cathedral, where they sell tinware, frightful shining German chromos and cheap gewgaws of black beads, such as are laid on graves. At the entrance to the grove of the Alhambra they stand in groups waiting for the stranger; they wait for him in front of the hotels frequented by foreigners, pursue him with bouquets of flowers, seize him by the hand and offer to tell his fortune, posture before him with swaying hips and ask to be permitted to dance for him.

Gypsy dancing and gypsy fortune-telling—whose heart does not beat romantically at these magic words? And yet these famous fortune-tellings have not even a trace of delicacy. "Monsieur, Madame is longing for you!" is their constant refrain, a refrain mumbled by all of them, children as well as old women. Their dance is a crude expression of a crude conception of the erotic. Men and women sit around in a circle clasping their hands, striking their thighs and singing. In the middle of the circle stands the "dancer," raises her legs a little and moves her hands indolently over her head, while all her temperament seems domiciled in her hips and pelvis, which move and writhe in vehement measure, with contortions that venture into greater and greater excesses under the heated calls of the onlookers. This dance, which does not move to a single line of beauty, but is rather to be counted with the unconstrained free expression of beasts, is frequently lauded by travelers and compared with the charming and ingratiating Andalusian dances. Distinguished English and American ladies who leave all sordid practical affairs to their husbands and dash through southern Europe in a mad hunt for romantic fertilizer with which to fructify the arid culture of their native lands, wander up to these caves in great numbers daily, escorted by their friends, in order to behold and admire these marvelous gypsy dancers.

You do not meet the men very often downtown, unless you find them playing their mandolins in the street, serving as artists' models, or as guides in the Alhambra. They are invariably less insignificant than the women and not so repellent; quite a number are tall and well-built with a bold look in their eyes—there is Andalusian blood in their veins. The most audacious and efficient smugglers in Granada are among the gypsies; and the two hundred or more *octroi* guards who form a cordon about the city day and night could tell many tales of the cunning tricks and dangerous exploits performed by these gypsies in smuggling goods, particularly liquor, into the city. The duty to be paid at the town gate is one franc for each liter, so that this smuggling is good business.

Each morning there is a long line of donkeys outside the gates of Granada waiting to discharge their cargoes of fruit. One fine day a donkey stumbles under his burden, and some of the beautiful green and yellow giant melons turn out to be containers of gayly painted tin, filled with alcohol. For some days to come, the *octroi* guards will carefully stick their lances into all large fruits, while an ox-cart daily moves unobtrusively into the city with its load of sawed planks; until it transpires that some of the planks have not really been sawed but are actually big boxes filled with alcohol. Or, a dried-up old gypsy man will trot over the bridge on a donkey that seems so gravid that the *octroi* guards crack their jokes about it, but the animal's hide is a double hide—and there is alcohol between the two layers.

The guards have now become so experienced and the penalties, as well as the rewards for stool-pigeons, are so large, that the business is about to die. But by night the gypsy continues to be active; he crawls down the hills to town with a flat tin container, holding as much as four or five liters buckled over his chest; he crawls along paths trodden only by goats. Directly under him, but many feet below, rolls the river, with the listening guard on the other side of it. A rolling stone or clod of earth will be sufficient to put the guard on his mettle, the gypsy will be caught and sent to prison, or he will make a bold effort at flight and be shot down. Sometimes he may escape, but he loses his wares. If he succeeds in getting through the lines, he has made a pretty good taking for one day, judged by Granada standards.

All day long the smuggler sleeps in the sunlight on the mountain slope, his head hidden under a fig-cactus; or he buries himself in his cave and plays cards. He is as passionate a gambler as any other Spaniard and frequently is drawn into quarrels with his partners. Then all "lights must be put out," that is to say, daggers are drawn to adjust the difficulties of the game. During the cleaning of wicks a light occasionally does go out, but the authorities do not like to intervene in matters concerned with life in the caves, and it would be of little avail, since the wounded or dying man is likely to take the side of his opponent and refuse to give any information.

The gypsies are still fond of self-aid and are of the opinion that feuds are a matter only for the persons concerned. In this, as well as in many other connections, they engage in a desperate struggle with the authorities, and the latter close eyes to much that goes on in the mountains. For if each court of law should intervene in the cases falling under its jurisdiction, there would be no persons left in the hills.

But whenever the gypsies extend their rules of life and attempt to apply them in the larger domain, they run their heads against a stone wall and the criminal statistics of Spain show how frequently this is the case. About thirty per cent of the prisoners in the jails of Granada are said to be gypsies, but they appear to be able to make the prison air quite compatible with their proverbial love of liberty. They often escape from jail and usually with greater success than the other prisoners; but their returns to prison are also more frequent. In spite of all this, great progress has been made in Andalusia—perhaps without the knowledge or desire of those concerned—toward the solution of the difficult problem of acclimatizing the gypsy. Nature itself appears here ready to perform what has been given up by a number of governments (including even the Norwegian government) as a hopeless task: the task of attaching the gypsies to a specific locality and thus accustoming them to a more regular life. Many of the gypsies, even some of the old ones, were born in this place and have spent all their lives in and around the caves. The caves have been the point to which they have returned after all their wanderings. This feeling of local attachment is even stronger in their children, and their uprooted tradition continues in them only as a sort of general unreliability in the continuous performance of labor. Many are themselves the owners of the steep slope that holds their cave; they plant *chumbo* (the Indian fig) and keep goats, whose milk they sell, down in the town. Some of them even hire out as field-workers and a number go so far as to move to town and become artisans. I am personally acquainted with a blacksmith who has a number of apprentices, is a member of the organized citizenry, and a respected individual. He has not many words of praise for his own race, but prefers to employ gypsies in his establishment, in order to make them acquire more orderly habits.

The gypsies of Andalusia are gradually becoming members of organized society. The task has been made easier for them in this country since society here does not make such stringent demands on its members as in the north. The concept of order here is itself so vague, and it takes little to let one live with a sense of comfort. The problem becomes even easier because of the great tolerance and the fundamentally democratic attitude of the present-day Andalusian. In Granada the population is more reserved toward the gypsy than in the region of Seville, but, on the whole, these tormented pariahs are treated better in Andalusia than anywhere else in Europe. And they seem to appreciate this fact.

The caves serve as a transition between the tent of the nomad tribe and the foundation walls of settled society. Hundreds of the cave-dwellers may already be regarded as established citizens, for they pay taxes, have the right of suffrage and serve their three years' military period. The once foot-loose gypsy is now often eulogized for his obedience and good discipline as a soldier. *Sic transit gloria mundi.*

It was a cold morning toward the end of January; it was Friday, the gypsy market-day. The snows on the Sierras had crept down during the night as far as to the upper edge of the town. There was a thin sheet of ice in the fountain-basin in Alhambra's Court of the

Lions. The spacious Vivarrambla, once the theater of dazzling Moorish games of chivalry, lay desolate.

But up at one of the corners of the market-place there was a bustle, and certain old gypsy women with their honey, their bric-a-brac, their tin vessels, warming their bluish fingers over braziers of charcoal held in their laps, emitted shrill tunes from time to time. They tugged at my ulster as I went by and asked me to buy. I declined, smiled benevolently the while, but was none the less made the recipient of a torrent of abuse: "Ugh, *Monsieur, qué feo es!* How ugly you are, ugh!" Repulsive dirty faces grinned from over their wares and ugly comments pursued me as I walked on.

In my eagerness to round the corner I stumbled over the naked wrinkled stump of the leg of a gypsy cripple, which he had just stuck out into the air to inspire sympathy.

"Hermano, hermano" (brother). "Give me a shilling for the sake of God's mercy!"

"I'll give you two shillings if you will cover your ugly stump with a stocking and not expose it so publicly. You will only provide yourself with pneumonia and others with a dubious enjoyment."

"Hombre que sí—no doubt you are right, Sir! But then people will give me nothing."

"I think they will give you more."

"No, for then they will not see anything and the people want to see something for their money. Don't people want to see something for their money in your country? They all look at my leg and then there will always be one of them who will put his hand into his pocket. The ladies see it too, but they only look side-ways, for they do not want to give me anything."

"You see, the sight is too bitter for them!"

"No, not that, but they are stingy like all women. But then I stick out my stump so far that they cannot help touching it with their dresses; then they become disgusted and throw me a coin, so that I may not do it again, for they think there is pus on it! So you will permit me to keep your shilling and keep my leg exposed anyway, brother, nobleman (*hermano, caballero*)?"

"Oh, yes, if you like, good-by, *amigo!*"

"Go with God, *señorito.*"

In front of the Cathedral staircase lay a donkey, all four legs stretched away from him, his neck lying on the pavement, his eyes closed. He had collapsed under too great a burden of charcoal. The driver did not take off his load but kicked the soft parts of his body with his heavy boot and shouted: "Be up and doing, ass, beast, hypocrite!" But the donkey would not stir, and now his driver began to weep. Two gypsies came along. They did not help the peasant, but vituperated the beast, deciding to utilize his master's desperation to purchase the animal for a song. The transaction was already well under way when a priest came down the steps of the Cathedral and ordered the peasant to unload the donkey. The donkey rose with great difficulty; he had wounds on his knees and chest, from his fall, and his back was lacerated from the unending friction of the load. If you poked at these wounds with a sharp stick, the donkey would gallop away and would not stop until he fell lifeless to the ground. He was a little donkey, a sweet little donkey, and now that he was once more on his legs, the peasant would no longer hear of any sale. But he sold the load of charcoal to the gypsies for a mere nothing—in order not to be obliged to restore the donkey's burden.

You may make a short cut by passing through the great Cathedral. Most persons do this, and as a result the soil on this side of the building is trodden flat. The priests kneeling before the altar are obliged to turn their heads every moment to the swish of rustling petticoats.

Then comes a long narrow alley, overhung with heavy balconies—it is the street of the correspondents. The scribes sit at their desks breathing on their frozen fingers; their work is not in demand. But at one of the desks there is a young girl who is dictating: *mil besos y mil cariños,* a thousand kisses and a thousand caresses; all this wealth is to be enclosed in a single envelope.

The middle of the street is an inaccessible morass, while shoemakers, tailors, joiners and many other craftsmen have established their workshops on the sidewalk. A mason is stirring his mortar on the bare pavement. You must step into it with your foot to get by him, and one pedestrian after another goes through this operation without a murmur. Here sits a shoemaker who is taking the measure of a young girl's foot, as she places it in his lap. There sit a whole family, devouring their meal, their feet resting in the gutter, their breakfast served on the sidewalk. Up against the house-wall, a man is changing his shirt while a woman standing in front of him spreads her petticoats in a desperate effort to screen him from onlookers.

The alley becomes narrower, finally disappearing under the horseshoe curves of the old Moorish gate of Elvira. Beyond lies the market-place of the gypsies, a long patch of sandy soil, tapering into a point that collides with the gateway of the arena for bullfights. On one side there are numerous wine-shops; on the other rises the mountain with the city of weaving women, Albaicin, and beyond are the caves of the gypsies.

There are intimidated peasants standing all over the square, sunken, frozen until they are blue, a drop suspended from the tips of their noses, holding by their heads the animals which they must sell at any price. Their consciousness of their hard lot, combined with the cold which has not yet been banished from the air, gives them a pitiful appearance. Watery-eyed gypsies stroll from group to group, noting the weak points of the animals and estimating the poverty of their owners, later to utilize both factors for their own advantage.

Middlemen also go their rounds, naïve Spaniards in long cloaks. They have arrived from the seaport towns by the morning train and seek to give themselves the appearance of skilled tradesmen. The peasants cast longing glances at them and signal to them to come and buy. "Buy something, from me, little friend," says a little peasant to a tall go-between, "so that none of us may be stung by one of these fellows."

But his wretched long-eared animals that have lived all winter on maize straw and dried mountain thistles do not easily captivate a purchaser, for at the other end there are the gypsies with their neat little donkeys clipped in delicate patterns, and enchanting little mules with red tassels over their brows. No Spaniard alive can resist this spectacle, though he may have learned to his cost a dozen times that appearances are deceptive. There is not a child that cannot tell you what optical illusions may be resorted to by a gypsy when it is important for him to sell an unsaleable animal to some one else. Here you can buy the nicest little donkeys and mules which later turn out to be nothing but patchwork and may be taken apart almost like sewing-machines. By the use of arsenic and secret herbs the animals are stimulated into assuming a well-nourished appearance, holding their heads high, prancing about in the presence of the purchaser. But on the next day they are like wet rags, dejected; their beautiful mouse-gray color comes off, leaving behind a dull gray speckled hide, great pieces of which fall off, since they have simply been pasted on to the wounded and worn spots. And as for the tail, it often can be taken off and put on again to suit your fancy.

When the gypsies, who do now impart a special color to the general scheme of life in Andalusia, have been completely absorbed by the rest of the population, they will undoubtedly be found to have contributed their marked talent for trade to the total impression.

In this regard the Andalusian proper has no gifts at all; he may be deceived twenty times before he learns by experience. He ascribes his undoings to the magic devices of the gypsy, which the devil himself could not cope with, no matter how wise he may be. The Andalusian completely lacks ability to estimate a general situation. All things are tinged for him in accordance with his personal feelings. He judges, ponders and acts in accordance with insignificant whims, according to the pro and contra of his own ego.

"I don't like his face; he shall pay so and so much for these goods!" is a statement often heard. Though a transaction may often depend on whether a certain face is sympathetic or not, the transaction will finally in each case be decided by the adversary's repartee. The Spaniard assigns to an animal whatever qualities are claimed for it by the loquacious gypsies. For in this lovely country great round words have the value of gold, and the strongest evidence is the most fluent.

The gypsy has less conscience and more persuasive power than a horse-dealer in West Jutland. He ambles about with a superior calm, his hands in his pockets; stopping at one place, he sells one of his animals to the middlemen; then he takes a leisurely walk over the square, to inquire about prices.

To judge from his derisive laughter, you would think the peasants were making shameless demands on him. One of them asks ten duros (about ten dollars) for a good little donkey; there stands the handsomest Andalusian colt for not much more than forty dollars. Poor lean beasts can be bought for very low prices.

A group has formed about the spot where several gypsies are engaged in wearing down a peasant's resistance. The gypsies stand about idly, with long whips in their hands; here and there one of them has his cattle-shears sticking in the back of his sash. After having said every vile thing possible concerning the animal to be purchased, the purchaser makes an offer and tries at the same time to worm a duro into the peasant's hand under any possible pretext. This is the handsel, and if the gypsy succeeds in making the peasant take it in his hand, the deal is made. But the peasant is agile enough to steer clear of it; no sooner does the coin touch his hand than it falls flat on the ground. Here come two lanky scoundrels, two gypsies; one of them takes the side of his kinsman, the other that of the peasant. They alternately push the two contending traders into each other's arms or berate both seller and buyer to the accompaniment of the most dreadful yells; or the representative of the purchaser takes both owner and customer by the neck and draws them aside, while the representative of the seller runs behind all three, clutching at their cloaks. The disinterested observer finds it a splendid spectacle; but the peasant reminds one of a dying man over whose head birds of carrion are circling.

The peasant still offers some resistance and the crowd moves on. Later it gathers again and there stands the peasant still holding his animal by the head, so discouraged and so deeply buried in his thoughts of taxes and imposts that you could pluck at his eyes without arousing his attention. His price has sunk and before night falls the gypsies will have bought his animal for one-third of its value.

If he likes, he may come back again on Friday next and behold his beasts, now tricked out to kill, shorn in lovely figures and with the very devil of energy in them, being sold at high prices to the middlemen. He will utter a *carramba!* pick up a cigar-butt, already chewed, will roll a cigarette out of its vitals—and forget trade. Next time he will fare no better.

Among donkeys and mules sits an old gypsy woman with no nose, her lap full of little red suckling pigs. They go like hot-cakes; every minute a pig is carried off with such lively squeaks that the donkeys squeal, too, and the slender Andalusian horses canter nervously. Back to back with the old woman sits a gypsy from the Sierra with naked feet and a horse-blanket round his neck, who is selling sharp-mouthed wolf cubs. The middlemen dash about with waving cloaks; the gypsies blink smilingly with their lashless eyes, and the water-sellers—the most indispensable creatures in Granada, next to the beggars—cruise over the square in every direction like swallows, glasses in their hands and carrying their cork-tanks on their backs. *"Agua,* here is *agua!* fresh clean water, snow-water, ice-water!" Only the peasants stand motionless with drops depending from their noses and holding the heads of their wretched animals; for the moment they have taken refuge behind a mute and persistent policy of resistance.

Up and down the road paces an iron monster, not unlike the portable engine of a steel threshing-caravan, drawn by five little donkeys in single file. On it sits a gypsy who eggs his donkeys forward with loud shouts, at the same time stirring a cauldron; behind which walks an old woman who pokes at the fire and sings out *"Caliente! caliente!"* Here you can buy a warm breakfast for a penny. Cuttle-fishes of as bright a red as new-born mice, bacon-rinds with the bristles still on them—a handful of each, dripping with luscious oil, and meant to be gulped down forthwith.

You can hear the looms rattling up in Albaicin, and still higher, in front of the rocky caves, walks an old gypsy woman hanging out red rags on the cactus to dry. The color stands out like a brilliant trumpet flourish against the light green mountain and blue sky.

I stroll into the park grounds on the other side of

the road, sit down on a bench, and gaze on the scurrying in the market-place. The noon hour is past. The sun shines so warmly that it entices beggar after beggar out of the damp streets. They walk over the square a few times, turn in my direction, and finally lie down in the grass to rest, their blankets wrapped around their heads. There they lie, snoring mounds of rags—a superabundance of poverty.

Granada has so many of them that they even beg from each other; and they are so proud that they invoke the blessings of God upon your head whether you give or not.

Here comes a distinguished-looking lady, leading a child by the hand. The child points to one of the sleepers and says:

"Mother, look, there lies a beggar."

"No, my child," answers the mother, "it is a brother, a poor brother."

The custodians do not even take the pains to chase them away, although they lie in the grass with their heads resting in the flower-beds.

The day draws to a close: the peasants, having at last yielded, prepare to start for home or disappear into one of the many wine-shops. The gypsies withdraw with their mutilated beasts and head toward their caves in the Mountain of Mercy, where the great transformation of turning decrepit and diseased beasts into fiery untamed animals is to take place before the next Friday comes.

Soon recruits begin to drill in the market-place, and chase away the few traders who remain; and here and there a poor devil of a dog digs in a heap of garbage.

Along the wall of the ditch running by the road a

few gypsy girls have taken their seats. They babble and distort their flabby features into broad grins and ape-like grimaces. They lay their heads in each other's laps, and while the busy finger-nails of their friends search for vermin they eye the passers-by, chew pine-cones and talk together in languishing tones. Truly they are like the monkeys in the zoo.

XII

THE BULLFIGHT

SPRING-TIME. Granada had had no bullfight for an eternity—not a single performance for six months. For a bullfight is an expensive business and the Granadinos are poor people. But do I really mean to say that there is a single beggar or an old discarded wretch, a poor tenant or cripple in all Granada who will not find means to get the fifty cents to pay for his admission ticket, if a bullfight is announced?

Certainly not; but Granada is only a city of the third rank, in which the great geniuses—the bullfighters by the grace of God, whose eyes never fail and whose hands never err—do not find it worth their while to appear in public.

Well, suppose it is—are we unreasonable in our demands? Do we insist on first-class art? Did we not swallow the affront when an animal announced in the program as black turned out to have a white speck? Did we not accept a bullfighter who struck the bull in his eyes instead of between the shoulders? And did we fire the stand for the kind of reasons they gave in Valencia and Barcelona?

No, but we did once bombard the Police Prefect with rotten eggs and drove both the bull and the bullfighter from the arena with our sticks, tore down the whole circus and finally raided the box office to get back our money!

We did. But think of our provocation! They gave

us bulls that kept their tails between their legs and bullfighters that ran after them and stuck them from behind. A blot on the honor of the nation.

But why have they given us no bullfights is the question long asked, in the cafés, in the market-place. Wherever two men have met the question has come up, gently, with resignation. But even an Andalusian's patience has its limits. The question became more bitter, became a murmur of public opinion that foreboded ill.

And their bitterness turned against the Prefect, the Mayor and Director of Police in one person, the man in charge of bullfights as well as of all other matters of public weal. He is no longer the favorite of the people; they no longer salute him in the streets but turn away their heads. They will not even beg from him. But the Prefect is stubborn—either that or pursuing some game of his own.

He is a poor ruler, they say. He is to blame for the fact that the city is going down-hill; it is his fault that the river Darro overflooded its subterranean bed and inundated a whole section of the city; he is to blame for the plant-louse and the plague of locusts. And now he will not even give them a single miserable bullfight! He hears words of abuse as he passes by; stones fall at his feet by day; by night they pass through his windows. But the Prefect is pig-headed, or clever.

All misery, every unhappy event is traced to his evil-doing and becomes doubled and tripled in magnitude in the minds of the offended population. They gather themselves together, all the humbled and poor in spirit, the injured and offended, hungry men join hungry men, sick men, sick men, jobless men, jobless men. In a great demonstration, they march to the house of the Prefect and shout: "Down with him!"; they demand food and health and work; they go down on all fours and begin to rip up the stones of the pavement. At last they have moved him! He steps out on his balcony, waves his hand and the masses listen breathless:

"There will be *corridas* before the month is over!" They begin to stir, they speak softly, at last they shout with joy. No longer are they hungry men, sick men, jobless men; they have been welded once more into a happy people. They scatter with laughter, smiling and babbling, to the various parts of the town.

But the days pass and the people begin to have misgivings and again become restless. Why was the day not set, so that they may know where they are at? Does he think the thing can simply be allowed to lapse, to die of inertia? At last one day! There stands the first yellow poster, gigantic, on the walls of the City Hall itself. It shouts its great word over the market place in monstrous letters: *Corridas! Corridas!*—at last! Already there is a crowd gathered about the poster and the market-place sucks its crowds from every adjacent thoroughfare. They come running, shouting, waving their hands: "When, when does it come off?"

"On election day!" is the answer.

Three bullfighters are depicted on the poster, lifesize; and behind them is a great steer dripping with blood. In the four corners of the poster are depicted small episodes of the arena: a horse prostrate; a duel between the bull and bullfighter, etc. The onlookers

recognize the portraits of the large picture and vie
with each other in shouting the names of the great
artists. Children are raised over the shoulders of
others so that they may see; old women stand on their
toes and grind their jaws together.

A bullfight has the ineluctable power of the absolute over a Spaniard; neither Papal bulls nor a modern
refinement of culture nor change of fashion lessen their
hold. It seems to be increasing not decreasing. These
fights in the arena are deeply rooted in the historical
consciousness of the nation; they are closely interwoven with its most primitive conceptions. The Spanish people have been brought up on bullfights, as it
were. A pregnant or nursing mother will attend the
bloody spectacle. The image of some celebrated
espada or other hovers before the eyes of the newly-
wedded, lost in their common dreams of the great future awaiting their unborn sons. The great bullfighter
has an altar in the heart of every single inhabitant, and
the sacrificial flame that burns in these hearts is never
extinguished. Children, as soon as they are able to
walk, may be seen playing bullfighter in the streets.
One boy holds a board to which two horns have been
nailed; he straps it about his forehead, while the other
boys anger him by waving their coats and finally slay
him with a wooden sword. The game is made as
realistic as possible; sometimes far too real.

One day when I was in Granada a crowd of boys
were playing bullfight and the boy who represented the
espada (the sword; the slayer) suddenly threw aside
his wooden sword and refused to play any more, "for
the bull must really be stuck in the neck so that he dies,
otherwise the whole thing is silly!" The boy who

played the bull was perfectly willing, and the little *espada* got out his father's dagger, provoked the bull to make an onslaught and killed him on the spot. Further games of this kind were prohibited by the police, but the boys still play it, for nothing is so impotent in Andalusia as a police prohibition. Even men play at bullfighting in the meadows on Sundays, and whenever an Andalusian traveling on a railway express sees an ox or a cow grazing, though the animal may be far from the window of the car, he will hiss and wave his red handkerchief at it.

All roads lead to the official pawnshop, once the day has been set for the bullfight. Everywhere there is calculation and general stock-taking. People stint themselves and beg until they have the price of a ticket. No one ever thinks of elections, of the insurrection in northern Spain, where the gendarmes have been shooting down defenseless women and children—all this has vanished from their minds.

"When do the bulls arrive?" That is the question! And on the day when the train pulls in with the six horned champions from the breeding ranches near Seville, the populace gather at the station to receive and accompany them on their last humiliating journey to the arena, where they are immured in pitch-black stalls, with not a ray of light. The Granadinos stand at attention along the gutters and fences. They lunge at the steers with pointed sticks, spit at them and call them vile names. The Spanish people oblige the national enemy to run the gauntlet in disgrace before they destroy him.

Any fair-sized city has its arena that will hold from ten to twenty thousand spectators. In Madrid, Seville, and Barcelona there are performances every Sunday during the season (in summer). The Spaniard is not interested in *corridas* during the winter, since the cold prevents the steer from showing the necessary aggressiveness; he cannot be so easily inflamed. In somewhat smaller cities these tournaments take place only once or twice a month; in cities as small as Granada they may be seen only on the great annual feast days: the Resurrection, the Ascension and certain holy days.

In the provincial places there are no arenas at all; and in such towns, perhaps two hundred and fifty miles away from the nearest spectacle, people will deny themselves and slave on a pittance for years, looking forward to the great journey they will one day make to the city to see the spectacle. Some succeed in making the trip once in their lives; some never make it. But the rumors of the *corridas* trickle down into the provincial villages through the most varied courses, making the whole population quiver. And when Easter brings the world-famous *corridas* to Seville, in the villages the peasants drive their most powerful bull to the village market-place, barricade with wagon-walls all the thoroughfares that radiate from the market-place and hold bullfights of their own. The bull has buttons at the tips of his horns, and sometimes around his neck a long rope, the ends of which are held by several men. The young fellows of the village, sometimes even the young girls, will dash at the bull, and provoke him by waving red cloths, whereupon they run away or are tossed by the bull. Few of these affairs end without broken arms and legs. On roofs and balconies, and on the wagons barricading the street, the onlookers are seated. They shout and roar, applaud and get excited quite as they would at a real *corridas*. The animal is adorned with garlands of flowers from head to tail; he is the recipient of much abuse and many beatings; and he is pricked by the long goads of the ox-drivers. But they do not kill him. They cannot afford to; he is too valuable. Plenty of those present would be glad to kill him and would be able to do it too! Besides the professional bullfighters there are thousands of men in Spain—and not a few women—who can manipulate a sword well enough to kill a steer; and there are many amateurs—young noblemen, bankers, and others, who do not suffer by comparison with the professionals themselves.

The bullfight, which was a game of chivalry among the Moors, a tournament, has now become a handicraft whose practitioners travel in groups (*bandas*) from arena to arena, sometimes even going off on tours to France, Portugal, or South America. Such a troupe or quadrille consists of ten or twelve persons, with four different functions: *los picadores* (the lance-bearers), *los chulos* or *las capas* (the players of the cape), *los banderilleros* (the bearers of the darts) and *las espadas* (the blades, the fighters). It is the latter who organizes the quadrille and pays them; it is in his power to cover the whole band with glory or disgrace by a single turn of his wrist.

The *picadores*, successors to the knights of the Moors, ride wretched mares worth not as much as fifteen dollars each. These men are supplied with lances, each held in its lance-rest; this they plunge into the bull's chest to arouse his rage. They wear iron greaves about their calves to protect them from the horns of the bull. Their sole function is to manage so that the bull slays their mount as dramatically as possible. Their trade requires no particular skill, merely brute strength, contempt for death, and bones of iron. They must be able to survive a most savage tossing, which often hurls them to the ground with a tremendous impact. They enjoy no extravagant admiration except among the middle and lower classes; but they get about one hundred dollars for a single performance.

The *chulos* and *banderilleros*. There are fellows for you! They are quick of foot and as swift as arrows! They must flit and dart before the bull's eyes like unstable shadows; they must tease and torment him with their red cloths and plant their motley arrows in his huge neck. The lives of the *picador* and the *espada* often depend on the swiftness and decision of the *chulos* and *banderilleros*. They are uneducated men, but well trained and sober in their habits. Their pay is not half as high as that of the *picadores*. They do not get more than seventy-five dollars for one performance; but they enjoy greater prestige. The young men of the nobility associate with them in public. It is from their midst as a rule that the *espada* is recruited.

La espada! He may be a priest who suddenly casts aside his hood and scorns the authority of the Church Almighty in order to take up the work of bullfighting as a simple apprentice with a village troupe; or he may be a student coming from an excellent family with a splendid career waiting for him. Perhaps he is simply an apprentice in a slaughterhouse who practices his new art by striking down the calves with his great knife while an associate drives them toward him. But they all feel the urge of the great vocation. They are possessed by the most wonderful and sublime of all arts; they are candidates for immortality.

The possibility of the boundless admiration of a population of twenty-five million persons preys like a nightmare on the youth of Spain. Hundreds of young men answer this call every year. Some of them work their way into the profession, become mediocre combatants and sooner or later succumb in the performance of their handicraft. One of them, perhaps, will master the art with all its delicate ramifications; he will take as his model some master of old, whose maxims he will carry out in every detail. For, once in each new century there arises an *espada* who develops an entirely new system and creates a school of his own. His name will never die, but will be spoken by every tongue in the nation; it will shine in the firmament of history; his biography will be written and rewritten again and again; his esthetic significance will be discussed in newspapers and periodicals. Pepe Illo, Montes, Lagartijo, were the shining stars in fame's constellation; in their light the divine Cervantes, the author of Don Quixote, pales to insignificance.

Some of them, perhaps, neither read nor write and may know so little as to fancy Catalonia near the North Pole. But they are permitted to associate with the first persons of the land; young counts and marquis hover in their wake. They have in their pay a body physician and a private secretary; they travel on special trains; some of them have private orchestras to wake them in the morning. Ladies of high station besiege them with fragrant *billets-doux* and beg to be granted a rendezvous.

These princes have a salary of two or three thousand dollars for each performance and if they live to be as old as forty they become millionaires. At every appearance in the arena, they are bedecked with gold and jewels of great value. But they carefully pick up the poor cigars which the people throw to them in their wild enthusiasm, and do a little side line yielding quite an income, selling these cigars. Nor is the manner in which they ordinarily come by their jewelry and other adornments exactly indicative of great delicacy of feeling.

Before the *espada* slays the bull, he customarily dedicates him to the fatherland, and the highest official in the audience—sometimes it is the King himself—accepts this dedication in the name of the nation and is obliged to reciprocate with a present. These compulsory gifts have been diminishing from year to year, and the *espada* has therefore hit upon the idea of dedicating the bull not only to the nation as a whole, but also to some very rich man in the audience. This is an extremely uncomfortable mark of attention, for the Spanish being as they are, it is impossible for one of them to retaliate with a lesser gift than a gold watch, a diamond stick-pin or a large sum of money. Foreigners also are often made the object of this ill-disguised bunko game. The bull was once dedicated to a Frenchman, present at a bullfight in Madrid, with the following words, spoken in the pure jargon of the streets by an illustrious bullfighter: "To *Mu* (Monsieur), *Mu* Wife, and all the little *Mus.*" The well-bred Frenchman, the honor of his wife and children being at stake, threw his purse to the famous protagonist, who pocketed it without turning an eyelid.

The bustle in the Spanish streets and market-places is epitomized in this the most national of all their popular amusements; the innate frivolity of the people, their passionate and capricious nature, are well expressed in the high light of the arena, and impress themselves indelibly upon one's consciousness.

The Spanish nation is as rich in ideals of liberty as any other nation; but it succumbs easily to hood-winking. To-day the elections are being held and the leaders tell us that the question at stake is one of freedom or bondage. But are not the Spaniards free men? The bullfight surely is taking place in response to the popular desire. Is not the people supreme ruler of the arena? The bullfighters must obey them. The gendarmes dare not budge; the Prefect himself is the submissive servant of the people and must swallow what they offer him. We have in the arena an apparent realization of the political dream of autonomy, here in the most important field of all. No doubt it is only a minor matter that the election returns last Sunday were manipulated to the advantage of the reactionary groups, and that to-day, on which another election is being held, several thousand voters will be absent from the polls because of the bullfight. A minor matter, but it may become quite a serious one if the bullfight should in addition be a poor one. Then the people will seek for some object on which to vent their rage and they will then recall even the minor circumstance.

And it is not impossible for a bullfight to fail of its effect. The bullfighter may be a wretched amateur, so mediocre that the onlookers tear off their cloaks and jump down into the arena to show him how a thrust

should be delivered.   Or the bull may be cowardly,
may have been unskillfully bred.   The breeding of battle bulls is a fine art, and in this domain, at least, the
Spaniards have developed one of the sciences connected
with agriculture.

Though it may even come to pass that the wildest
of bulls becomes timid and cowardly when facing the
thousand-headed monster that occupies the seats of the
arena.   In such cases little charges are inserted in the
darts of the *banderilleros,* which explode on being inserted in the animal's neck, and these drive him mad
with pain.   If he continues to show a tendency to run
away, the crowd will yell for the half-moon, which is
a sickle attached to the end of a long pole, and the
calf-muscles of the bull are severed with this instrument.   No decent bullfighter will have anything to do
with an animal so disgraced, and it is dispatched from
behind by a stable attendant, the bold public meanwhile
expressing their most fastidious contempt.   But if it
should turn out that not only the first bull but also the
second, and perhaps even a third, is a failure and unfit
for the combat, the Prefect should be prepared for the
worst.

The day has come; the people flock to the arena, a
large circular amphitheater that can hold eleven thousand persons.   The great central space is covered with
sand, with a fence about five feet high all around it.
Outside the fence is a narrow passage, the outer wall
of which is a barrier seven feet high from which the
rows of benches rise in ever-expanding circles up to
the top of the encircling outer wall.   The sky is blue
above.   About half of the seats are shaded by the

encircling wall; the others are in the sun. These are respectively the seats of the rich and the seats of the poor. Contrary to the usual rule, the poor have their place in the sun. But they have had to sacrifice for it, having arrived at one o'clock to get as much as possible for their money. The performance begins at three.

Happy and carefree is this human swarm; in fact, they begin to bustle about on the white sunlit giant steps, in their mantles draped in many folds, their abbreviated jackets, their red sashes and shirt sleeves, barefoot or in laced sandals or in tight patent leather shoes; bareheaded, or with their handkerchiefs wound about their foreheads like turbans, or with rakish broad-brimmed Spanish sombreros. All these types are mixed at random, but all are free, careless, putting no restraint upon their expression of feeling, or on any impulse that comes along!

"Toros! Toros!" (Bulls) they suddenly roar in unison, although it will be more than an hour before the performance begins. They sing whistling signals to the empty box of the Prefect and greet with shouts of applause a dog who runs across the arena. Why? Just for the fun of it! They enjoy their power as a Nero; they dictate laws and pronounce judgments by the simple method of sticking all their ten fingers into their mouths and whistling. The whitewashed rows of seats shine dazzlingly bright in the sun, a ceaseless bustle passing over them; soldiers, peasants, women, ladies nursing their children with no sense of embarrassment, Spanish dandies with sunken cheeks, blazing feverish eyes and moistened coal-black locks, *filles de joie* carrying expensive fans, proud Spanish beggars in brown horse-blankets, young artisans who express all

their pride in the provocative slant of their head-gear, street boys who have sneaked in, and more. In the arena, where the bulls will soon be slaying and being slain, cake-sellers walk about with big baskets, crying: "Rolls, Rolls!" Large wine-pouches are passed from hand to hand across the rows. The people insist on having something to nibble. They howl and shove out an arm as a signal, and the cake-sellers hop about like frogs, jumping and throwing their wares; the rolls fly in all directions, rising even to the uppermost rows, where they are caught in their flight with equal skill. Money is thrown downward and intercepted in its course by the tradesmen who work like rubber balls, jumping, throwing and catching with motions that follow one another like the strokes of a skilled tennis player.

"Toros! Toros!" The racket suddenly increases; the people are attacked by a veritable frenzy of whistling, stamping and hissing. They bite into their rolls and throw them back again without paying for them; the brass band strikes up a tune to quiet them, but its music is drowned in the general noise. They stamp their feet to a new rhythm and oblige the orchestra to start playing the Toreador March from "Carmen." Suddenly there is complete silence: the Prefect has pushed aside the velvet curtains of his box. He makes a sign. There are a few breathless seconds. The gates fly open as far as they can; the band indulges in a great flourish.

Two heralds dressed in the ancient chivalrous Spanish manner, all in black velvet, gallop into the arena. Each trots around one of its semicircles, and both meet again under the box of the Prefect, where they bow

low in salutation. The Prefect throws to them the key
of the bull pen, and off they gallop again. *"Toros!
Toros!"* is the roar, increasing in volume, proceeding
from ten or twelve thousand throats.

The band plays a subdued march and a splendid procession moves into the arena. Two by two, the bullfighters enter, dressed in silk, embroidered with gold;
then the columns separate and each proceeds to its
own side, single file, as in a folk dance. The first couple
are the *espadas,* who are to take turns in slaying the
beasts; the following six couples are the *banderilleros*
and *chulos;* then come the *picadores,* on horseback,
and last of all two beautifully caparisoned teams of
four mules each, which are to drag out the beasts after
they are killed.

All smile happily, assured of victory, at the assembled public, as if the whole business were a grave
form of trifling. But in their course they reach a little
chapel under the circus, where a priest administers the
sacrament to them; a stretcher is held ready under the
circular passageway, and in a little hospital next to the
circus stand two surgeons with their instruments ready.

The procession has saluted the Prefect and the
audience; the mule teams and the *espadas* have retired
to their places; the rest of the bullfighters stand around
in groups, conversing nonchalantly. The cake-sellers
have not yet all left the arena; the last of them are
still picking up their wares; all seem inclined to believe that there is still time. Suddenly a horn is
sounded; a barn door flies upward; the bull dashes
into the arena. The swift-footed *chulos* barely have
time to jump aside and seize their red blankets; here
and there on the fence a cake-seller is still clutching in

a mad effort to scale it. The last of them was obliged to leave his basket behind him; he tries again and again to get over the fence with it, but in his excitement always falls back into the arena. The bull sniffs at his basket and finally delicately applies his horn to the man's seat, helping him over the fence quite adroitly, to the general satisfaction and applause. The Prefect has played his cards well; the bullfighters are furious; but the people are enthusiastic over the sudden admission of the bull.

The *chulos* assumed their places long ago. They have thrown their gold-embroidered cloaks to the more aristocratic seats, the occupants of which eagerly combat for the honor of guarding them during the bullfight. Now they stand with their dark red cloths waiting for the bull. But he does not see them; he is still dazzled with the sunlight and the unfamiliar crowd, and is rushing hither and thither like a mouse looking for a hole, having been confused by the shouts and the racket rising about him on all sides. A *chulo* trips forth lightly and holds his provocative red cape under the bull's nose. The animal stands dazed for a moment at this audacity and then goes for him, plunging his horns through the cloth. He stops and makes a movement as if he were about to throw some very heavy object many feet in the air. He shakes his horns astonished—there is nothing on them. A new *chulo*—a new attack by the bull, with the same result. The bull, disappointed, gores his horns into the ground and rips it up; he feels a desperate need of seizing something tangible. Again he makes a furious onslaught on a *chulo,* only to be once more disappointed.

Every time he imagines he has one of them on his
horns and makes a gesture to toss him to the sky, he
finds he has nothing to toss! He feels the futility of
possessing a neck that could support a millstone without bending, and horns that measure five feet from tip
to tip, in this ridiculous combat with phantoms.

The bull tires of this game and wants to go home;
he runs around the inside of the fence, looking for an
exit. There is no exit. Then he places his chin on
the edge of the fence, moves back his hind legs and
begins to work his way over the fence. The spectators
crowd toward him from all directions, they abuse the
bull, beating him with their canes and hats. The
twenty or thirty policemen who have been on guard in
the circular corridor forget their dignity and turn
somersaults over the fence to get down into the arena.
They run about insane with fright while one *chulo*
after the other waves a red blanket before their noses,
as if taking them for bulls. The public shouts, "He's
coming! He's coming!" to terrify the policemen still
more. At several points in the fence there are little
gates which, when opened, block the passageway.
Through one of these gates, the bull again reaches his
proper habitat, and the gendarmes again execute their
humiliating maneuvers, in the opposite direction, to
the accompaniment of an ear-splitting jubilation. In
the arena, a *picador* stands impatiently awaiting the
vagrant bull who makes for him directly, and before
the man has had time to assume a defensive posture,
both man and horse are hurled into the air and drop
to the ground like felled trees. The *chulos* entice the
bull away. The stable man comes jumping over the
fence and pulls out the *picador* from under the horse;

the horse is set up on his legs, but falls again at once; the *picador* is led out limping.

The second *picador* succeeds in facing the bull with his horse head on and sits, on the defensive, with his lowered lance resting under his right arm. The bull moves forward, slowly, determined, his head lowered; then he stops and paws up clouds of sandy dust.

He moves forward and plunges one horn into the horse's chest, at the very moment when the *picador* pierces the bull's shoulder with his lance. The horse trembles; a thick jet of blood stands out from his chest, like water from a pump—the horse falls.

The third *picador* sits on his horse, waiting, full of eagerness to sacrifice his animal. But the horse standing with eyes blindfolded, like the other horses, manages to scent the danger; it snorts and jumps timidly to one side. But the bull now means business; he pushes his head under the horse's belly and slowly draws it back, the entrails encircling his horns; he weaves them in a long thread over all the arena until they rip. Another signal from a horn—the first act is over.

Once more the arena swarms. The quick-footed *capas* and *banderilleros* dance about the bull like gay butterflies. Now one of them dances forward; he has no cloth behind which to shield himself; but in his hands he has two red arrows, each a yard long. He prances about the arena, swinging his arrows like two conductor's wands, one in either hand. The bull dashes toward him; the *banderillero* stops. And while the bull appears to be goring him with his horns, the *banderillero* sticks the two arrows into the animal's neck—one over each shoulder blade—and lightly moves off again. The bull snorts and shakes his mane in order to be rid of the painful adornment; he whirls up the sand of the arena in a thick cloud and bellows. But the arrows are provided with hooks like those of harpoons, and they continue to project from his neck like two consecrated candles.

The bull finally makes up his mind to make a clean sweep of these unclean spirits; but it is love's labor lost. They hide behind their red blankets, and if he selects one of the wretches and attempts to tire him by a brisk chase, the creature will merely jump over the fence, into the planks of which the bull may plunge his horns. Under the fence a horse is writhing in his death throes. The bull picks him up, carries him a few paces on his horns and then sets him up again, the horse's four legs spread wide apart. The horse staggers on for ten or twelve paces, then falls and rolls over on his back dead.

A second *banderillero* steps forward, equipped with two green arrows; he assumes a challenging posture. The bull now knows that every one of these arrows has a devil in it; he foams as he makes for the man; the arrows are implanted, one on each side, perhaps three or four inches in front of the other arrows. And the third *banderillero* comes and plants his arrows also. These men work with all the calm and certainty of fate; but the bull has lost his last powers of cool reflection. He dashes about blindly, raging with pain, while the arrows swing over his neck like the masts of a ship in the storm; and the people shout with joy. Another signal—and the third act is ready to begin.

But let the reader turn aside with me for a moment —from this springtime in Granada's circus, to another springtime in Madrid.

It is the same circus; it is the same motley crowd of persons, at first glance like a huge wreath of pansies in a great pasteboard box.

The third act has just begun; the fourteen thousand faces are fixed motionlessly on one and the same point. Down below is the focus of all their glances, a slender page toying with a blade in his hand. His shoes and stockings are of silk; his knee-breeches and his tight-fitting doublet are embroidered in gold; from the back of his head sticks out a little rebellious whorl of hair. Opposite him stands a great black bull, head lowered, delving into the sand of the arena with his hoofs. The bull lowers his horns and the page aims at the bull with the tip of his sword, and so they stand motionless for a long time. The whole scene would be as peaceful and quiet as a living tableau if it were not for the dead horses lying at one side, their chests gored and their bellies ripped.

Suddenly, the bull makes a lunge. He moves like lightning and the page's sword flies through the air, landing somewhere among the onlookers in the upper seats; the page himself runs lightly over the sand of the arena, while the spectators whistle and hiss. After the page has gone a few steps, he throws himself flat on the ground, face-downward, and weeps; but the bull runs across the arena to a dead horse and moistens his horns in the horse's intestines. His head covered with blood, he begins a desperate man-hunt on the swift *chulos;* the page, however, continues to lie, face-downward, still weeping, until the spectators cease their hisses and a few of them shout encouraging words to him. Then he jumps to his feet like a rubber ball; they give him a new sword; again bull and bullfighter stand posed, their weapons ready to strike.

This time it is the *espada* who makes the first thrust. His motion is as short and fast as a stroke of lightning! In fact, you cannot tell that he has moved at all. He stands three yards away from the beast, right opposite him; but his blade sits well planted between the animal's shoulders. Only the hilt may be seen. He is a light agile little page who has just paid his respects to an obese, well-padded Queen and now waits respectfully, his eyes turned towards her. The bull also regards him, long and intently, as if transmitting a last sigh in the direction of his youthful outlines, in order to impress them unforgettably on his memory. For a few breathless seconds the bull stands thus, then falls to the ground, dead, coloring the sand all around him. And the young *espada* skips out gayly with but little applause, not forgetting to collect on his journey the cigars that have descended to the arena from every direction.

A new bull comes in, and while the bull dutifully performs his first two acts, we shall pay a little attention to the young page.

Only eighteen years of age, he is already the hero of the province. His father was a butcher; the boy was studying theology when suddenly two years ago he felt the irresistible call of the vocation. The nation has given him a serious handicap. It has called him the Tiny Little Lizard; and the Little Lizard, his uncle, is one of the most famous bullfighters of the present day. The Lizard himself was one of the greatest of all, crowned among the immortals like Frascuelo and Pepe Illo.

These men are dead and gone, the famous men of the past, and all the greater is the attention and hope with which the nation follows the steps of this promising youth. Only Madrid has as yet failed to approve him. He has come to conquer the capital; and to-day for the first time the Tiny Little Lizard appears in order to win a decisive applause. If the approval is given, if he really is a person of as much promise as rumor would have him, the world is a splendid oyster which his sword may open; his name will be a glory to his own generation and to those that come after. But if he fails—!

The popular mood has already cooled a little; the eulogies of the province have made the capital reserved; furthermore, his first appearance has been a little awkward. If he ever weeps again, his tears will not save him from shame.

But there he stands! His childlike face is radiant with confidence as he salutes the Prefect and the people, dedicating the bull to them. Like a reckless page he glides over the arena, his shining blade concealed coquettishly under his little red scarf, which is held in his left hand. And again he stands opposed to the bull's lowered horns, his own sword lowered and his little tuft of hair rebelliously standing out from his neck. He toys with the monster, obliges the monster to lunge for him; pretends to make a thrust of his own, and leads the bull all around the arena to do his will. The whole scene is like child's play, it seems to move so neatly; only the trembling calves of the page's legs show you what is at stake—and the dead horses lying on the sand.

The Tiny Little Lizard plays in the sun, golden

fringed and silken and filled with vibrating youth. The applause makes him bounce about like a ball. The hearts of the capital are inclining in his favor; he determines to take them by storm. He challenges the bull impetuously, and as the bull makes for him, he plants his sword far in between the shoulder blades, terminating the thrust with a pirouette. The spectators this time applaud before his magnificent maneuver has been concluded; the applause has already burst when the young man is seen quivering in the air, impaled on one of the bull's horns, which has entered far into his left lung. But the sense of life has been raised to such a pitch in his body at this moment, and he is so completely dominated by the desire to succeed, that he extricates himself from the bull's horn, hops down on to the arena and executes a few ballet steps with a smile and a gesture of apology to the public. Then he falls down on his left arm and great roses of blood spread their petals in the sand under him. They contrast curiously with the snow white forehead of the young man. He is borne out amid deathly silence; the capital has really not seen enough of him to be able to judge him fairly.

XIII

A VISION OF SUDDEN DEATH

I N the mountains of Spain you sometimes meet a curious creature. From afar it resembles a gigantic beast, which, presenting a pointed tail ahead of it and dragging a great yellow head behind, dashes in and out down the crooked mountain paths, the dust rising in clouds about it. On closer view it turns out to be a great omnibus rocking along behind a team of as many as fourteen mules, head to tail in long procession. Only the two animals closest to the vehicle are paired, the rest are in tandem.

On the first mule of the procession rides *el delantero,* the outrider. This man guides the course of the long file and in ancient days, when there were no railroads, he was often obliged to sit in the saddle for three days and three nights running. There is quite a distance from the outrider to the omnibus. On the seat of the omnibus sits *el mayoral.* He holds the reins of the two wheel-mules and with their aid guides the vehicle, which, owing to the sharp curves of the mountain paths, is often going in a direction opposite to that of the outrider. The *mayoral* also has the important duty of applying the brakes, besides being responsible for the entire outfit. He has a lash with a short handle and a long tail, which can reach the third animal ahead of him; and besides, he has *el zagal,* a boy fourteen or fifteen years old, who runs by the side of the carriage and prods the lazy beasts with his stick. Sometimes the vehicle is double-decked, with seats above, in the open air, accommodating three or four persons, their legs dangling free in space. These airy vantage-grounds, as well as the second story, are accessible by means of a rope-ladder. Such an omnibus can accommodate about thirty persons, and is divided into three classes, like the railroad trains. Until not so long ago there was always an armed convoy for protection against robbers, and I am told that such a convoy is still found in remote places.

Of the large cities, only Granada is still connected with the outside world by means of these old-fashioned vehicles. Granada is encircled on all sides by the great arteries of traffic which connect Madrid and northern Spain with the southern part of the country and the shores of the Mediterranean; they pass within several miles of Granada and turn aside as if repelled by the proximity of the city. A little branch line runs from Granada to the south, but you must spend a day in an omnibus if you wish to leave it in any other direction, in order to reach a more modern means of transportation.

We were going to Madrid; we could choose between three post-roads, each going in a different direction. We chose the most difficult and the most interesting: the route over the highlands of the Sierra Nevada to Guadix.

On the day before our departure I took a shoe to be repaired. The cobbler was a janitor in an aristocratic house and sat all day long on the sidewalk in front of the lovely portal of the palace, working. I asked him when I might call for my shoe.

"I'll start on it at once. You can have it in an hour."

"But you must get it done to-day without fail, I am leaving early to-morrow morning." He looked at me in astonishment.

"But did I not tell you that you may have it in an hour?"

After the hour had passed, the shoe was not done; the man's mother-in-law—it was explained to me—had died in the meantime. But he would surely come to my house by evening.

He did not come; I found him sitting at his table on the sidewalk, reading his newspaper. No, the shoe is not done; but it would have been done had it not been for his mother-in-law; no one else is to blame but this mother-in-law! It was bad enough while she was alive, but now that she is dead she is comporting herself ten times more inconsiderately; she simply cannot be gotten under the ground. If I am married, I must surely understand the situation. The fact is she had once been married to a Protestant, a Frenchman or African or something like that, and now the priests are not sure that she has a right to be interred in Catholic soil. He has had a lot of running about to do on this account. But to-morrow morning for certain. The Holy Virgin and the Sacrament are called upon to witness that he will have to work all night merely because of this cursed mother-in-law; and my shoe shall be the first object touched by his hand: "You may rest assured, Señorito!" and he laid his hand on my shoulder.

Early the next morning I banged the knocker on his door for half an hour. Finally the man came out half dressed, his eyes tearful with slumber. I told him I came for a shoe.

"A shoe? Yesterday, you say? Promised it for to-day?" And the man whom I had seen sitting here on the sidewalk every day and who had even occasionally had the honor of polishing my shoes insisted that I must have made a mistake in the address of my shoe-maker. But he soon abandoned this untenable posi-tion and by imperceptible stages gradually trans-formed himself into a great master-shoemaker who could not be held responsible for all the promises made by his employees—conditions being as they were, un-fortunately, in Granada.

"But it was you yourself, Sir; my God, you know it was. You even told me into the bargain that your mother-in-law—"

He listened attentively; the entire expression of his face betrayed his zeal to get at the bottom of this curious position. Suddenly a light seemed to dawn in his mind: "Then it must be my brother you were talk-ing to! He said his mother-in-law had died, didn't he? And that he had a lot of trouble about the funeral? Why, the matter is very simple, I see it all now!" He laughed heartily and was so delighted with his solu-tion of the enigma, that he felt obliged to repeat the whole story through a little window to his wife, inside the house.

"Yes, that was my brother," he again turned to me. "He is the spitting image of me, well, well! That's the way things go! But why are you so anxious to take this rickety omnibus? Why don't you hire a car-riage to drive you over to Daifontes? And you can catch the train and you need not leave here before noon."

"So you think a little difference of about five dollars in the expense will be all the same to me?"

"My God, five dollars, is such a sum even worth talking about? Can you consider such sums at all, traveling about as much as you do? And you could wait until to-morrow morning. Your tickets will be good until then. Then you will have time enough to catch your breath; and we can devote all our attention to your shoe. And you will save the five dollars, which, after all, is a matter not to be despised. You don't want to miss the carnival? Bah, the carnival of Madrid doesn't look like thirty cents! If you must see a carnival, why don't you stay and see the Granada carnival the day after to-morrow?"

I preferred, however, to have my shoe delivered to me, and this was finally done after I had paid a small fine of one franc for having violated obligations previously assumed by me. A policeman, who was called to adjust the dispute, confirmed the fact that the fine was in order, to assure the proper conduct of business intercourse. And the man, no doubt, earned his franc. In one-half the time taken for his prattling, he might have mended the shoe, and he might furthermore have spared himself all these fabrications. But he preferred to hand out the shoe. And I am sure that, had he been the Omnipotent himself, he would undoubtedly have set in motion a bridge disaster, a pestilence in Madrid, an insurrection in Andalusia, and other harassing incidents of the same type, in order to compel me to remain until the shoe was mended. Whatever might have been required from him, he would have done it to favor me, just in order to mend my shoe; how dare we call such people lazy!

We reached the country coach just at the last moment, and it rolled upward with us through the narrow

streets. It was six in the morning; day was breaking.
There were two other passengers in the coach with us:
a fat woman and a little boy. The coach had two compartments and was a single-decker; but its roof was
loaded with freight of all kinds. It was a rickety old
boat with weak springs and a tendency to careen to
either side, as if animated by a desire to break down
the encompassing walls of the road.

There was an ear-splitting noise, caused by the
rattling windows, the loose parts of iron banging
against each other, the coach-springs, which slapped together at short intervals, and the brake, which ceaselessly ground against the wheels although we were going up a steep hill. The sleepy windows of the houses
descended obliquely past us; likewise their roofs. Terrace after terrace, the city dropped away beneath us.
We ascended as in a liquid which becomes clearer and
clearer toward the top. Looking up in the air, we saw
the pavements of many narrow little streets beneath
a murky darkness with only the upper halves of the
houses in the light.

We had only six animals ahead, two wheel-mules
and four others in tandem. We had no *delantero*
(outrider); but we had a *zagal* who knew how to
wield his goad. His blows fell on the unhappy beasts
and they humped their backs, and managed to drag us
up the steep path. The brake ground ceaselessly
against the wheels.

Before us rose a wall of hills, seemingly inaccessible.
The highest ice summits in the Sierra Nevada, Mul-
hacen and Picacho intercepted the first rays of the sun
from the Mediterranean and scattered them in space,
while the morning twilight advanced like a fiery blush

over the white snowfields. Beneath us lay the city, dozing in the face of twilight. The mighty Vega, enveloped in a white vapor, resembled a long bright mountain torrent eating its way deeper and deeper into the encircling wreath of snowy mountains.

We climbed ceaselessly through the twilight, entering into the cold sparkling sunlight of the mountains. We got down from the coach and persuaded our fellow-passengers to do likewise, but without any apparent effect. The animals continued to creep up the road, their backs humped into a sharp curve, as if their vertebræ might burst through their work-worn gray skins. They used the edges of their hoofs like claws to grip the mountain and the coach staggered drunkenly after them. The *zagal* dashed about flogging the mules. The *mayoral* slept on his seat. I woke him and called his attention to the fact that the brake held the wheels so tightly that sometimes they did not turn.

"It's broke," he said with a shrug, "but it's not so bad going downhill."

"Yes, but now we're going uphill!"

"Oh, you can't have all things in this world," he answered with a yawn.

He considered this matter a domestic affair concerning the mules and the post coach. But when I insisted that we must do something about it he got off and stopped the vehicle. Down on his back under the coach in the dust of the road he propped up the heavy brake spring with his feet while I tied it to the floor of the carriage.

The hills to the east of Granada have an uncanny baldness. The only vegetation is a stiff grass and a few thistle-like sharp plants with yellow blossoms. The road has been cut through and great walls rise on both sides, cutting off the view, while the land begins to pile up behind. Only within the silhouette of the sides of the road is there a glimpse behind of a bit of the Vega and a small gray shapeless speck which is Granada.

We left our walled road and the coach and explored the surrounding heights. In some places were entrances to uninhabited caves. An overgrown path led away from them, disappearing a short distance ahead. There were no human habitations, only naked pinnacles all around; but when we ascended the nearest height a black abyss opened at our feet. The steep slopes were covered with fruit-trees; at the bottom a white river wound in and out through a group of houses; voices rose from below, and the trumpet neigh of a donkey. It was a little world of its own surrounded on all sides by massive mountains.

It was nearly nine o'clock when the *zagal* came running up and begged to get in. At last the road was level and the animals, having rested, started on a sharp trot. They rushed along as if they had just been taken out of the stable—forward, then around a sharp corner and down into a deep valley. The beggars showed some spirit! The coachman applied the brakes through force of habit, though he knew they did not work. The animals broke into a gallop. We rolled downward with increasing speed like a diminutive avalanche; but at the next bend the grade came to an abrupt end. There was a frightful creak in the old tub, and we jolted complacently into the village.

Once more we ascended. It was uphill and downhill like a great seesaw that threw us from pinnacle to pinnacle every two or three miles, rising all the time, while the earth all around dropped away, wider and wider. The Vega, at an elevation of 2,300 feet above sea-level, seemed almost hidden in the abysses. Even its white wreath of mountains fell away; Sierra Elvira, Sierra Alhama, the gloomy cleft far across the way near Loja. All the mountain-tops dropped lower and lower until the entire landscape seemed boundlessly great; only the battlements of the Sierra Nevada still protruded.

At the stagecoach office they had told me that the route made the connection with the Madrid express which passed through Guadix at three o'clock in the afternoon. The *mayoral* was greatly astonished to learn this, and proved to me that the schedule time of arrival for this coach was five o'clock. This meant that we should not be able to leave Guadix until the slow night-train which took twenty-four hours to reach Madrid. I promised the *mayoral* a duro if we could make the express train at Guadix.

This was the signal for a mad dash. The *mayoral* rose in his seat and lashed his mules with a shrill yell: "Y—aa! Y—aa!" The *zagal* dashed forward beating the animals with his stick and throwing stones at them. He ran and yelled and beat them until their course became so furious that he was almost left behind, being obliged to cling to the running-board. We had just scaled a ridge and were again descending at a furious pace. The bells jingled, the coach bumped, bounced into the air, swayed to one side—but on it went—on! Down into a deep gully, then over a glen by an old wooden bridge, and up over a steep slope at the same dashing speed.

In the sharp turns the lead animals of our train were

running in a direction opposite to that of the coach. It looked as though they would drag us over the precipice, but we made the turns with only a bad shaking. On we went in our mad rattling downward course into uncanny depths, a perpendicular rocky wall on one side, with the precipice on the other. The coach was an old one; the brake did not work; the *mayoral* could control only the wheel-animals. The others were guided only by shouts. They ran as they willed, squeezing themselves against the cliff or edging over to the precipice to dodge the missiles of the *zagal*.

It was about a thousand feet, perhaps fifteen hundred, to the bottom of the cliff. The figure is a matter of indifference, for the result would have been the same. But, strangely enough, I should prefer to be dashed to pieces at a depth of one thousand feet rather than at fifteen hundred. After all I am a Dane, and the small nations do not do things in a large way. An Englishman would have desired the other figure. Far below us the gully ended sharply and rose on the opposite side, being only a few hundred feet away, to such a height that the sunlight did not reach us, although it was nearly noon. Goats hung in breakneck positions on the tremendous bluish wall staring after us, shaking their beards, and making crooked leaps over the sheer surface.

We smiled at each other with rather forced smiles and sought a peculiar consolation in taking firm grasp of the carriage-cushions and looking as brave as we could. The fat woman on the outside would surely have caused the vehicle to turn turtle if I should have offered to exchange places with her. *I* don't mean that I ought to have changed places with her. I bore the full responsibility, both legally and morally, for my wife also, and therefore I had no right to sit with my back to the abyss. In fact, it would have been quite correct for me to have jumped off while there was time; I owed it to my children. But we are cowards, after all; and the fat woman snored as if there were no dangers. Her fat made her sleepy.

Again we went uphill, with undiminished speed. My promise of a duro seemed to have bewitched even our mules. The bells jangled amidst the ear-racking noises of the carriage; the window-panes hummed like angry insects; the galloping mules whined and kicked out from behind whenever the *zagal* leaned forward from the carriage to beat them. "Y—aà! Y—aa! Go on! Go on!" We shot past huts and over mountain brooks, up and down in a great seesaw. Every five minutes we thumped over a culvert with a bump to make the heart fly out of the throat.

Beneath us the road disappeared around a gable of rock, leaving only a dizzy depth behind. It reappeared as a detached fragment on the other side of the declivity and hung there like a remnant of a small cornice, again to disappear around a sharp corner. This was the road we must go, and at this same crazy speed! The *mayoral* was standing on his seat shouting and lashing away, while the reins swayed slackly between the two shaft-animals.

But all things are in flux. A few hours later we were again breathing freely. We abandoned our worries as to life and limb and enjoyed the landscape. This was the highest point of our journey. On either side little glaciers sparkled in the light; cold clear brooklets gushed forth—no wider than a finger—and trickled downhill. These were the first indications of some river or other. There were folds and wrinkles and scars; great frost-bluish gnarls and sulphurous yellow pates; huge crusts of blood and menacing brows. The earth lay below us like a gigantic maltreated face, its features distorted in pain and hatred. But when viewed from the next ridge, it was a placid smile; gleaming waterfalls over rocks standing like huge organ pipes in the valleys below, pillar-like cliffs rising on the battlements like great monuments, with birds wheeling about their peaks in narrowing circles.

At times the landscape expanded into a world of battlements and long ridges, limited only by the blue ether in every direction, a highland floating lonely in universal space. And then it closed around us again, narrowing into a cleft between two steep walls of rock. Or, a semicircular chain of mountains rose like a mighty lower jaw above it; from out the jaw project black rocks, broken off and intermingled with sharp splinters and broad scars. Very appropriately this spot is called the "Old Women's Teeth." At this elevation there was not a human being, not an animal, not a single habitation. But far above, hanging as it were between two yellow rocks, clung a parcel of cultivated soil—a signal to the sky that the earth is tilled even at such altitudes—like a brown ragged patch on a silken robe.

I asked the coachman how high we were.

"Oh, I suppose about fifty or sixty fathoms," he answered reflectively, and with a face that seemed to express a belated fear that he might have exaggerated.

We left the fat woman and her son at an old inn, taking an hour's rest, and then dashed on. Now we

went steadily downhill. The trickling streams flowed
with our course, while the mountainous masses gradually piled up above and behind us. Before us a luxurious valley gradually unfolded, with villages and blossoming fruit trees. Through the valley there ran a
broad stony river. On the other side the land rose
again, with an impress of infinity and harmony, through
blue and purple, out into the wide world, where it was
lost in the endless snowfields of the Nevada. Finally
we were down in the great valley, at its end. Great
hills lay behind us, and the valley itself was only an
incision in the rocks. In front of us our glance fell far
below to flat country, a marshy basin many miles wide,
which, shut in on both sides by highlands, moved along
in unrelieved flatness, until it finally merged with something in the distance—perhaps the sea. At least so it
seemed to us from so high up; but when we reached the
bottom, this apparent marsh-land was also a mountainous landscape, on a smaller scale and built up of loam.
A mighty layer of loam must at some previous time
have risen from the sea, but so cautiously as to have
preserved its horizontal surface. Then the waters
descended from the Sierra Nevada and cut up the surface, transforming it into a confused labyrinth, but
leaving thousands of spheres and knolls and combs of
loam standing. All their tips are at the same level,
and it was this that afforded from a distance the spectacle and the impression of an arm of the sea that
had been shut in.

We rumbled down into this droll landscape, the assembled units of which seem to have been executed on
a crude lathe. For about a mile a water-course took
possession of the road, and we drove through the

water up to the hubs. In this loam, which is as hard as stone, nothing but vines grow. And since the vineyards had been cut down, the landscape had a disconsolate appearance. Not even a bit of grass covered the yellow crust. We peered about for dwellings, but saw nothing but occasional entrances to caves along the slopes. Gradually these became more numerous and we lumbered through a village consisting of nothing but inhabited caverns. I counted a hundred such entrances as we drove past, most of them with masonry doorways. But there were also aristocratic caves with panes of glass and neat brick façades, terminating above in a cornice of red bricks. Some of the mountain cones were inhabited to the very top, and a trail wound up the mountain like the course of a snail, to the "mansard." Such caves may be seen everywhere in Guadix in great numbers. Half of the ten thousand inhabitants of the city are said to live underground.

A few miles this side the city we heard a sharp locomotive whistle and observed the express snorting away to Madrid. But the *mayoral,* whose zeal had diminished considerably during the last few hours, rose in his seat and lashed the beasts like a madman. We ended our long drive of some forty miles as we clattered up to the hotel at Guadix. The *mayoral,* proud of his work, came to ask for his gratuity.

I looked at him astonished.

"Well, didn't I drive like the devil?" he asked, relating to the bystanders the arrangement that had been made between us and describing the manner in which he had been driving.

"He drove like the son of a Spaniard," they confirmed his statement, "and he has deserved his duro. You must admit it, Señor Foreigner!"

And one of them took me by the arm as he pointed to his watch: "He has arrived an hour and a half ahead of time. You have had some fine driving and you must pay."

"Yes, but how about the result!" I interposed. "The point for me was to make the express!"

They shrugged their shoulders and turned their backs on me. The expression of their backs clearly pronounced the word "Quibbler!"

"It's always that way with foreigners when they are expected to live up to their agreements," one of them said aloud. I took counsel with myself swiftly and paid the duro.

Of course the others were right and I was wrong; for we were in Spain, not at home, and my fierce indignation was mere Nordic pedantry—though for a Nordic I do not suffer excessively from moral pedantry.

There was the case of an Andalusian waiter who was supposed to give me some small change. Among the small coins returned to me there were three or four that were worth nothing. I pushed them across the table to him as his tip. He shoved them gently back and said laconically:

"No, not these, Sir, these are really no good." And I gave him others without protest, pocketed the counterfeits, to place them later furtively into circulation.

It was still a long time before midnight so we strolled forth to take a look at the neighborhood. All sorts of fruit as well as grapes grew near the town; wherever human hands had been active, the arid earth seemed to have yielded. But nothing could grow of itself here, not even thistles or cactus. The soil, a sort of composite of loam and rocks, was too hard for a plant to strike root in, though soft enough to manipulate with hoe and pick. At several points we were able to see the people digging out homes in the cliffs. First the substance of the cliffs had to be chopped loose in blocks, to be carried away by donkeys. Then the walls and ceilings were smoothed by cutting away with sharp iron tools. A considerable portion of the furniture is manufactured by simply leaving some of the material standing in its place and cutting out its outlines—window frames, benches, bedsteads; sometimes even tables.

It is by no means only poor people who inhabit such caves, whose construction often costs more than a house of the same size. We visited in an aristocratic cave dwelling occupied by the owner of an estate, a habitation of eight lovely rooms, lying in three successive rows. Although the inner rooms obtained their light from the front rooms, you found light enough to read by even in the second tier; in the last two rooms, only, which were used as bedrooms, was there constant twilight—so strong is the daylight in a southern country. Behind the dwelling there were stalls and granaries. The whole establishment extended far into the earth, terminating in a great yard, which was open to the air. This yard had been cut fifty feet down into the rock and was connected with the outside world by a narrow passage.

It became dark about six o'clock. The city had nothing of interest to offer at night, being simply a great village. There was not even a comfortable place in which to sit and talk; only cold and dirty wine-cellars, and we were very chilled and tired. Nor was the waiting-room of the station very appetizing; furthermore, it was closed after the departure of each train. So we dragged ourselves through the streets in bad humor, with the prospect of spending our time uncomfortably until midnight. We cursed the lying owner of the post-coach, we cursed the inefficiency and unreliability of Andalusia, and became quite enthusiastic remembering the comforts and dependable habits in our home country—the sandwich buffet, and the upholstered seats in the waiting-rooms, and the incomparable trustworthiness of the population. Then we dropped into a dirty wine-shop—at least to enjoy the discomfort of a wooden bench.

Gradually a few workingmen gathered in the place; most of them had musical instruments with them. They were in their working dress, but their hats and boots were as elegant as they always are with the Andalusians. I assumed at first that it was an amateur orchestra; but it turned out that it was a quite accidental meeting. Most of the young men of Andalusia play the guitar and in remote places like Guadix they usually take their instruments with them when they go out looking for entertainment in the evening.

Each of them ordered a glass of wine, some of them leaving it standing before them for a long time. Then they alternated in singing love songs to their own accompaniment—these sad Spanish *coplas*, which all sound alike to the ear of the northerner. They have no complicated melodies of the kind we like, nor have they any songs with more than one part. But three of them—common workingmen—played very charmingly in unison on guitar, mandolin and lute. And one of the railway-stokers had an inexhaustible supply of *coplas* to recite, which he was able to make more lively by including references to those present. At last he roused the most extraordinary enthusiasm of the others by improvising a song about the two fair-haired foreigners, who came from the distant north way down to Guadix—way down to beautiful Guadix! His listeners threw their hats at his head as a sign of applause and pounced upon him in boisterous delight. We, the foreigners, expressed our pleasure by ordering wine all around. The stoker competed with another fellow in a tournament of song, each improvising his own verses.

The evening passed. Before we were aware of it, midnight had come. The train drew up at the station, and a moment later we were pulling out of the little town of Guadix—out of Andalusia.

Days in the Sun!

THE END

Frie - Von Temske